J Kegley

Sept. 2019

SUBJECTS THAT MATTER

SUBJECTS THAT MATTER

PHILOSOPHY, FEMINISM, AND POSTCOLONIAL THEORY

NAMITA GOSWAMI

Published by State University of New York Press, Albany

Printed in the United States of America

For information, contact State University of New York Press, Albany, NY
www.sunypress.edu

Library of Congress Cataloging-in-Publication Data

Names: Goswami, Namita, author.
Title: Subjects that matter : philosophy, feminism, and postcolonial theory /
  Namita Goswami.
Description: Albany : State University of New York Press, [2019] | Includes
  bibliographical references and index.
Identifiers: LCCN 2018043673 | ISBN 9781438475677 (hardcover : alk. paper) |
  ISBN 9781438475684 (ebook)
Subjects: LCSH: Feminist theory. | Postcolonialism.
Classification: LCC HQ1190 .G67 2019 | DDC 305.42—dc23
LC record available at https://lccn.loc.gov/2018043673

10 9 8 7 6 5 4 3 2 1

For Papa

Contents

Acknowledgments

It is never easy to come to the end of a journey no matter how difficult it might have been. Yet, I am not really certain I can pinpoint when this project began. Inklings of it seem to have always been there while the rest of me needed to catch up. Now that the book is moving into the world, I can only gesture to those who made it possible—you are part of a lifeworld that cannot be captured on a page. These people buttressed my ability to live to fight another day, often by the skin of my teeth.

If there is a lesson to be learned in any transcribing of "what it actually takes" for a story to be told, for me, it lies in a paradoxical recognition that this book could not be what it is without being what it was. And so, in the words of Emily Dickinson, "It's all I have to bring today— / This, and my heart beside."

I want to thank SUNY Press, and in particular, Andrew Kenyon, for standing with this project for more years than I would like to count. His diligence and his faith are irreplaceable. I must add that I am incredibly grateful for SUNY's readers and their invaluable feedback.

If we must assign beginnings, then all of this begins with Richard Werner. His was the first philosophy class I ever took, and it has always stayed with me. Thank you for being my mentor, my teacher, and my friend, when I was a newly arrived international student at Hamilton College. I have also always had excellent brilliant woman karma, and without Chandra Mohanty, Deepika Bahri, Beverly Guy-Sheftall, Cynthia Willett, and Tina Chanter, I would not be who I am today.

A most affectionate nod goes to my former graduate students (you know who you are), including those in my two Spivak seminars and my seminar on postcolonial theory. Some of the material herein was first presented to these students who surprised me every day with their smarts and creativity. I witnessed firsthand their courage, maturity, and ferocious intellect; you will always remain a part of me.

I am indebted to those who held out their hands when it seemed impossible to go further: Charles Mills, Kristie Dotson, Henry Schwarz, Alison Bailey, José Medina, Sarah Hoagland, Falguni Sheth, Azadeh Erfani, O'D Johnson, Mary Rawlinson, Eric Nelson, Russell Ford, Tommy Curry, Mickaella Perina, Robin James, Tyler Williams, Matt Roberts, Lauren Guilmette, Linda Martín-Alcoff, Emily Lee, Kathryn Sophia Belle, Kyoo Lee, Yitian Zhai, Maeve O'Donovan, Lisa Yount, Franklin Perkins, Mary Jeanne Larrabee, and Ann Russo. I miss you, Darrell Moore.

My students at Indiana State University (you also know who you are) show me why we must persist. You made this venture easier with your humor, sincerity, and fortitude. My colleagues at Indiana State University, including those in the Department of Philosophy, the Department of Multidisciplinary Studies, and the College of Arts and Sciences, have always provided the requisite resources and *bon homie*. Thank you.

So much of life happens as a project comes into being. I must register how my family *got me through* while also being in the crucible alongside me. There are no words that will ever suffice to impart what Brendan William Corcoran means to me. Without you, I would not be here today. As my partner, best friend, and fellow traveler in every way, your sacrifices, efforts, patience, and love are inestimable. The privilege is all mine. Diarmuid Dhruv Corcoran, there is nothing that makes me prouder and happier than being your mom. Your songs, beaming smile, biting wit, goodness, fierce intelligence, curiosity, kindness, and compassion bring pure joy. You are everything.

Samir अब उस वक़्त के साथ क्या करें? Thanks for sticking it out with me भाई साब. My mother's wicked humor, let's-get-on-with-it attitude, and fearlessness helped immeasurably during many an impasse. You were there at every step. I can only hope that I am my mother's daughter. My mother-in-law undauntedly provided unconditional love and taught us all to cherish life. Having come to hold his new grandson a week after he was born, my father-in-law died before holding him ever again. I still hear his bellowing laughter and try to feel gratitude, as he did, for each new day. (Thank you for listening to me and reading my missives as I called to you when exploring Ireland's landscapes.)

This book is dedicated to my father who passed away two months before his only grandchild would visit India for the first time. पापाजी आप इतना जल्दी चले गये। It is your integrity, untiring discipline, humility, and goodwill that are my example. Although nothing would be better than giving this book to you in person, I know that you always understood. Your sacrifices and love are the bridge this immigrant daughter walks on.

An earlier version of chapter 3 was originally published as "Europe as an Other: Postcolonialism and Philosophers of the Future" in *Hypatia: A Journal of Feminist Philosophy* 29:1 (Winter 2014): 62–78.

An earlier version of chapter 4 was originally published as "The Second Sex: Philosophy, Feminism, Postcolonialism, and the Race for Theory" in *Angelaki: Journal of Theoretical Humanities* 13:2 (August 2008): 73–91.

An earlier version of chapter 7 was originally published as "The (M)other of All Posts: Postcolonial Melancholia in the Age of Global Warming" in *Critical Philosophy of Race* 1:1 (January 2013): 104–20.

An earlier version of chapter 9 was originally published as "Among Family Women: *Sati*, Postcolonial Feminism, and the Body" in *Phenomenology, Embodiment, and Race*. Ed. Emily Lee. Buffalo: State University of New York Press, 2014. 79–102.

Introduction

What Tradition Tells, Tradition Wanted: Subjects That Matter

> Views are implicit from the direction taken by the subject-matter itself, its entire freedom to move, and freedom of our thought to follow it.
>
> —Theodor Adorno, "Why Philosophy"

> It is the matter . . . that brings us to dialectics.
>
> —Theodor Adorno, *Negative Dialectics*

> There are no new ideas. There are only new ways of making them felt.
>
> —Audre Lorde, *Sister/Outsider*

> We excel our ancestors only in system and organization: they lied as fluently and as brazenly.
>
> —C.L.R. James, *The Black Jacobins*

The subject matter of this book is heterogeneity. The book uses this subject matter to challenge Eurocentrism, which prevents postcoloniality as a historical era and distinct conceptual accomplishment from truly making a difference in how we understand subjectivity and agency. This interruption of Eurocentric identity politics is oriented by the following three questions: 1. Is it the subject itself or the disciplinary framework that brings this subject matter to life—that really matters? 2. Does understanding heterogeneity as a common subject matter of philosophy, feminism, and postcolonial theory allow the nonidentitarian value of these disciplines to emerge? 3. Can a

1

conceptual continuity between philosophy, feminism, and postcolonial theory enable a non-antagonistic understanding of difference? I suggest that only by understanding difference as inherently oppositional and antagonistic can Eurocentrism retain hegemonic insistence. Eurocentrism's identitarian value, which prioritizes not the subject matter to be understood but the worth of its practitioners, is used to caricature non-Eurocentric conceptual frameworks as mere politics and ideological advocacy. The book, therefore, considers heterogeneity, which is diversity not dissonance, as a conceptual continuity between philosophy, feminism, and postcolonial theory. It posits this particular conceptual continuity to foreground philosophy, feminism, and postcolonial theory's essentially historical co-implication in understanding the world in which we live. Their nonidentitarian value as disciplines—that is, the proportionality of their claims to our *actual* lives, rather than their supposed generalizability—makes them subjects that matter.

Why heterogeneity? For two reasons: 1. The book suggests that a non-antagonistic understanding of difference may interrupt interdisciplinary identity politics. If philosophy is the general frame towards which non-Eurocentric disciplines ought to move to be taken seriously, then philosophy and its geopolitical determination mean the same thing: philosophy is identity politics. As Theodor Adorno emphasizes, "What tradition tells, tradition wanted" (*Negative* 47). Because philosophy *uses* its subject matter to render non-Eurocentric disciplines belated and marginal, a proportional footstep by Eurocentrism's practitioners, who presume to be the standardbearers for what counts as thinking, may impede the sanctioned ignorance gussied up for the proverbial *hoi polloi* as the philosophical.[1] A proportional footstep breaks Eurocentrism's claim to the constructive frame by not stopping short at where a perspective comes from, but by privileging where we are going, *for the sake of the subject matter*. This mutually implicated understanding of the promise of philosophy considers the marginalization of feminism and postcolonial theory as their historical privilege: our struggles to find what is worthy about philosophy, amid those who would take this belongingness for granted, ask philosophy to live up to its creed precisely because philosophical understanding is worth fighting for.

2. This book invokes heterogeneity in response to a historical moment defined by the extraordinary collapse of species-life and the destruction of the physical environment. Any postcolonial project must be situated in the frame/arena of anthropogenic climate change, which challenges the standing, roles, and meanings of all disciplines, especially in the humanities, and changes everything about how we think into, and about, our world.[2] A force multiplier, climate change puts the lie to Eurocentrism as heterogeneity is the very basis upon which terrestrial life, human civilization, and human thought

depend. The localized readings contained herein juxtapose how heterogeneity works in philosophy, feminism, and postcolonial theory specifically when we are facing a devastating *loss* of heterogeneity. Part of this attempt to rejuvenate certain aspects and/or premises of these conceptual frameworks involves reckoning with the scale of climate change. In place of a comparative analysis of climate change discourse in these disciplines (and, relatedly, discourse of the animal, posthumanism, or biopolitics, for example), the book reinvigorates heterogeneity as a tenet and tool. If all critical discourse must somehow be situated in the frame/arena of anthropogenic climate change, what are the implications of valuing heterogeneity in a catastrophically challenged world?

The discretionary reference to extant scholarship is the result of following a common thread in philosophy, feminism, and postcolonial theory to learn about heterogeneity. I do not pit these disciplines against each other, but try to understand the concept of heterogeneity in the work of various scholars. I also do not put forward the somewhat idiosyncratically defined textual selections as representatives of "good" philosophy, feminism, and postcolonial theory. In pursuit of what Adorno calls an "intellectual experience," which must necessarily remain "grounded in the subject matter" (*Lectures* 29), the book's lovingly orchestrated moments of exegetical exchange, between traditions and their sacred texts, focus on small moments of affinity and disappointment to confound and limit our habitual disciplinary lexicons.[3]

Advancing heterogeneity as a conceptual continuity between philosophy, feminism, and postcolonial theory undermines what is conventionally and/or traditionally deemed feminism's and postcolonial theory's diagnostic and/or corrective stance vis-à-vis philosophy *tout court*. Feminism and postcolonial theory, which are already in dialogue with the rich tradition of European thought, evince how disparate experiences cannot be grasped with *only* our usual conceptual apparatus. By taking their derivative and marginal rank for granted, Eurocentric identity politics ignore the contributions of interdisciplinary scholarship towards an understanding of our heterogeneous world. As just one example of a common subject matter between philosophy, feminism, and postcolonial theory, heterogeneity allows the nonidentitarian value of these disciplines to emerge. Such fluid family resemblances seem especially salient to reinvigorate heterogeneity as ideal and instrument from within the frame/arena of anthropogenic climate change.[4]

Notwithstanding the book's aspirational trajectory, I give prominence to disciplinary debates occurring in the western academy. These are the debates I have been privy to, and I have lived some of them. My education in philosophy, feminism, and postcolonial theory began in the United States when I arrived as an immigrant for undergraduate study. During the fall semester of my sophomore year in college, I took my first philosophy class as well as my first course in nonwestern feminisms. It was then that I noticed how these different fields take up similar questions about truth, justice, and the good life. Prior to my arrival at the age of eighteen, I had already lived in various countries such as Libya, Canada, Venezuela, Greece, and Poland, which complicated any claim to a so-called Indian identity. I am obliged, however, in the United States, to adopt the identity of a woman of color. I can say that this book is written from the perspective of an Indian citizen who is a woman of color in the Euro-US academy.[6]

What this perspective means beyond the categorial is perhaps illustrated in the texture and feel of the readings themselves because the exegetical exchanges orchestrated in this book are meaningful. They are an attempt to grapple with that unspeakably vile power that defends reason with anything but reason: this fight is never fair; no low is too low; the Great Game usually wins. Just as Hortense Spillers reminds us, we are still struggling to define our object, as the revulsion, brutality, and malice we encounter in the name of tradition can only be called racism on a lazy day (*Black, White* x, xii).[7] Violent repetition of identity's categorial discharge turns rhetoric into reality by contracting living, vital heterogeneity into mere oppositional antagonism for gratuitous destruction. A relentless narrative devoid of substance—the nihilism of entitlement is obviously soul destroying—ensnares heterogeneous, historical life by obliging its victims to prove a negative. Even the few herculean victories against this real (not cogitative) power rarely seem to change the comfortable social world that is the Euro-US academy. By laboring for the rational and humane, contra the performative cruelty of prolonged categorial prestige, this book attempts to make real the abyss between effortfully created (silent) meaningfulness and effortlessly repeated (noisy) stereotype.

While the protocols of Eurocentric identity politics recommend enlisting a "daddy text" to be considered philosophical, this is a postcolonial book. To whom it may concern: I am not an Adorno scholar in the traditional sense; he figures as a useful fiction to make a philosophical point. I do not use Adorno to reconstitute a critical genealogy of the postcolonial (that is, Adorno as proto-postcolonial) but engage postcoloniality in two ways: as a historical era and as a conceptual accomplishment. The first approach purposes Gayatri Spivak's claim that there is no postcolonial*ism* as long as colonial devastation refurbishes itself as globalization and development. Considering the manifest importance of postcolonial theorists' multifaceted analyses of capitalist exploitation's durability, the book attempts to make postcoloniality real as a historical moment. To this end, I explain how Eurocentric identity politics prevent extremely hard-won historical achievements from making a difference beyond the superficial and perfunctory. Thwarting Eurocentrism requires us to convey and uphold the subject matter and not insulate the inveterate disciplinary framework at hand. This is the postcolonial move of the book. Its locus is heterogeneity as it emerges as subject matter, and how this subject matter may be reinvigorated from within the frame/arena of climate change.

In terms of postcoloniality as a conceptual accomplishment, the book does not conflate postcoloniality with cultural criticism *par excellence* but focuses on its philosophical dimension. Postcolonial theory and cultural criticism when coalesced lead to a vaguely articulated critical posture that appropriates and displaces other discourses (for example, African-American feminism) and reduces postcolonial theory to the applied version of postmodernism and deconstruction (which is very different from Spivak's "setting to work").[8] If the particular concentration of understanding known as the concept is at the core of a Eurocentric sense of exceptionalism, then the book takes the conceptual turn to provide an understanding of the philosophical in different terms.[9] I define postcoloniality as the striving for a non-antagonistic understanding of difference. (This simple definition with all its utopic implications clashes with the violent history of colonialism and neocolonialism and creates a sort of ironic and melancholic stage for the readings the book conducts.) The possibility for the encounter with heterogeneity—that is, for what Spivak terms "the experience of the impossible" (*Aesthetic* 341), heterogeneity being at once utterly omnipresent and out of reach—is exegetical. Assembled at the subject matter of heterogeneity, philosophy, feminism, and postcolonial theory do not rehearse a categorial discharge, but set forth the value of postcoloniality as both a historical era and conceptual accomplishment.

Any analysis of subrepted material conditions of philosophical inquiry begs the question of the *place* of the exegetical, especially because Eurocentrism's closed circuitry hinders the qualitative variety of experience necessary to change one's mind. Yoking heterogeneity to postcolonial possibility also runs the risk of facile demands for representation to mirror reality, even if by albeit a more tortuous route: the epistemic strategy of particularization via essentially historical categories of identity. Granting that heterogeneity is empirical reality, it still cannot be apprehended directly, as the heterogeneous does not await revelation as the unsullied.[10] Whereas Eurocentrism's peremptory stellar strut showcases the specular solidity of the (as proclaimed) singularly conceptual, I seek an exegetical rigor that may instantiate postcoloniality's qualitative divergence from cursory grievance-based censure. As distinct from onomatopoeic contrariety (the "post" in postcolonial), the homology between postcoloniality and philosophy may foster precisely the speculative moves that can bring heterogeneity into possibility. Philosophical speculation in turn gives rise to an apocryphal—not Eurocentric identity politics-based—critical genealogy on account of taking difference seriously.

This book, therefore, does not approach philosophy from the outside to diagnose and/or correct its failures because, as the striving for a
non-antagonistic understanding of difference, postcoloniality is an intrinsic
part of philosophical understanding. An exegetically created encounter with
heterogeneity, with heterogeneous life entering into a concept meant to
understand living, may lead to *sincerely* earned negativity: it is the difference
between experience and its description that permits us to actually *learn* about
our historical inadequacy. Attentiveness to whether our conceptual frameworks are adequate for the historical moment in which they are needed may
be helpful in connecting the dots between philosophical speculation and a
politics of struggle, for understanding difference as inherently oppositional and
antagonistic runs the risk of repeating in political struggle the very premises
that led to the injustices in the first place. Only the brush with heterogeneity
makes self-reflection possible, and facilitating self-reflection is the common
responsibility of philosophy, feminism, and postcolonial theory. In a catastrophically challenged world, these disciplines must accompany one another
for the sake of the very heterogeneity that makes them subjects that matter.

Postcoloniality:
A Non-Antagonistic Understanding of Difference

I conceived of postcoloniality as the striving for a non-antagonistic understanding of difference in graduate school when I began my dissertation with Gayatri
Spivak's "Can the Subaltern Speak?" (1988).[11] The dissertation sought to answer
one question: who was Roop Kanwar? Kanwar was a nineteen-year-old widow
immolated (*sati*) on the funeral pyre of her husband on September 4, 1987, in
Deorala, India, in front of five thousand spectators. No matter what scholarly
tradition I used to understand her experience—philosophers such as Theodor
Adorno, Immanuel Kant, Michel Foucault, Friedrich Hegel; postcolonial theo-
rists such as Homi Bhabha, Edward Said, Frantz Fanon, Partha Chatterjee;
postcolonial feminists such as Ann McClintock, KumKum Sangari, Mrinalini
Sinha, Rajeswari Sunder Rajan; critical race theorists such as Paul Gilroy, Aimé
Césaire, Sander Gilman, Lewis Gordon; African-American feminists such as
Patricia Hill Collins, Toni Cade Bambara, Beverly Guy-Sheftall, bell hooks;
feminist philosophers such as Judith Butler, Eva Kittay, Uma Narayan, Iris
Young—I battled contradiction and unknowability. Consequently, I stated in
the introduction that the project was about a specific person whose experience
evokes horror. But also, the project did not seem to be about her.
     When deliberating on my own failure to answer the question my dis-
sertation raised, I did not comprehend why Spivak's concept of subalternity

in "Can the Subaltern Speak?" was assessed as synonymous with sheer victimization. Notwithstanding postcolonial feminist disapproval of Spivak's putative silencing of the subaltern, the essay's money line (if you will) is the acknowledgment that the "subaltern *subject* is irretrievably heterogeneous" (284).[12] To refute the normalization of silence, Spivak's titular question lends the lie to any proxy (*Vertreten*) or portrait (*Darstellen*) that undertakes verisimilitude. At that time in the Euro-US academy, the aggregate ontology of the colonized female body stood in stark contrast to the condition of philosophy that proffered an unknowable subject. Against this desire for authenticity, Spivak interjects her notorious lament that "the subaltern cannot speak" (308).[13] It may be worthwhile to briefly reread how she got to this statement, especially since "Can the Subaltern Speak?" entered its thirtieth year of publication in 2018.[14]

In her essay, Spivak demonstrates the geopolitical determination of discourses that declaredly vitiate the sovereignty of the western subject but in fact rehabilitate this subject's hegemony by ceding the intellectual as a transparent vehicle of the other's transparent voice. To garner actual avenues for subaltern women to speak, Spivak aims for a more nuanced understanding of ideology that can dispute subaltern women's reputed accessibility. First, the beneficent impulse to transmit the other's authentic voice presupposes a "monolith [. . .] [called] 'women' . . . whose unfractured subjectivity allows them to speak for themselves" (278). The subject is typified as fragmented and dispersed (subject rather than Subject) while the oppressed are valorized as unified and whole (for example, "the workers' struggle" [271]). Second, she is mindful of the intellectual's constitutive contradiction: any claim to represent the oppressed evades the representer's complicity in the international division of labor (272). Third, integrating consciousness with knowledge relinquishes the intricate terrain of desire, interest, and subjectivity traversed by ideological production (286).[15] Irrespective of disingenuous self-abdications as endowed by the state of philosophy, the sovereign subject's geopolitically determined normativity is the noumenal ground upon which the other's presumably self-conscious identity is promulgated (279–81). But, the intellectual cannot forsake its responsibility to represent (292); it cannot jettison its responsibility to history upon surmising a *sui generis* west; and, it cannot waive its responsibility to ethnography, as incriminated by the (un)canny extraction of its own itinerary via wiping out the other's (291).[16]

Spivak thereby shifts the burden of proof by cautioning that being on the exploiter's side of the international division of labor substantially incapacitates our philosophical agendas (287). Critical discourse cannot simply ferret out the other's purity of consciousness but must limn *how* subalternity is produced. By tracking the "*mechanics* of . . . constitution" (289), the intellectual "*systematically* 'unlearns' female privilege" (295) to avert the subaltern's displacement, appropriation, or idealization. On the contrary, the affective and ethical challenges faced by "the female intellectual as *intellectual*" (295, emphasis added), as she excavates an itinerary of unknowing, arbitrate an aporia (302). This is because whether subject or object the "subaltern *subject* is *irretrievably* heterogeneous" (284, second emphasis added). After defining subalternity as structurally produced silence, Spivak moves to her case study of *sati* (*suttee* is the colonial British spelling of *sati*), which exhibits epistemic violence in the narrow and general sense: colonialism serves as an "imperfect" (287) example of the violence intrinsic to establishing an *epistemé*. Colonial and postcolonial debates on *sati* oscillate the woman between subject- and object-status because they adhere to theoretical conceits like veracity (the voice of the woman) and radical subjectivity (the will of the woman). Spivak balks at these discursive constructions and in their stead moves further back in the opposite direction.

At that time in Euro-US postcolonial studies, she returns to the archive of antiquity, the Hindu texts of the *Dharmasastra* and the *Rg-Veda*, wherein she cannot come across the subjectivity of the widows who were burned, and, hence, have the makings of a "counter sentence" (297). When compared with culturalist accounts of *sati* that hypostatize false positives—western culture gives women the right to choose (to live); nonwestern culture gives women the right to choose (to die)—her scrutiny of the *Dharmasastra* and the *Rg-Veda* confirms that subject- and object-status actually mean the *same* thing: the widow's self (in outline) is a structural effect. Retroactive facsimiles of her voice or will culturally predestine the widow regardless of whether *sati* is ritual or crime. Postcoloniality in turn becomes mired in "a foreshortened history of female victimhood" (Hortense Spillers's phrase) because the widow's cultural lineaments are left intact. In place of the seductive expedience of veracity and radical subjectivity, Spivak characterizes the intellectual's charge as "measuring [the] silences" (296) by which the allegedly nonpareils obliterate their utter contingency. She scrupulously "plots a history" (297) of how structures recuperate the heterogeneity they resist as sexual difference: the woman is either a victim or heroic. Per Spivak's concept of subalternity, to want postcoloniality (the intricate terrain of desire, interest, and subjectivity) is to want heterogeneity at the site of that violence where meeting the gendered subaltern is the experience of nothing.

In an interview with Elizabeth Grosz, Spivak states that "the limits of . . . theories are disclosed by an encounter with . . . [the] other. . . . So, I am fundamentally concerned with that heterogeneity" (*Critic* 11). The systemic machinery of identity and difference blots (out) this heterogeneity in the interest of its own self-sustaining trajectory: any proper name can be inserted here. This heterogeneity's very irretrievability sets the course of the

postcolonial critic who tracks a process of unknowing that effects the subaltern's subject and object ventriloquist functions—that is, either the woman
wanted to die (*sati*), or the woman was forced to die (*suttee*) ("Subaltern"
297). The knowing and unknowing that so transpire are not contradictory
but aporetic. Spivak elaborates that

> one is haunted by the ghost of the undecidable. . . . When we find
> ourselves in the subject position of two determinate positions, both
> right—or both wrong, of course—one of which cancels the other,
> we are in an aporia which by definition cannot be crossed. Yet, it
> is not possible to remain in an aporia. It is not a . . . dilemma, a
> paradox, an antinomy. It can only be described as an experience.
> It discloses itself in being crossed. . . . In the aporia to decide is
> the burden of responsibility. ("Moral" 105–6)[17]

The fundamental concern with "that heterogeneity" instigates the experience of
crossing an aporia whence the synonymy of knowing and unknowing makes
ethics "a problem of relation rather than a problem of knowledge" (105).[18] *In*
this place of undecidability, we accede to "an experience of the figure"—that
is, "of that which is not logically possible" (105).

I suggest that the experience of the figure, of crossing an aporia, of
the burden of responsibility, is only viable when we bear a non-antagonistic
understanding of difference. An understanding of difference as inherently
oppositional and antagonistic repudiates the very heterogeneity that makes
any relationship possible. If we are defined by identitarian conceptual cultures,
whose administered systematicity is self-perpetuating, then self-preservation
perforce involves killing off our freedom to be responsible. Few are willing
to pay the price for responsibility in an upside-down world that makes liars
of us all *by virtue of category alone*. If postcoloniality is the pursuit of the
irretrievably heterogeneous, then it strives for that non-antagonistic understanding of difference that lets heterogeneity be.

Section One: Heterogeneity

The first section of the book is "Heterogeneity." The five chapters that comprise
this section introduce heterogeneity as a common subject matter of philosophy,
feminism, and postcolonial theory. The first chapter uses the bridges built by
postcolonial theorists' varied engagements with Theodor Adorno to suspend the
conventional and/or traditional dialectic of the western philosopher and (their)
postcolonial critic. As these scholars have already challenged Adorno's Eurocentrism, I concentrate on reorienting postcolonial theory from a diagnostic

and/or corrective standpoint to the philosophical charge of its enterprise. I conceive this philosophical charge to be the striving for a non-antagonistic understanding of difference. What is at stake is making postcoloniality real as a historical era and conceptual accomplishment so that it may truly make a difference in how we understand subjectivity and agency.

The second chapter reads the "Introduction" and the "Concepts and Categories" section of Theodor Adorno's *Negative Dialectics* (1973) to stage what may be called the postcolonial Adorno. I do not regard Adorno as a postcolonial critic *avant la lettre*, but indicate how negative dialectics such as postcoloniality is the striving for a non-antagonistic understanding of difference inimical to the inexorability of identity and difference. I recognize this germ of postcoloniality in Adorno's conceptual framework because he poses for philosophy an essentially historical task: to convey and uphold the heterogeneous. His philosophy and anti-philosophy at once honor the subject matter to be understood against an identity-based philosophical practice that forgets why its tradition brought this subject matter to life.

In chapter 3, I revisit Spivak's concept of subalternity as a placeholder for heterogeneity by reading portions of the "History" section of *A Critique of Postcolonial Reason: A History of the Vanishing Present* (1999). Specifically, the chapter follows Spivak as she trails imperial proceedings that dispense the role of agent/implement to the Rani of Sirmur for the changeover of an *epistemé: from* tradition *to* modernity. (Rani is the Hindi word for Queen. A fuller biography of the Rani is provided in the chapter itself.) The Rani's figuration in the colonial archive shows *how* identitarian conceptual cultures turn colonialism into civilizing mission. I suggest that Spivak's venture to experience "relation with" instead of "knowledge of" the Rani is important for three reasons: 1. Rummaging for the colonizer and colonized via an antagonistic understanding difference depreciates their heterogeneity. Both emerge ready-made. 2. These proper names cordon off what could *only* have been a historical relationship *in* colonialism between those identified. 3. Postcoloniality as the striving for a non-antagonistic understanding of difference upends precisely this legacy of Europe and its Others, which is still used to sheath Eurocentrism's practitioners notwithstanding its utter contingency.

Having located heterogeneity as a common subject matter of philosophy and postcolonial studies, I move in the fourth chapter to feminist theory. It reads Barbara Christian's iconic essay, "The Race for Theory" (1987), which received much opprobrium upon publication. Although Christian's statements were stereotyped as boosting minority identity politics, the chapter suggests that Christian's concept of the race for theory subverts the logic of major and minor traditions: since major theorists lack the cultural competency necessary to provide a meaningful understanding of difference, they cannot combat the actual historical challenges at hand. Major discourse abrogates this historical inadequacy by relegating non-Eurocentric traditions to perspectival roles in knowledge production without any general implications. In light of the *actual* course of history, however, Christian charts how major discourse erases *that* race for theory that black women will (always) have been.

Any postcolonial project in the Euro-US academy must acknowledge how certain strands of postcolonial theory are complicit in minimizing black women's works. At the time that Barbara Christian published "The Race for Theory," Eurocentrism pitted postcolonial theorists against older minorities by portraying the former's knowledge production as a model minority discourse. In response to this supersession, Spivak posits the African-American experience of negotiated independence as the paradigmatic case of postcoloniality in the United States. Spivak's analysis centers on South Asian migrancy for aspirational class advancement, but the chapter uses Spivak's description of Euro-US postcoloniality to make two suggestions: First, by challenging the antagonistic understanding of difference that prolongs major discourse's hegemony, black women's works are paradigmatically postcolonial. Second, black women's exercitation of the heterogeneity dislocated by the diminution to minor status makes black women's works exemplarily western. Inasmuch as the difference from the normative is underived from Eurocentrism, this tradition demonstrates the historical inadequacy of major discourse's conceptual cultures. The heuristic metonymy—black women's works are paradigmatically postcolonial and exemplarily western—brings Eurocentric identity politics to crisis: if the metaphysics of presence is no longer the only knowledge the west has to offer, then black women's works are essential for a philosophical understanding difference.

Section Two: The Resurrection of the Flesh

The first section of the book addresses heterogeneity as a common subject matter of philosophy, feminism, and postcolonial theory. It identifies this common subject matter to refute practitioners of Eurocentric identity politics who presuppose thinking to be their exclusive purview. These chapters delineate how a non-antagonistic understanding of difference prioritizes the subject matter rather than the theoretical framework at hand. In the second section, this postcolonial move of the book—not using the subject matter to sustain a tradition's sanctioned ignorance and hegemonic posture—brings these disparate conceptual frameworks together to confront climate change. I begin with the recognition that the sheer scale of climate change and its associated threats defy the book's operational logic of using heterogeneity as a value and tool to set a frame and facilitate the action. At issue is whether our understanding of postcoloniality as the striving for a non-antagonistic understanding of difference is adequate for a historical moment defined by a staggering *loss* of biological heterogeneity amid the ongoing and further anticipated devastation of species-life with the physical environment.

In Percy Bysshe Shelley's poem "Ozymandias" (1818), "a traveler from an antique land" describes his encounter with "Two vast and trunkless legs of stone / [that] Stand in the desert . . . [and] Near them, on the sand, / Half sunk a shattered visage."[19] The traveler observed this ruined, almost lost visage, "whose frown, / And wrinkled lip, and sneer of cold command, / Tell that its sculptor well those passions read / Which yet survive." He further recounts an inscription on the pedestal beneath the trunkless legs: "My name is Ozymandias, King of Kings; / Look on my Works, ye Mighty, and despair!" Whereas surety in our exceptionalism entitles us to presume a recipient of this ancestral injunction, Shelley ends his poem with a truer prospect: that "Round the decay / Of that colossal Wreck, boundless and bare / The lone and level sands stretch far away" (870). Shelley does not reassure the reader of the continuity of an intelligence who receives the admonishment because the "sands" subsume the human remainder. The extension of these sands around the almost entombed artifacts of disintegration—and then beyond the scope of the imaginative eye—undermines the posterity figured by hearsay: a speaker who relates to the reader what the traveler related to it.

In the middle distance of a humanized world, our grasping the possible impossibility of our self-preservation seems to require some future intelligence that gazes comprehendingly at flooded cities, whose towers and skyscrapers are hopefully at least nesting sites for colonies of seabirds. Yet, climate change is the ultimate context that imperils all that we presume and are. In lieu of an intelligence receiving an antecedent's warning, our geologic legacy may be met by illimitable silence. As the apotheosis of our life as a species, climate change takes us over a threshold: it mocks the "[h]alf sunk . . . shattered visage" of human exceptionalism. When nothing remains to interpret our oblivion, why the merciless infliction of *this* forgetting of our actual proportions? The very vastness and intimacy of climate change calls into question the prospect of exegesis, for there may be no apocryphal genealogy of a nameless traveler who saw the "Works" of a nameless sculptor who left a mark "on . . . lifeless things." It is *this* sculptor who made the "frown . . . and sneer" that "well . . . read" the abject silliness of a "King of Kings" whose decapitated head, lying askance, half-buried amidst "boundless and bare . . . sands," proclaims itself among his peerless "Works" (870).

The chapters in the second section do not necessarily refigure the absurdity of human hubris but follow the logic of scholars whose disputations of cultural determinism reiterate rather than rupture human exceptionalism. From within the catastrophic frame/arena of anthropogenic climate change, these readings garner how the striving for a non-antagonistic understanding of difference is historically inadequate when grounded by the nature and culture dualism. I chart the route that culminates in subalternity to arrive at that aporetic juncture where we might gain a cosmogonic peek at how a world is (un)made. At this moment of exegesis, we witness *how* nature's heterogeneity is cut (out) from our sacred texts *for* the functional concept of nature, which keeps nature itself in the penumbra of an exceptional species. *This* heterogeneity is experienced as the crossing of an aporia because cultural overdetermination manufactures nature as the signifier of irreducible human difference.

This section's chapters scuttle the logic of a humanized world that deflects its utter contingency by dint of a benighted cultural identity for which nature and culture actually mean the same thing: they are the result of conceptual cultures that fortify human exceptionalism. I suggest that because of the bloody brutality by which we damn nature—a history of theft, cruelty, and murder that (now) calls itself postcolonialism—the nature and culture dualism is no longer the exclusive provenance of western culture. The possible impossibility of our self-preservation as a *species* exposes the unrelenting silence that awaits us all. In keeping with our traditional doggedness and eternal hope, at least when it comes to lost causes, we may assume the risk of our further debasement in our equivalence with nature to embolden culture. Against this doctrinal casuistry, postcoloniality as the striving for a non-antagonistic understanding of difference allows explanations to come "from all sides" (Spivak, "Culture" 360). These explanations of culture—that is, of how *this* explanation of culture came to be *the* explanation of culture—invalidate cultural continuity fomented by an antagonistic understanding of difference.

I would like to return to that aporetic juncture wherein knowing and unknowing mean the same thing: both are an encounter with irretrievable heterogeneity. Spivak creates a "relation with" (not "knowledge of") the gendered subaltern to avoid what she terms her "moot decipherment" (*Critique* 309) as either subject or object, while I stage the experience of crossing an aporia quite differently. When exegesis shows us how nature is turned into its mercenary concept, we may experience the crossing of an aporia as what Adorno terms "the resurrection of the flesh" (*Negative* 207) to aver the actual suffering of subjects immured by the systemic machinery of identity and difference. The proper names conferred by this kind of conceptual culture are products of abstraction that turns what is alive into what is ancillary.

Marshaling Adorno's call for resurrected flesh, I turn the aporetic juncture into a kind of zero degree: here, knowing and unknowing take us to a potentiality of embodiment that is heterogeneous. The crossing of an aporia,

when experienced as the resurrection of the flesh, fills (in) what is hollowed
(out) to conjure an exceptional human being. *In* the place of the undecid-
able, where flesh is both itself and its own opposite—everything and nothing,
matter and form, nature and culture, animal and human—its resurrection is
when a decision must be made: if culture is "its own explanations" (Spivak,
"Culture" 360), then *who* are we going to be? Postcoloniality as the striving
for a non-antagonistic difference resurrects the flesh of an *anomalous* species
venerated for its *lack* of self-preservation to create "a solidarity that is transparent to itself and all the living" (Adorno, *Negative* 204). This philosophical
understanding of difference may provide a cosmogonic peek at how to suture
the King of Kings to the world in which we actually live.

In the second section, chapter 6 reads Adorno's lecture, "On Dying
Today" in *Metaphysics: Concepts and Problems* (2000). This lecture criticizes
metaphysics that confuses the absolute abstraction of human experience with
transcendence of cultural determinism. Adorno criticizes those metaphysical inquiries of death that recapitulate the dehumanization and functionalism modernity inflicts as naturalized culture. He posits dying *today* as the
object of metaphysics, as opposed to the side of being turned away from us,
because the concept of death should be adequate to the manifold ways in
which people actually die, today; otherwise metaphysics relegates people to
the same nothingness wreaked by capitalist culture. In this lecture, however,
Adorno makes an offhand comment that in comparison with all other species,
humans are singularly aware of our biological floor. But, how can we ever
know? The chapter tracks how it is possible for a species constituted by *lack*
of self-preservation to be nonetheless singularly aware of its biological floor. In
response to Adorno's swift dismissal of *all* other species, the chapter contests
the radical humanization of death by figuring our species as animals. At this
aporetic juncture, where all other species are present and absent, known and
unknown, self-preserving and unaware, this figuration is proportional to our
actual predicament. Anthropogenic climate change, our dying, *today*, extends
a cosmogonic peek at how effortless generalization extracts nothingness from
heterogeneity for the sake of human exceptionalism.

In chapter 7, I read Paul Gilroy's Wellek Library Lectures at the University
of California, Irvine, that were published as *Postcolonial Melancholia* (2006).
In these lectures, Gilroy invokes Adorno's negative dialectics to call for a vital
planetary humanism, which is modeled on the demotic multiculturalism of
urban spaces. Their organic and unruly forms of *bon homie* create a negative
dialectics of conviviality that can tackle ongoing environmental catastrophe.
The chapter suggests that Gilroy's recoding of liberal humanism as planetary
humanism dislocates the planet itself: though the planet is radically humanized, this humanized planet is radically urban. Such a naturalized evolution

progressively expands the scale of liberal humanism's alleged provenance: human→ urban→ planetary, which reiterates the nature and culture dualism that obliges a vital planetary humanism in the first place. Gilroy argues against an explicitly racial logic via the congruity between the planetary and urban culture—that is, by valorizing the demotic multiculturalism of a space categorially defined by the absence of nature. At this moment of undecidability, when the planetary is simultaneously urbane and natural, city and earth, concrete and galactic, the chapter figures the planetary as nature. In other words, I move in the opposite direction from Gilroy's naturalized evolution: if postcoloniality truly matters as a historical era and conceptual accomplishment, then for a vital planetary humanism, today, empire's first victim is the animal.

Although Spivak addresses problematic representational claims made by Foucault and Deleuze in "Can the Subaltern Speak?," chapter 8 focuses on contemporaneous postcolonial accounts of sati, which deploy an epistemic strategy of particularization via essentially historical categories of identity. I suggest that particularization may provide a better representation of the widow's predicament but this strategy also yields her readability: as sign of history, bearer of sanctified culture, exemplar of good wifehood, manifestation of the goddess, individual free will, honorable family woman, etc. These explanations lead to an aporia: the widow is culturally saturated yet also in possession of authentic voice and free will. The widow's ability to embody professedly exclusive narrative arcs signals these explanations' utter contingency: when we attempt to know her, she recedes further from our grasp. I provide these contemporaneous discourses on women's victimization because they capture a particular moment in postcolonial theory's institutionalization: while one exemplar of postcoloniality was harnessed for antagonistic cultural scripts by Euro-US multiculturalism, the other ignominiously lamented the subaltern's irretrievable heterogeneity for unevenly decolonizing space. These analyses provide the context for Spivak's reading of Bhuvaneswari Bhaduri's sati/suicide, whereupon she submits the intellectual's responsibility as to conceive radical alterity, discussed in the following chapter.

In "Postcolonialism's Archive Fever" (2000), Sandhya Shetty and Elizabeth Bellamy reread Spivak's reading of Bhuvaneswari Bhaduri's sati/suicide. Chapter 9 shows how this rereading cedes heterogeneity to sexual difference. Shetty and Bellamy state that the section on ancient Hindu scriptures in "Can the Subaltern Speak?" holds the key to subalternity: women are written-in into the archive as an exception to the general rule of suicide, which is prohibited except for men who reach a particular form of self-knowledge. This is the way subalternity is produced: written-in only as the good wife, she is irretrievably heterogeneous. Shetty and Bellamy agree with Spivak that Bhuvaneswari flips the script of sati when she hangs herself while menstruating.

(Menstruating women are barred from ascending the husband's funeral pyre because they are unclean and inauspicious.) As an addendum to the archive, Bhuvaneswari is the exception (menstruating) to the exception (good wifehood) to the exception (male self-knowledge) to the general rule (of suicide). The chapter suggests that their rereading of her menstrual blood does not flip *sati*'s principal conceit of good wifehood because Bhuvaneswari's *sati*/suicide preserves this teleological potentiality: she is not an unsanctioned mother. At this instant, when menstrual blood is actual and potential, auspicious and inauspicious, clean and unclean, the chapter figures menstrual blood as the erasure of sexual difference. Upon her hanging, Bhuvaneswari is cut (out) from our sacred texts to leave behind (her) menstrual blood: "she" is (now) utterly contingent. For the heterogeneous, Bhuvaneswari annuls her symbolic integrity. In this upending of the antagonistic difference that ensconces both colonizer and nationalist, she makes outside what is inside: a horizon of potential embodiment—that is, of all that life can be.[20]

Chapter 10 reads Hortense Spillers's essay, "Mama's Baby, Papa's Maybe: An American Grammar Book" (1987), which was published a year before Spivak's "Can the Subaltern Speak?" In this essay, Spillers remarks that American feminism's "foreshortened history of female victimhood" ignores the particular cultural logic that establishes New World domesticity: due to the slave-holding civil codes, which installs the curious interchangeability of "black women" and "it," black women breed property not children. Spillers's search for these missing persons takes her to The Middle Passage when tools of the trade (whips, chains, knives, etc.) must (first) make black women into flesh and blood entities to (then) turn them into unsanctioned mothers. Black women so *un*gendered bear the hieroglyphics of an impossible futurity that orders all (else) that follows. In Spillers's revision of an American Grammar, however, gendered and *un*gendered come to mean the same thing: sanctioned motherhood, as she maintains sexual difference as the ground of culture. Since the heterogeneous possibilities available for pre-view on board the slave ship are *already* human in outline, Spillers misses the *other* flesh and blood entity listed in the logs of commercial enterprise: livestock. The radical humanization of the planet manifest in *this* oxymoronic name thwarts our recognition that to have bodies ripped apart, torn open, seared, mutilated, divided, is what it means to be (an) animal. A prior ordering of nature and culture, therefore, is the essentially historical condition of possibility for making a slave. In this aporetic predicament, when the flesh and blood entity is gendered and ungendered, live and stock, human and animal, the chapter figures the flesh and blood entity as that unsanctioned Mother who is the (only) possibility for (a) culture.

In the conclusion, the book's accruing a sense of scale moves from flesh and blood, rural and urban, animal and earth, to the planet. Spivak's concept of planetarity dislocates human exceptionalism with a para-galactic alterity by depositing us as a planetary accident. Understanding life as accidental (for example, but for the meteor sixty-six million years ago . . .) is an imaginative endeavor because radical alterity, as underived from identitarian morphologies, eludes our conceptual cultures. To this end, the conclusion is modeled after Spivak's canonical essay, "Three Women's Texts and a Critique of Imperialism" (1985). In this essay, Spivak reads *Jane Eyre* (1847), *Wide Sargasso Sea* (1966), and *Frankenstein* (1818) to limn the limits of feminist individualism, which occurs at the expense of the native subaltern. My conclusion supplants what Spivak terms "soul making" (248) (the colonial imperative to humanize the globe) with the planetary (the postcolonial imperative to dehumanize the planet). It reads three women's texts that model how to provide a cosmogonic peek at our not-quite-not-a-relation with radical alterity. The shift in perspective, from cultural saturation to the utter contingency of living, does not rely on an antagonistic understanding of difference, but stages how a world is (un)made from the heterogeneous to condemn us all to an illimitable silence. In this time of consequences, these women's texts affirm that learning to take proportional footsteps may lead the way home.

PART ONE

HETEROGENEITY

Chapter One

Objects Behaving Like Subjects

Because We're Way Past the Post

Was my freedom not given to me then in order to build the world of the *You*?

—Frantz Fanon, *Black Skin, White Masks*

[H]ow does *our* sense of the West distort *our* sense of ourselves and of *our* traditions?

—Emmanuel C. Eze, "Toward a Critical Theory of Postcolonial African Identities"

I'm the last Jewish intellectual. . . . The only true follower of Adorno. Let me put it this way: I'm a Jewish-Palestinian.

—Edward Said, *Power, Politics, Culture*

[D]o not accuse, do not excuse, make it 'your own,' turn it around and use.

—Gayatri Spivak, *A Critique of Postcolonial Reason*

I. Past-ing the Post

As Edward Said attests, postcolonial scholars find Adorno to be a kindred spirit because of his criticisms of modernity. They use his work to further questions of identity and contemporary global reality while also challenging Adorno's Eurocentrism, which sustains a violent and hegemonic western culture. This chapter builds on these versatile conversations with Adorno by reorienting postcolonial theory from cultural criticism to the philosophical charge of its enterprise. It tries to get past the reversal implied by the "post" by unsettling the conventional and/or traditional dialectic of western philosophy and postcolonial criticism, which allots to the latter a derivative and marginal rank. The chapter reads postcolonial works that enlist Adorno to confront a post-independence era marked by continued depredation via globalization and the international division of labor.[1] I suggest that this compelling and bridge-building recruitment of Adorno nevertheless dispels postcoloniality to a diagnostic and/or corrective standpoint in relation to the former's apparently self-evident claim to the constructive frame. Affixing postcolonial criticism to a diagnostic and/or corrective standpoint maintains postcoloniality's adherence to belatedness and marginality, and cements a critical stance that runs the risk of leaving one of Eurocentrism's fundamental premises untouched: difference as inherently oppositional and antagonistic. Postcoloniality gauges how identitarian conceptual cultures ward off heterogeneity to secure jurisdiction *by virtue of category alone*. As the striving for a non-antagonistic understanding of difference, it confounds and limits our habitual disciplinary lexicons, and, hence, is an intrinsic part of philosophical understanding.

II. Adorno and Postcolonial Theory

In *Exotic Parodies: Subjectivity in Adorno, Spivak, and Said* (1995), Asha Varadharajan carries out a postcolonial analysis of Adorno's conceptual contributions. She makes a comparison between Adorno, Spivak, and Said possible by characterizing the formidable scope of their work as differing cultural approaches to subjectivity. For example, she uses Adorno's criticism of progressive dialectical synthesis to resist fixed definitions that automatically serve colonial interests (xxii). Simultaneously, she protests that the postcolonial theorist is coy about her attempts to avoid a political encounter with the subaltern, even as this political encounter is inevitable (xxv). The postcolonial theorist is subject to a Manichean (not aporetic) fate: she struggles between her alleged political fidelity to her "origins" and her felicitous adroitness with major metropolitan theory (xvii). In Varadharajan's challenge to metropolitan interests, which continue colonial interests in a postcolonial guise, the polarity she creates between fidelity and adroitness is a rendition of the colonial/postcolonial divide: instead of the native in the colony, the site of this battle is the metropolitan feminist in the Euro-US academy. And, the inaugural paradigm, in her estimation, of this newly minted academic's coyness about avoiding a political encounter with the subaltern, is the work of Gayatri Spivak.

Varadharajan suggests that Spivak neglects the privileges that allow the metropolitan feminist "to roam the corridors of power at will, all the while proclaiming her marginality" (85). She asks whether Spivak's emphasis on women "[without] access to the culture of imperialism as objects of knowledge . . . impl[ies] that resistance can only come from those lucky enough to be 'shuttles' than victims" (85). (The distinction she makes between shuttles and victims is unclear because the shuttling in Spivak's account produces the victimization.) Be that as it may, she warns that Spivak's focus on the subaltern assumes that victimization necessarily leads to awareness and action (xxvii). She criticizes Spivak, moreover, for not recognizing that sheer survival requires the subaltern to evaluate social, political, and cultural *epistemés* and their concomitant truth-claims (86). To sum up: subalterns resist; victimization does not automatically prompt rebellion; and, survival itself drives victims to be perspicacious. With these somewhat impuissant pronouncements that rely on positivistic notions of representation, Varadharajan alleges that Spivak's distinction between shuttle and subaltern turns the latter into the insubstantial object of theory. She may be objecting to the presumption that the subaltern is of such epistemological interest that she *can* be made to shuttle between subject- and object-status, but she registers Spivak's effort to track *how* subject- and object-status enact silence as the subaltern's further curtailment. This stunting of subaltern insubordination—that is, a politically motivated disregard for actual subaltern defiance—allows for self-indulgent musings on theory's inevitable groundlessness (xxiv). On the basis of this *other* category of subaltern victimhood, which has not materialized owing to Spivak's concept of subalternity, Varadharajan brands the migrant Euro-US feminist academic as the native subaltern's metropolitan nemesis.

Against Spivak's recalcitrance in light of this *other* subaltern's dissent, Varadharajan puts forward what can be described as a determinate-philosophical approach versus a theoretical-postcolonial approach (each attributed to Adorno and Spivak, respectively). Observing that the postcolonial theorist in her depiction is caught between fidelity and adroitness, she begins with the object's political desire: if theory is inevitably groundless, why did the object suffer (20)? To answer this question, she applies Adorno's philosophy to Spivak's politics to betoken Adorno's conceptual contributions as far more politically valid than what she surmises as postcolonial theory's claim to universality. Thanks to her valorization of substantive rather than theoretical discourses of subjectivity (27), Varadharajan ratifies a conventional and/or traditional dialectic: philosophy is universal, postcoloniality is particular; philosophy's universality yields substantive politics, postcoloniality's particularity yields theoretical inconclusiveness. By virtue of these predications of universal (substantive politics) and particular (theoretical inconclusiveness), which oust postcolonial theory from the realm of knowledge production and ideology critique, Varadharajan applies Adorno's "(merely) philosophical discourse" (82)

to the specific case of a masculine Eurocentric Self and its feminine Ethnic
Other: the feminist academic secures metropolitan interests (in cahoots with/
via mimicry of a masculine Eurocentric Self), but the feminine Ethnic Other's
ontological negativity questions the dualistic process of definition (83).[2]

At this point in Varadharajan's narrative, the feminine Ethnic Other
(interchangeable with the native subaltern) holds the metropolitan feminist
accountable for her suffering through an actual political encounter between
them. (She does not explain how this political encounter takes place.) Irrespective of this profession of her political desire, however, the feminine Ethnic
Other still seems to shuttle between a constitutive silence (radically other)
and a derivative sameness (negatively other). Varadharajan rebukes Spivak for
ignoring subaltern resistance to buttress her position in the Euro-US academy
(89) without considering how her own differentiation between radical otherness and negative otherness mirrors Spivak's differentiation between alterity
and identity, respectively. Varadharajan can only dispute the ethereality that
ensues from the metropolitan feminist's avoidance of a political encounter
with the feminine Ethnic Other by an overt politicization of subaltern subjectivity. The feminine Ethnic Other's doubtlessly transparent and readily
accessible political interests counteract the metropolitan feminist's disavowal
of culpability when the latter reduces subalternity to a theoretical problem *par
excellence*. To resuscitate this abstract subaltern via an infusion of determinate
politics, therefore, she cannot grant any substantive basis to Spivak's concept
of subalternity, when political interests (colonial *or* metropolitan) generate the
subaltern's ethereality in the first place. Varadharajan applies the determinate-
philosophical to the theoretical-postcolonial for the feminine Ethnic Other's
political desire to gain priority over metropolitan interests precisely because
Spivak's reputedly self-interested discourse eclipses subaltern protest.

Having established a distinction between the substantive subaltern
(universal determinate-philosophical) and the abstract subaltern (particular
theoretical-postcolonial), Varadharajan reinstates a gendered subaltern whose
body is the site of political remonstration against historical processes. Since
this seemingly fit to purpose subaltern signifies radical otherness *and* negative
otherness, she embodies the immaculate (radical) *and* the immanent (negative);
the radical has the quality of pristine other-worldliness, the immanent the
quality of destitute this-worldliness. This tension is resolved by recourse to the
heterogeneity of both materiality and subalternity, which allows for surprise
(99, 101) and epistemological dissent (108). In this manner, Varadharajan's
subaltern becomes the locus of an immaculate, radical, pristine materiality
and an immanent, negative, destitute materiality. Contra progressive dialectical synthesis (Spivak sublates the subaltern's political force by rendering
her theory's insubstantial object), negative dialectics produce refusal: of the

determinate and the theoretical, the substantive and the abstract, the negative and the radical, the immanent and the immaculate, and the political and the inconclusive.

Varadharajan contends that Spivak ignores counterhegemonic ideological production when she holds the political encounter with the subaltern in perpetual abeyance. In fact, she goes even further and suggests that Spivak infantilizes the subaltern, as she makes the experience of oppression itself a "matter of gullibility" (95). When Spivak extols the vertiginous potential for cultural explanations released by theory's inevitable groundlessness (93), she annexes subaltern activism to an ineluctably metropolitan point of reference. The feminist academic's identity-based pursuits, which include a theoretical understanding of constitutive privilege, supersede the problem of subaltern subjectivity (95). She censures Spivak's susceptibility to a "jargon of authenticity" (97), a particularly low blow because Adorno used this neologism to criticize Heidegger's genocidal romanticization of German identity, despite Varadharajan's own admission that political action inexorably has ambiguous outcomes (96).[3] Spivak is reproached for procuring her third world bona fides by dissipating the "particularity of the subaltern woman in the seeming inexhaustibility of the category" (98–99)[4] to the effect that theoretical-postcolonial practice unlike determinate-philosophical politics becomes an exotic parody of liberal humanism.

In her critique, Varadharajan rightly regards Adorno as a valuable resource for postcolonial criticism because negative dialectics, as a utopic mode of substantive cognition, aims for particularity without recourse to the dogmatic or arbitrary—that is, particularity underived from the façade erected by identity and difference. What remains unclear is why she charges postcolonial theory with lack of substantive content given that concrete engagement with material realities (including those that mediate its own existence) is one of postcolonial theory's hallmarks. Discounting postcolonial theory's characteristic rejection of discursive detachment to assert Adorno's exemplarity undermines the critical force of Adorno's conceptual contributions against a long standing European philosophical tradition. It also projects this long standing European philosophical tradition's worst impulses—abstraction, political irrelevancy, tribalism, culturalism, occlusion of material conditions, etc.—onto postcolonial theory. Even so, Varadharajan's use of Adorno to check postcolonial theory's theoretical proclivities presumes a coherent and identifiable subaltern. This positivistic move permits her to sidestep the representational issues that institute subalternity. To accuse Spivak of delivering the feminine Ethnic Other to the very metropolitan interests that orchestrate her insubstantiality, she must conflate irretrievability with inexhaustibility. She must also distill negative dialectics into a postcolonial—that is, *not* metropolitan—feminist practice that plucks the subaltern out of obscurity so that she may prevail over her subject- and object-status by (finally) professing her political desire.

Her poignant essay, " 'On the Morality of Thinking,' or Why Still Adorno" (2007), similarly applies Adorno's conceptual contributions to postcolonial criticism but, here, postcoloniality results in (pejoratively understood) politics and not philosophy. To counter Adorno's relative absence in postcolonial theory in comparison to other philosophers, Varadharajan fuses postcolonial practice with thinking or the philosophical. She takes at face value metropolitan efforts that either subject Adorno to a hermeneutics of suspicion due to his Eurocentrism or apply Adorno's criticisms of modernity to the political problem at hand, which, in turn, is abbreviated to an almost singular preoccupation with the politically exhausted but unsuitably represented issue of difference and minority (317). This exhaustion-cum-unsuitability can be rectified if postcolonial theory were to dedicate itself to eradicating suffering *globally* (319): the insularity and parochialism of identitarian squabbles must give way to global cultural politics that facilitate opportune deterritorialization from local political agendas "if only because the global face of culture . . . wears [colonialism's] scars" (318–19).

Such compliance with Eurocentric identity politics' diminution of postcoloniality not only presumes postcolonial theory's lack of philosophical valence but also runs the risk of corroborating an insidious stereotype: philosophy transcends via thinking, postcoloniality placates via identitarianism. Varadharajan's prescription for political exhaustion is postcolonial theory's transformation into a global cultural politics, which is envisioned as the postcolonial instantiation of Adorno's understanding of thinking. In addition to being allotted a derivative and marginal rank, postcolonial theory is stripped even of a diagnostic and/or corrective standpoint irrespective of its innovative and multifaceted assessments of European thought. This narrative obscures the actual historical record of postcolonial opposition to some of European philosophy's most codified premises—that is, of what its inheritors regard as thinking or the philosophical. Postcolonial politics must instead become more global rather than continue to challenge Eurocentrism (which is why "still Adorno"). Aside from the questionable wisdom of such a course (a process of displacement, appropriation, or idealization that Ato Quayson terms "postcolonializing"), the global in Varadharajan's framework becomes synonymous with the philosophical.[5]

Neil Lazarus's essay "Hating Tradition Properly" (1999) similarly allots postcolonial theory a derivative and marginal rank by coupling Edward Said, Homi Bhabha, and Gayatri Spivak with Foucault, Lacan, and Derrida, respectively. These purportedly representative thinkers establish their credibility at the expense of Marx, as the accentuation of discourse analysis shortchanges the negative potential of modernity (23). Lazarus seems to suggest that concentrating on Marx will allow us to hate tradition properly,[6] which credits postcolonial theorists as inheritors of modernity but still apportions them a diagnostic and/or corrective standpoint. Of course, Lazarus's disquiet about Marx cannot be adjudged as entirely misplaced, as postcolonial scholars such as Aijaz Ahmad, Frederic Jameson, Benita Perry, Partha Chatterjee, Ranajit Guha, Sumit Sarkar, etc. have also confronted the elision of material analyses since the early days of postcolonial theory's Euro-US institutionalization. In keeping with Lazarus's concern, Keya Ganguly's "Adorno, Authenticity, Critique" (2007) abjures the Eurocentric linguistic and psychoanalytic turn of postcolonial theory, but she remains vigilant about the one-sidedness of historical materialism. She also relegates Marxist postcolonial criticism to a diagnostic and/or corrective standpoint because it apprehends processes that remained in the shadows for Adorno's Eurocentric perspective (254).[7] While the usefulness of Marx, Foucault, Lacan, Derrida, etc. for postcolonial theory is beyond dispute, we must not stunt the latter's genealogy and methodology to European philosophy and its applications, respectively.[8]

Alongside its dependence on Marx, Foucault, Lacan, and Derrida, Fred Dallmayr characterizes postcolonial theory as a variety of postmodernism, which in his estimation has Adorno as its precursor (34). As postmodernism has transformed philosophy from a "sequence of school doctrines into an again open field of inquiry" (33), the changes it parleys create a "transgressive mood" (33) that refutes Eurocentrism with genuinely global and multicultural contexts. Dallmayr's account, however, relies on an overestimation of postmodernism's putative transgressions of doctrinal philosophical practice. He typecasts postcoloniality as a benign cultural component of postmodernity, which neutralizes its critical force as a historical era and conceptual accomplishment. For example, he declares that Edward Said's nomadic intellectualism, drawing its inspiration from Adorno's concept of nonidentity, prioritizes the diasporic intellectual's aesthetic production (35).[9] When the crux of the relationship between counter-identity and no-identity is the diasporic intellectual who is located "everywhere and nowhere," real life agonies are obscured (44). In fact, Said renews the dichotomy between Orient and Occident, as the Orient still functions as a particularizing counterweight to the Occident, or as an indistinct demimonde for Occidental denial (46).

Insofar as Said's version of nomadism is not entirely faithful to Adorno's version of homelessness, his oscillation between counter-identity and no-identity does not fully realize the tangible traction-based possibilities of negative dialectics (51–52). Dallmayr may fault Said for overlooking the true critical potential of Adorno for postcolonial criticism, but he grants the capability for attaining substantive content only to negative dialectics. Said's application of

Adorno—that is, of the postmodernism that has Adorno as its precursor—unlike Adorno's work, obscures real world agonies. According postcoloniality a predominantly Eurocentric genealogy (Hegel, Descartes, Deleuze, Lyotard, Foucault, etc.) leads to remarkable results[10]: no matter the *actual* course of history, postcolonial theory deters substantive content; Eurocentric postmodernism creates genuinely global and multicultural contexts; and, Edward Said's concept of nomadic intellectualism promotes Orientalism. It is Europe that has de facto thought of everything: philosophy *and* postmodernism, Eurocentrism *and* global and multicultural contexts, diasporic intellectual *and* real-world agonies, school doctrines *and* open fields. Shorn of even a diagnostic and/or corrective standpoint, postcoloniality as an extremely hard-won historical achievement seems to teach us nothing.

III. The Philosopher and the Postcolonial Critic

I would like to return to Neil Lazarus at this moment to provide an example of how the conventional and/or traditional dialectic of the western philosopher and (their) postcolonial critic obviates possibilities for change imparted by postcoloniality as a historical era and conceptual accomplishment. The coupling of western philosopher and postcolonial critic enables the latter to acquire a global conceit whereby postcoloniality becomes virtually tantamount to criticism of any injustice anywhere. This kind of universality stems from a collusive interdependence that stages oppositional dialectics as a critical stance. As the striving for a non-antagonistic understanding of difference, postcoloniality delimits the consolidation of proper names on dualistically predetermined ground for a sincerely earned negativity. In lieu of a myopic view of history that cordons off what can *only* be a relationship between those so identified, small moments of affinity and disappointment release the heterogeneity that confounds and limits our habitual disciplinary lexicons.

In "Modernism and Modernity: T.W. Adorno and White South African Literature" (1986), Neil Lazarus criticizes Adorno's philosophy of history for its universalism in spite of his own diagnosis of this philosophy's incompleteness (135). Lazarus applies this philosophy of history to the prospective cultural instance of a post-apartheid white South African literature. Arguing that contemporary white South African literature is unequivocally modernist, he also solicits an alternative understanding of modernity (150). For Lazarus, Adorno undermines meaningful change as a practical possibility because of his unmitigated sense of resistance and acute negativity (146). He explains this lack of practical possibility by drawing an inverted historical parallel: the contemporaneous presence of revolutionary black masses for white South

African writers reflects the contemporaneous absence of proletarian resistance for Adorno.

For this modified understanding of modernity, Lazarus criticizes the "evolutionary mood" (153) he attributes to Adorno. For example, he says that Adorno's argument against committed art is contingent and political and not aesthetically and abstractly motivated, for in modern South Africa committed art can still have cultural valence as a meaningful strategy. Adorno's understanding of modernity, therefore, cannot countenance resistance in the non-European world. But Lazarus also presents contemporary white South Africa as a "still recognizably *modern*" (143) space by providing a moving analysis of white South African modernity, which seems condemned to a fetishistic obsession with waiting (131). This fetishistic obsession demonstrates the oneiric conformity of majority white opinion (134). (One could argue that this fetishistic obsession with waiting, its unpopularity among a majority of white South Africans, keeps the actual implications of post-apartheid South Africa at bay.)

To establish white South Africa's indubitable modernity, Lazarus compares anti-apartheid white South African intellectuals with their European counterparts (143). He uses a political frame to discuss literature—even utopia is described politically as a "socialist collectivity" (142). Since Adorno's examination of fascism makes Eurocentric historical sweeps—he goes from Hegel to Hitler without a sideward glance at imperialism—Lazarus tenders the white South African example to demonstrate Adorno's historical incompleteness (135). Lazarus's quarrel with Eurocentrism is obviously appropriate but it remains unclear how he can criticize Adorno's historical sweeps and his historical incompleteness simultaneously, as the latter charge seems to suggest that Adorno's historical sweeps were simply not far-reaching enough to cover imperialism as well. He characterizes Adorno's response to Marx in the introduction to *Negative Dialectics*, moreover, as a political explanation for the historical possibility of fascism, which omits that this rebuttal also comprises the "opening sentences" (143) of a painstaking philosophical (not just historico-political) argument.

In fact, Adorno's rejoinder to Marx takes Hegel, Heidegger, Kant, etc. as its interlocutors *before* it arrives at the Holocaust, which is more explicitly discussed in the much later section on metaphysics. Lazarus's constriction of this conversation to a political explanation may lead to another historical parallel (in excess of white South African writers and their Adornian counterparts): if the philosophical can be cast as the political, which, in turn, is equated with Eurocentrism, then postcoloniality, too, loses any philosophical valence in bucking Eurocentrism. Any postcolonial exposition is reduced to a political critique at the expense of elaborating how postcoloniality is an intrinsic part of a philosophical understanding of difference. Lazarus's attempt to dispute the historical adequacy of Adorno's understanding of modernity appears to discount Eurocentrism's cost to the philosophical, a political over-determination that confuses the intellectual's context-specific effectiveness with its *entire* historical burden. Lazarus shortchanges the implications of postcoloniality—philosophy and postcolonial criticism sustain each other as antagonistic political discourses—yet he specifies an intellectual who must be politically viable while also respond in humanity's name against the undue instrumentalism of rationalized society (144).

Adorno's critical intellectualism expresses itself in the language of salvation because of the absence of proletarian resistance, unlike in the post-apartheid era, when white South Africans witness a "militant, self-possessed, disciplined, increasingly powerful force for revolutionary change—the black working class, 'the masses,' 'the people' " (144–45). After actual history expended its historical alibi of ontological primacy, the whiteness contemporary South Africans live comes across as stultifying. (Lazarus does not say this explicitly but provisional whiteness looms as misfortune; it is not greeted as a marvelous instance of historical luck.) Following its lack of historical viability, white writers cannot use ontological primacy to confer moral or representative authority upon themselves; they kowtow to their irrelevance (and concomitant pain) in accordance with the restricted nature of their competence or ability: "to the extent that their writings are representative, they are representative of enlightened white opposition to apartheid, no more and no less" (145).

Even though Lazarus's modification of Adorno is ascribable to the coincident vitality of black revolutionary masses, it is white South African writers who, notwithstanding their ennui and stasis, are "still recognizably *modern*" (143). Lazarus's diagnostic and/or corrective standpoint appropriates and displaces the *actual* agents of change with a Eurocentric genealogy, which grants a *recognizable* modernity to white South African writers. No mention is made of the potentialities for non-white supremacist *relationships* with the black masses (now) released by an extremely hard-won historical achievement: the post-apartheid era. Lazarus's genealogy of modernity prevents the "essential gesture" (155) (Nadine Gordimer's phrase) made possible by actual history: whiteness is a choice; it is not ontological. I do not think Lazarus would dis-agree with this line of argument but he presents a series of comparisons that amplify Eurocentrism. First, he criticizes Adorno's dogmatic sense of complete resistance and absolute negativity (146). Second, he contrasts Adorno's outright idealism with white South African writers' ambivalence. Third, he contrasts white South African writers' ambivalence with the revolutionary idealism and hopeful optimism of black South African theorists and activists (147).

Why would white South African writers feel "much closer" (146) to their Adornian counterparts than to contemporaneous black South Africans?

Lazarus describes a modernist vanguard that is marked by inconsequentiality and self-consciousness (148) but remains committed to truthfulness (140), which predominant white opinion considers a cultural betrayal. Just the same, by accepting white South African writers' socially positioned "extremity" (147), could Lazarus be dissimulating an unwitting racial solidarity as a shared melancholy? Could this publicly consecrated self-abnegation-as-respectful-waiting place the burden of history on apartheid's victims and not its beneficiaries—that is, on those black masses that were already the actual agents of change?[11] This suspicion is heightened when Lazarus minimizes the resolution of this respectful waiting to a question of genre: "as a discourse . . . [contemporary white South African writing] is so *ethically* saturated, so *humanistic* . . . so concerned to *represent* reality, and so *rationalistic* that it would be quite inappropriate to describe it as *postmodernist*" (148). Avoiding the intellectual's responsibility to build non-white supremacist relationships, white South African writers give the impression of anticipating a future built only by others. Lazarus reifies white South African writers' perceived lack of "cultural options" (148) by fashioning a writer's genealogy that removes those black bodies on which the battle for modernity was waged: Lazarus can tweak Adorno's philosophy of history because of their modernist struggles in the first place.

A paradoxical form of hope for white South African writers is being historically recognized on account of black South African militancy, self-possession, discipline, and power. Although the post-apartheid era is rife with openings to dismantle black difference, Lazarus acknowledges that post-apartheid whiteness reconstitutes the "protocols of imperial legality" (150). This is a whiteness that, as with Coetzee's magistrate in *Waiting for the Barbarians* (1980), remains tied to a progressive narrative of western civilization. But why does Lazarus suggest that the doubled alienation of white South African writers (from the black masses and other whites) is most fittingly apprehended by the "antinomies of Self and Other" (149), especially since he qualifies Adorno's philosophy of history? He recognizes Adorno's glaring omission of imperialism in his explanation of fascism but still describes the white intellectual's "predicament" in post-apartheid South Africa as "*unambiguously* modernist" (150, emphasis added). He rushes to fill in the "space of *historical* realization" (150) with a categorial genealogy that turns our gaze to Europe, not to actually decolonizing terrain. (For example, this sentence dazzles: "To read Coetzee is to understand why, in the years after World War II, Lukács was to reverse himself and to begin celebrating Kafka as a *realist*" [150].)

Lazarus appreciates that his call for a "*potentially* sacrificial . . . trust" (150) that rejects the instrumentalism emblematic of Manichean battles deviates from Enlightenment discourses. Yet, even as this paradoxical form of hope is being historically recognized, the black masses do not emerge as inheritors of these Enlightenment discourses (being its victims). Here, a historical sleight

of hand permits whiteness to automatically stand in for an always-complete
Europe regardless of the particularities of South African history. Lazarus
cites Breytenbach's emphasis on dilution, ongoing change, "losing control,"
and dealing with "whatever mass organizations the people may throw up"
(151), but the absence of a named author or leader among the masses, or
a sustained reading of black literature and theory, unlike that of European
harbingers and influences, smack these worries with an *anachronistic* longing
for the transhistorical cultural valence of an *exceptional* (white) intellectual
consciousness. (Indeed, one could read waiting white South African writers'
self-abdication following their historical obsolescence as the surreptitious
recoding of this exceptional [white] intellectual consciousness.)

Brushing aside his admission that a "catalogue of functional similari-
ties" (151) cannot make white South African literature modernist in Adorno's
sense, Lazarus asks whether Adorno's theory of modernity is flexible enough
for the "cultural instance" (151) of white South African literature, or would
it "dissolve" local particularities due to Adorno's "evolutionary mood" (153).
Adorno is chastised for Eurocentrism because of his universal historical sweeps,
but, at the same time, his theory of modernity is also unfavorably evaluated
for not being total (flexible?) enough in its relevancy. Adorno could construe
only very rarefied differences between fascism and bourgeois democracy
because he understood modernity as a historical dialectic between progress
and regression, which becomes seamlessly configured in its evolutionary
movement. Still, Lazarus commends Adorno's insights into the continuities
between fascists and the bourgeoisie before relating that his philosophy of
history cannot "explain [. . .] the vitality of oppositional culture and politics,
not just in South Africa, but *globally*" (152, emphasis added).

From there, Lazarus's criticisms become increasingly stronger: for
Adorno, history is an "undifferentiated story with intensifying violence as its
sole motif" (152); "[w]hat has happened in history is treated by Adorno as
the only thing that could have happened" (153); Adorno conflates reification
and rationalization, which allows him to treat social struggle as compulsorily
lagging (153); and, he unequivocally inoculates his theoretical apparatus from
social struggle "not in the center but at the margins of the world system"
(153). Surprisingly, we arrive at such a nihilistic verdict irrespective of the
connection Lazarus establishes between white South African writers and their
Adornian counterparts, albeit with the former in a better position because
of revolutionary black South Africans. (Perhaps what white South African
writers and predominant white opinion are contending with is the wretched
banality of poverty, racism, disease, genocide, exploitation, ethnocentrism,
AIDS, refugee crises, homophobic patriarchy, etc. now that post-apartheid
blackness cannot be contained as an existential threat, which requires a

defensive dramatic posture unlike the suspended animation of waiting for "whatever mass organizations the people may throw up.")

Be that as it may, Lazarus concludes his essay with a brilliant move. He cites a particular passage from *Minima Moralia* (1978) in the footnotes to support his claim that Adorno regards Auschwitz as a "categorical break in the flow of history" (154).

> Auschwitz cannot be brought into analogy with the destruction of the Greek city-states as a mere gradual increase in horror, before which one can preserve tranquility of mind. Certainly, the unprecedented torture and humiliation of those abducted in cattle-trucks does shed a deathly-livid light on the most distant past, in whose mindless, plan-less violence the scientifically confected was already teleologically latent. The identity lies in the non-identity, in what, not yet having come to pass, denounces what has. (*Minima* 234–35; quoted in Lazarus, "Modernism" 154)

This depiction of Auschwitz as a categorical break in history's flow is "enough to suggest the possibility of its [directional and evolutionarily historical] dialectical opposite" (154). When the historical sweep from Greek city-states to Auschwitz is broadened to include imperialism, Auschwitz becomes a normalized horror imported to Europe from the colonies. In other words, Auschwitz's nonidentity in identity reveals modernity as "heterogeneous and differentially layered" (154).

Heterogeneity not only empowers the intellectual to muddle the binary of flow and break but also divulges modernity's nonidentity in identity as a "vital and nonracial legacy" (155). But, in his denial of evolutionary history, Lazarus awards the intellectual with a very different itinerary: postcolonial theorists have the charge of salvaging modernism—no less—from Adorno's evolutionary system. Adorno's schema

> impose[s] its universality on their particularities, its totality on their phenomenalities, *inexorably* transforming all local developments into side shows [that] . . . would *only* serve to confirm . . . a dialectic of defeat[.] . . . [H]istory would be able to teach it [world spirit] *nothing.* (153, emphases added)

Adorno's understanding of modernity cannot explain vital politics in South Africa much less globally because the coherence of struggles initiated in the marginal spaces of the multiple world system —first, second, third, etc.—would not quell its defeatist trajectory (152–53).

Lazarus effectively erodes modernity dependent on ontological differences between west and nonwest via modernity's heterogeneity. But when he tasks intellectuals with modernity's salvation, he reverts to the conventional and/or traditional dialectic of the western philosopher and (their) postcolonial critic. He quickly fills in the extremely hard-won historical achievement of the *post*-apartheid era with (nothing but) oppositional dialectics: the western philosopher (Adorno) and postcolonial critic (Lazarus); center (Europe) and periphery (South Africa); world system (philosophy) and third world (postcolonial criticism); solitary modernist intellectual (Adornian counterparts) and the minority (white South African writers) (152–53). He restores whiteness and blackness as inherently oppositional and antagonistic just as the black masses materialized non-white supremacist possibilities in post-apartheid South Africa.

IV. Adorno as Postcolonial Theorist

Adorno's postcoloniality was first conceptualized by Robert Spencer in "Thoughts from Abroad: Theodor Adorno as Postcolonial Theorist" (2010). His Adornian analysis of J.M. Coetzee's novel *Disgrace* (1999) clarifies that *how* Adorno thinks makes him a postcolonial theorist *avant la lettre* and *sans pareil* (208): "The constructive (as opposed to self-indulgent or despairing) practice of self-critique is what makes Adorno a postcolonial scholar" (209). He proffers a beautiful examination of his ethos of "thinking humanely" (213). Postcolonial theory becomes Adornian when introspective and empathetic, which by definition is inimical to the gratuitous cruelties and apathies of imperialism qua capitalism. Spencer states, "An Adornian postcolonial theory would keep in mind at all times the conditions of those millions whose blighted lives facilitate the superficial and restricted prosperity of neoliberalism" (214). The philosophical project (suffering) and the postcolonial project (imperialism) converge in Spencer's narrative to facilitate a Marxist self-examination, which affirms "the rejoinders . . . and . . . retorts of distant voices" (219). Postcolonial literature assists this Adornian Marxist postcolonial theory (colonial discourse substitutes for philosophical idealism) because it teaches readers to recognize the actual costs of neoliberalism (neoliberalism forthwith substitutes for colonial discourse). When readers are moved by the fate foisted onto others, postcolonial (all?) literature can bring closer those who are distant (210, 215).

Spencer duly commends postcolonial literature's persuasive abilities (what Spivak terms an "*uncoercive* rearrangement of desires" ["Righting" 526]) in the context of a metonymic conjunction—philosophical idealism/colonial discourse/neoliberalism, but he truncates this literature's aesthetic dimension to a socio-political goal: Adornian Marxist self-critique. This socio-political aesthetic dimension appears to place the entire historical burden of "blighted lives" onto postcolonial authors alone and casts an undifferentiated pall over the indistinct millions that must always be kept in mind. Actualizing Adornian (just?) principles of introspection and empathy may bridge the great divide between "retorts" and their recipients, except actual agency is granted only to postcolonial authors who can reach neoliberalism's beneficiaries. Insisting on Adornian Marxist self-critique delimits the creative capacities for changing minds that any aesthetic production may realize.

Whilst Spencer is accurate in his assessment that "[i]t is a very short step from Adorno's dialectical philosophy to postcolonial theory's eschewal of ideologies and systems" (220), an intermediary role (like Sir Thomas Macaulay—to be discussed later) between remote hailers and attendant readers reprises a perilous stereotype: the latter produces philosophy, the former produces literature, which, in turn, centralizes the disposition of privileged readers. Spencer's effort to merge philosophical and postcolonial projects via accountability to belittled, nugatory, and expendable life is worthwhile. But, why does postcolonial theory need Adorno as a prototype of self-critique to extol introspection and empathy as the crux of *any* critical enterprise? Allowing that literature is usually recognized as postcoloniality's salient intervention in the Euro-US academy, Spencer valorizes postcoloniality as an exemplar of Adornian values yet forgets that self-critique is pivotal to any postcolonial endeavor—not just of its own presuppositions and methodologies but also of the various disciplines it engages.

Contrary to Spencer's approbation of postcolonial literature's ability to close yawning gaps between the beneficiaries of neoliberalism and those it condemns, Deepika Bahri addresses postcolonial literature's depreciation as a transparent text that stands in for the third world *tout court*. In *Native Intelligence: Aesthetics, Politics, and Postcolonial Literature* (2003), Bahri draws on Herbert Marcuse, Walter Benjamin, and Theodor Adorno to recoup postcolonial literature's "nonidentitarian understanding of the value of aesthetic expression" (6). Giving this particular genre of literary production a documentary function permits first world scholars to forfeit the arduous work of close reading demanded by literary texts (deeming this work a new-fangled genre implies faddishness not artistic merit). Readers are also able to avoid the difficult research (including language training) needed to grasp the complexity of third world realities.[12] Postcolonial literature's Euro-US institutionalization exhibits criticism's "inadequate resistance to the status quo logic of exchange society" (7).[13]

The crudity ensuant from withholding normative scholarly standards contracts the third world into a nodal point of contact with the west, which "disciplinary politesse" (10) makes palatable to a transnational readership. Primarily first world diasporic elites are endowed with an instant credibility, as tokenism comes with the burden of representation.[14] Their "aggregate Third Worldliness" (18), whose "migrant-centered ruminations . . . constitute . . . a beguiling *soufflé* of identity, without substance or the staying power necessary for a meaningful postcolonial resistance" (162), leads to a "synecdochic fallacy" (37). Posing as a quixotic battle contra empire's ambiguous legacy, a profligate failure of anamnesis is inducted into postcolonial canonicity (163). The isomorphism of mimesis and realism mistakes "the representational for the representative, the artistic copy for the exact replica, the particular for [the] undifferentiated" (123) to enervate the very aesthetic dimension of postcolonial literature that could prevail over these prohibitive politics.

Bahri's examination of the institutional trappings of the postcolonial novel led me to think about postcoloniality's philosophical dimension. As Bahri emphasizes, postcolonial literature's "historically grounded readings are parsed in so localized a way as to leave it no larger ground . . . to reveal, for instance, . . . what it means to be human . . . [in the] new millennium" (14).[15] Postcolonial scholarship is patronized as merely political precisely so that the politics intrinsic to the work can be dismissed as polemic.[16] If this work were recognized as philosophical, its multivalence would place the politics endemic to any work (its structure, style, narrative, language, etc.) in a *human* context, which renders postcoloniality's exclusion from philosophical inquiry virtually unthinkable. And so, via the rhetoric of rigor and standards, versus putative jargon-y (subaltern, hybridity, mimicry, identity, etc.), grievance-based, modish trends, we arrive at postcolonial theory's lack of theoretical sophistication *by virtue of category alone*.

In her introduction, Bahri asks, "What 'third' world nonaligned with conventional rationality and identity thinking is suggested by these [postcolonial] texts?" (9). This chapter neither asks postcolonial scholars to reconsider Adorno to acknowledge his "true" contributions nor argues for a concerted conceptual engagement simply to enhance postcolonial theory's stature. Roiling the façade erected by a conventional and/or traditional dialectic between the western philosopher and (their) postcolonial critic perhaps broaches a qualitative variety of experience in their encounter.[17] Accepting our historical co-implication via lovingly orchestrated moments of exegetical exchange invites a glimpse of the heterogeneity that "exists neither in the present, nor existed in the past, [but] must continuously be unforgotten" (246).

Chapter Two

Without Sacrifice, Without Vengeance

The Postcolonial Adorno

I will suppose that all I see is false.

—René Descartes, *Meditations on First Philosophy*

In fact no philosophy . . . can paste the particulars into the text, as seductive . . . paintings would hoodwink it into believing.

—Theodor Adorno, *Negative Dialectics*

By claiming to be an all-embracing system, philosophy . . . risk[s] . . . crazy delusions . . . [If] it . . . gives up the idea of crystallizing all truth within itself, it denies the whole weight of its own traditions. This is the price it must pay in . . . linking reality with reason.

—Theodor Adorno, "Why Philosophy?"

To want substance in cognition is to want a utopia.

—Theodor Adorno, *Negative Dialectics*

I. The Philosophical Adorno

As discussed, Robert Spencer suggests that postcolonial novels hold their audiences liable for the privation inflicted on remote others by playing an intermediary role. Using Adorno's criticisms of systems and ideologies, an Adornian Marxist postcolonial theory persistently recalls the residuum of neoliberalism, which refurbishes imperialism for continued exploitation and impoverishment. This chapter reverses Spencer's technique to stage the postcolonial Adorno. In imagining postcoloniality anew in a philosopher from the past as a space clearing gesture, I suggest that negative dialectics and postcolonial theory commonly strive for a non-antagonistic understanding of difference.[1] The imperative to create a qualitative variety of experience, in *this* meeting between philosopher and critic, for a postcolonial—that is, philosophical—practice is reality, not tradition.

II. The Picture of Dorian Gray

As Oscar Wilde's novel tells us, life is always borne by real people. Ultimately, Dorian Gray's putrid and dissolute life caught up with him. People and not the system pay the price. If we concede that philosophical systems are meant to give expression to our best natures, whence the real life they vindicate? If actual living disappears into the void outside the schema, how can we reckon with even one life? How do we ever tell our story? The project of *Negative Dialectics* is to crawl back to the living. This striving for the heterogeneous entity trapped in the stranglehold of the system's logic is what this book regards as Adorno's postcoloniality.

Adorno begins by admonishing Marx: philosophy is *most* salient when it fails to provide a historically adequate understanding of reality, for failures are expressly how our systems brush up against heterogeneity. Given that negative dialectics do not sustain the particular identity that maintains overall logical coherence, happening upon the world in which we actually live reminds us that difference is not inherently oppositional and antagonistic. In fact, the ability to reference something *in* its heterogeneity is the mechanism to gauge the validity of how we think. Mistaking as reality the ahistorical and abstract object identity effects into being carries a terrible price paid by the substantive entity the system sought to relate. Philosophy's failure to change the world (Marx's accusation), therefore, empowers us to comprehend how our conceptual apparatuses are ever insufficient for the historical challenges at hand. Negative dialectics attend to this historical inadequacy by fostering an essential gesture of negativity (qualitatively distinct from a systematically derived logical and/or categorial negation).

Notwithstanding that we use conceptual systems to posit objects of thought, or, what's *there*—that is, *here*—mere repetition of an object's identity predetermines what can be (understood as) our world. By telling us what an object *is*, the strictures of logical coherence foil substantive interpretation. Because (all) objects (must) cohere, the world's complexity loses its emphatic force and can no longer exert a felt influence upon us, whoever identity construes us to be. Only as alien or trespasser can difference intrude upon our reality, as edified by our theoretical armature. I believe that Adorno's response to Marx is relevant today. Negative dialectics' diligent affirmation of substantive interpretation and emphatic objects may be understood as an allegory of postcoloniality, a hermeneutics of the gratuitous destruction of the rational and humane.

Adorno directs our attention to those thoughts that are happening in real time, which he terms "what I am thinking" (5). What I am thinking is heterogeneous, as my thoughts are not perennially commanded by the conceptual system's categorial performance (for example, philosopher, feminist, postcolonial critic, etc.). As thinking constitutes the horizon of what *is* there, my living thoughts, compressed via an antagonistic understanding of difference—that is, their difference from the system is *all* there is to know (about them)—disappear into the void outside the schema that organizes life. The conceptual system's repertoire of categories allows me to *function,* but it also reinforces my consistent *sense* of nonidentity in identity (6). (What is not functional can be sensed not known.) My heterogeneous thoughts, wherein lie all possibility for self-reflection, relate (to) reality. Thus, my consistent sense of *nonidentity* in identity is essentially historical in its negativity.

When pitched into the void outside the schema, this *consistent* sense of nonidentity in identity is identity's "remainder" (5), which is not functional, and, hence, remains undifferentiated. The negativity that is nonidentity's emphatic, living force eludes the system's totalizing mechanism of absorbing (all) difference. *This* heterogeneity—or subalternity (8, 19)—is the impossible yet necessary object of negative dialectics. Negative dialectics spur the full profusion of the essentially historical, for the conceptual system's useful but identity-based parapet only *seems* to have an explanation for everything.[2]

III. Negativity: Remainder→ Nonidentity→ Nonconceptuality→ Subalternity→ Heterogeneity→ Postcoloniality

In animating and legitimating the heterogeneous remainder, negative dialectics is a postcolonial movement of thought. As the condition of possibility for what is (or can only be) a negativity that is essentially historical, heterogeneity is not a logical and/or categorial negation. The dissonance the brush with heterogeneity yields between (an) experience and (its) description allows for meaning and hopefulness: insofar as my consistent sense of nonidentity in identity is inassimilable, we catch a glimpse of the life immobilized by identity's double bind—it is both semblance and necessity. Here, at this aporetic juncture, where a decision is made *for* a concept meant to fathom living, we may understand heterogeneity as the "apocryphal dregs" (204) imperative for substantive interpretation.[3] The categorial discharge decreed by the conceptual system (that presupposes its own identity-based negation) obliterates the fragile, temporal substance of diversity, complexity, plentitude, variety, or multiplicity.

If the philosophical is engendered by negative dialectics, then heterogeneity's entropic counter-pressure propels a postcolonial movement of thought: forsaking identity thinking may occasion truthfulness. An understanding of difference as inherently oppositional and antagonistic, however, erects what I term a "false positive infinite totality of non-contradiction." And so, Adorno (first) *negatively* begins by recalling that the object always leaves a remainder. When *something* is conceived, it enters into (its) concept and becomes an object; the concept substantiates what was conceived, but the remainder eschews the truth of identity between (an) object and (its) concept, as the concept cannot exhaust what was conceived. By presupposing the identity between (an) object and (its) concept, thinking assembles the order of things that acts as a screen for all that is conceived. The conceptual system is (a) semblance, but thinking proceeds by identifying; the conceptual apparatus so embodies truth and artifice, simultaneously: to think about something, we identify that something; when we identify something, we posit a semblance of that something (5).

These introductory pages of *Negative Dialectics* lay out how a conceptual totality becomes both appearance and reality: (all) concepts cover (all) objects; (all) objects cover (all) things conceived. Since the logical whole operates as though concepts exhaust what was conceived, the nature of (all) objects is determined by logical necessity. Preserving (a) logical totality becomes the ground for deducing (all) relationships between objects. This conceptual totality may be mere appearance, but anything heterogeneous differs in quality from (what functions as) reality. Even though what I am thinking, my consistent sense of nonidentity in identity, does not accord with logical necessity, to identity thinking, whatever is different is oppositional and antagonistic, as nonidentity contradicts identity. Variety, complexity, and diversity shrivel into nonidentity that does not fit into identity, and, consequently, their truth content is nullified. An identity-based conceptual system, therefore, induces a double bind: the untruth of identity thinking is equated with contradiction; the truth of identity thinking is equated with reality (5). Reality is no longer heterogeneous but (a) semblance that preempts heterogeneity as mere contradiction, undeterred that heterogeneity is the source of identity thinking *and* of its untruth.

The upshot of difference becoming "null and void" (128), and bereft of the emphatic force indispensible for substantive interpretation, is "stupidity"

(34).[4] In this way, (the) semblance turns into a false positive (and *eo ipso* imagines false negatives as negations), which posits (an) infinite totality. Adorno's postcoloniality enters the rift between system and thought, semblance and truth, concept and object, and description and experience, to return to what is "divergent, dissonant, negative" (5). This heterogeneity lives in/as the essentially historical immanent possibilities of negativity, which will (always) have exceeded the repetition of identity. While an identitarian conceptual system enforces cynical (and nihilistic) industry standards, to actually think about something is to look (out) for the apocryphal "imprint."[5] Accordingly, Adorno's postcoloniality strives for a non-antagonistic understanding of difference because our (only) possibility for substantive cognition is reality.

IV. Shock and Awe

The previous section explains why negative dialectics' diligent affirmation of substantive interpretation and emphatic objects may be understood as an allegory of postcoloniality, a hermeneutics of the gratuitous destruction of the rational and humane.[6] As a postcolonial movement of thought, negative dialectics convey and uphold a nonidentitarian understanding of the value of philosophy. By virtue of *this* obligation to heterogeneity, postcoloniality is an intrinsic part of a philosophical understanding of difference.

This section takes Adorno's rendition of the spiritualized coercion of subjects (aka objects) to define cruelty as that gratuitous performance of identity that trades nonidentity for "blinders" (4), which by enjoining substantive thinking may beholden subjects to efficiently administered lives, but forfeit reasonable living (6, 7).[7] In contempt of heterogeneity's naïve contravention of any power claims, semblance's substitution *for* reality leads to disproportional footsteps. What officiates as the world in which we live ensues from an impoverished sense of (our) commonplace (4): "*that*, ready formed in every detail, . . . [and] taken, as if from a shelf," is an object already *there*.[8] Concepts perform like currency in a simple barter economy (3): this payment (*of* difference) is the cost of living (*in* identity) in a market economy (*a* semblance) that presumes to be whole (*the* system).

Our strictured yet also incommensurate existence, whose stupidity is "not a cogitative law[,] . . . [but] real" (6), manufactures conceptual cultures that forego historical adequacy *for the sake of* tradition.[9] Identity thinking stages an instrumental calculus, even as heterogeneity (not conceptual totality) allows philosophy to *be* philosophical.[10] In that the actuality of (our) objects is *this* emphatic insistence of (their) heterogeneity, an identity-based conceptual system does not embody palpable reality, but is the result of "pre-philosophical activity" (9). For the reason that nonidentity, nonconceptuality, subalternity, heterogeneity—that is, postcoloniality—*are* the basis on which (alone) things can be conceived (at all), life in the false positive infinite totality of non-contradiction conditions subjects to unknowingness. Adorno states,

> The system is . . . one of the most conditioned spirit. . . . The subjective preconception of the material production process in society—basically different from its theoretical constitution—is . . . the part unreconciled with the subjects. Their own reason . . . establishing identity by barter, remains incommensurable with the subjects it reduces to the same denominator: the subject as the subject's foe. The preceding generality is both true and untrue: true because it forms that "ether" which Hegel calls spirit; untrue, because its reason is no reason yet, because its universality is the product of particular interests. *This is why a philosophical critique of identity transcends philosophy.* (10–11, emphases added)

In the semblance, everything is its own contradiction: even the façade contradicts itself (as façade), as it negates the difference between being (as itself) and functioning (as itself). The mode of consummation of this semblance—what *works* as reality or as conceptual capacity—negates objectivity and subjectivity (both actual, heterogeneous).

The patina, as formed by identitarian objectivity preempting heterogeneity, remains unresolved in subjectivity, and lingers preconceived to determine (our) immanent subjectivity. A vertiginous, infinitely inverted reality mass-produces (an) immanent subjectivity that shirks self-reflection: again, a subjectivity that is (its own) contradiction. Reduced to the same common denominator, reason becomes averse to what allows "life to go on at all" (10)—heterogeneity, which is ineluctably real.[11] Our seemingly manic indifference towards living, vital heterogeneity overdetermines our own ineffectiveness (22); objects behaving like subjects unthinkingly tread over the world where life actually takes place.[12] Adorno's postcoloniality breaches the shock and awe of identity by miming nonidentity: *how* do conceptual systems make their ghosts? Any insights reaped from these remainders arise from a yearning for reconciliation with our subject matter: the heterogeneity that led to the thing being conceived in the first place (15).

Those scouring for the heterogeneous find sanctuary in "ephemeral objects" (40) that paradoxically have the emphatic force needed for substantive prudence. Ephemeral objects, as remainders of paths not taken by understanding, are "neither [part of] a system nor a [system-derived] contradiction" (11).

Not yet decreed by identitarian intentions, these fleeting objects brook close contact with difference (17). Inasmuch as the conceptual system allegorizes societal systems of production, an administered world expunged of qualitative content is an essentially historical world evaporated into nothingness. Resigned to our historical fate, we conceive of difference as incommensurable with the lawful. What is alien is expelled as extraneous, insubstantial matter that haunts our *stolen* self-consolidation. Nothingness's "negative objectivity" (20)—it isn't real—discredits the heterogeneous, but the conceptual system's failures, deficiencies, and lacks nonetheless break "rationalization—[the mind's] own spell" (23) by aiding and abetting self-reflection.

V. Thinking Things

Adorno's postcoloniality sustains particularity, difference underived from the systemic machinery of identity and difference, to transmute the philosophical into an absolute entitlement (24). Precisely due to difference's oppressiveness, tradition appropriates and displaces individual moments of substantive insight via hostility to what defies unanimity:

> The "rational animal" . . . must find a reason. . . . The animal to be devoured must be evil. . . . Idealism . . . gives unconscious sway to the ideology that the not-I, *l'autrui*, and finally all that reminds one of nature is inferior[.] . . . The system is the belly turned mind, . . . akin to misanthropy: leave nothing unchallenged. (22–23)

The more semblance renounces (its) utter contingency, the more semblance is bounded to delusion in a world that withstands cohesion. Nonidentity survives identity's integrative force because of discontinuous instances of immanent connection, which may be availed as gateways for reconciliation with our subject matter (25).

In that qualitative variety of experience is tenable only via effortfully established immanent connection, postcoloniality is "historical . . . through and through" (26–27).[13] *For* the philosophical qua (our) entitlement, immersion in the subject matter unseals the "speculative power" (28) of nonidentity's emphatic, living force to debilitate the rehearsed category's predominant fixity (30). Being as heterogeneity provokes essentially historical multitudinous reactions, the designated categorial standpoint cannot provide "answers to everything" (31). Monopolistic cultures put (all) things in their (proper) place, but, in contrast, philosophical understanding rebuts "proximity, home, security" (33) with substantive insight, which is not the product of effortless generalization. It is instead an extremely hard-won historical achievement. Questioning the intelligibility of the dominant frame leads to inconclusiveness, even if the conceptual system's power cannot be belied, as negativity chafes what "one-track minds" (33) use to guarantee consensus. Superfluous claims ensure the "omnipotent impotence" (34) of the conceptual system because nothing (can) happen(s), unlike the philosophical insights gained by negative dialectics, whence the encounter with heterogeneity is qualitatively an emphatic and decidedly unpredictable experience. *Ideological* machinations engineer homogeneity to ensure that tradition gets what it wants, all along.

The (now) utterly contingent *a priori* is maintained by categorial discharges that demand scapegoats for self-certainty, an objective falsehood that squanders living, vital heterogeneous life.[14] Bereft of self-expression, subjects must defer to (totalitarian) stupidity, which expels the heterogeneous (the exotic object, so to speak) to shirk accountability for what difference *means*. What difference *entails* is disclaimed as what difference apparently *characteristically* intends: contradiction, antagonism, opposition, trouble making. But, the conceptual system fights against its own phantoms, for heterogeneity is "objective, not plausible" (41). Adorno's postcoloniality, therefore, conveys and upholds more subjectivity, not less, to detract from the façade accepted as the (given) world, and, hence, as the (given) conditions of philosophical inquiry.

In *that* reality, western philosopher and postcolonial critic must acquiesce to their subject matter—the heterogeneity of the world in which actually we live.

VI. Exit Strategy

Adorno's postcoloniality strives for those small moments of affinity and disappointment, where stuff really happens, to disavow the "wrong state of things" (11). A laboriously constituted meaningful relationship delivers a haven for subjective reactions that comprise the substantive aspect of cognition because of their historical density (42, 45, 47–48).[15] Negative dialectics move in reverse direction toward what can be saved from the concept's prerogative: the subject mimes the dross that roils the concept's autarky, all the way to its "internal composition" (4) and "immanent truth" (4), for a referential passage to the object's nonconceptual side (12). In contrast, identity's law compels ataraxy: the subject stays indifferent to the very social conditions from which it is derived as its own construction (141, 143–44, 146). Here, in *this* place, the subject works to experience what is not there, but what is despairingly hoped, will (always) have been, there. Only an *exemplary* reader's perspective (not usurped universality) can yield a concrete example just negative enough to negate identity's negation (52). Against the heteronomy unleashed by the false positive infinite totality of non-contradiction, the abject nonsense that seals the subject's function, negative dialectics creates an encounter with heterogeneity.[16] Adorno iterates,

> Philosophy rests on the texts it criticizes. They are brought to it by the tradition they embody, and it is in dealing with them that the conduct of philosophy becomes commensurable with tradition. This justifies the move from philosophy to exegesis, which exalts neither the interpretation nor the symbol into an absolute but seeks the truth where thinking secularizes the irretrievable archetype of sacred texts. (55)[17]

Identity seizes capital standing by vilifying the remainder: it is irrational, fraudulent, angry, incompetent, uncollegial, violent, oppressive, etc.

On the grounds that sacred texts are essentially historical *acts* of self-reflection, however, philosophy becomes commensurable with tradition when it makes possible that exegetical labor that "follows the impulse to transcend . . . delusion . . . without sacrifice and without vengeance" (141). For the sake of the subject matter, a reader's perspective disintegrates the foreground world to garner something impossible when that something shows itself (151–53, 158–61).[18] An identity-based conceptual system reduces everything to "all-conceptuality—from the beginning" (160), but understanding the "I" as a historic entity is the placeholder for thinking on a human scale. While the autophagy of belly turned mind dissembles the defining universal as the epitome of subjective significance, self-reflection, as the secular—not traditional, not European—element of philosophical experience, by turning to nonidentity, curtails the sway of (a) hegemonic description (149, 176).[19] Adorno maintains that "negative dialectics calls for . . . self-reflection. . . . [I]f thinking is to be true[,] . . . *today* . . . it must also be a thinking against itself" ("Meditations" 88, emphasis added).

The vulnerability necessary to take a proportional footstep on the ground, in lieu of shock and awe to terrify from up above, is cognition's utopic task, as creating a referential passage to our inexorable limitation is to *have* a philosophical experience. Adorno insists that "shame bids philosophy not to repress [the] insight that its history shows amazingly few indications of the sufferings of human kind" (*Negative* 153). An understanding of difference as inherently oppositional and antagonistic prevents dialectics from staying philosophical; as it loses, at least, the subjective in its outcome, the conceptual system is "blinded to the point of madness by . . . whatsoever will elude its rule" (172).

And so, it hustles hard to maintain the house of cards.

VII. The Postcolonial Adorno:
Philosophy→ Historical Dimension→
Postcoloniality→ Qualitative Variety of Experience

This chapter exemplifies its understanding of postcoloniality as the striving for a non-antagonistic understanding of difference by discerning what is conceptually postcolonial in Adorno's philosophical framework. By bringing philosophy and postcolonial theory together at a point of crisis, this concrete example lends the lie to Eurocentric identity politics. As a postcolonial movement of thought, negative dialectics provide a qualitative variety of experience—that is, of difference as not inherently oppositional and antagonistic, but as the togetherness of diversity. To seek historical adequacy, to countenance how our categories are ever inadequate for the historical challenges at hand, is a postcolonial gesture of negativity.[20]

The homology between philosophy and postcoloniality does not nolens volens sacrifice the empirical, expressly since empirical analyses by marginalized traditions are innovative and meritorious. As the shadow of the Eurocentric subject, the postcolonial subject covets precise imagination of the actual course of history via a reader's perspective (not as what is read) to vindicate the viscerous life entrapped within realities that are (really, not cogitatively) irreconcilable.[21] This incapacitated subject, found on the brink of an aporia, follows through, beyond the diktat of the categorial discharge, on the truthfulness of an autochthonous connection between the western philosopher and (their) postcolonial critic, at ground level. *This* is how we make postcoloniality real as a historical era and conceptual accomplishment.

Pursuant to the import placed on the concrete example, I would like to conclude with two textual moments in Adorno's work that perhaps capture the grief of an exemplary interruptive force. In some ways, these moments seem to be what Adorno is talking about in his discussion of negative dialectics. No matter our historical distance from Adorno, we should recognize these day-to-day realities in the identitarian conceptual cultures of the Euro-US academy. And, in both examples, Adorno turns to nonidentity—a dead man and a philosopher—to make his claims.

The first example occurs quite literally on the first day of Adorno's seminar on *Negative Dialectics*. The reader chuckles when Adorno complains about how teaching and committee work have kept him from his research, which is why the course lectures are "from a voluminous and somewhat burdensome book that [he has] been working on for six years . . . with the title 'Negative Dialectics'" (*Lectures* 4). But, before we get to this point, the lectures begin with a eulogy and a moment of silence. Adorno informs his students about the death of Paul Tillich. He first speaks about the debt he owes to Tillich for his own future during the rise of fascism. He then describes Tillich's "truly unique" (3) quality of character as an unprecedented open-mindedness. Adorno is not just referring to the ability to engage contrary viewpoints; what is crucial is that regardless of this receptiveness, Tillich did not respond to the overtures made by the National Socialists: "when what was at stake was the need to show whether or not he [Tillich] was a decent human being . . . in [a] particular historical context" (3), he was a decent human being. Adorno tells his students, moreover, that what Tillich was able to do as a teacher because of "actual human contact" (4) and his "living initiative" (4) cannot be grasped in his writings.

This concrete example is significant for two reasons. The first reason is that Adorno begins his lectures on negative dialectics with a negatively dialectical interruption of the ubiquitous business of academic philosophy. He reminds his students that unlike certain other philosophers, Tillich did not use his considerable philosophical acumen to justify being on the wrong side of history. 2. Secondly, emphasizing that Tillich was a decent human being, when being decent came at a cost, reminds us that there is no natural link between expertise and professional standing and *being* rational and humane. (Adorno also talks about this presumed link in the second example.) The accent on actual *human* contact and one's *living* initiative warns of mistaking career advancement with strength of character and merit. If we follow Adorno's inversionary logic, actual, not inherently oppositional and antagonistic, difference calls a bluff: how does the academic ground game make us humanly stupid?

This, too, is philosophical experience.

The second textual moment is also not without its humorous aspects. Early on in his lectures on Hegel, Adorno speaks about philosophical speculation and the necessity to broaden what we understand as experience. He uses the example of committee work to make his point: unless one completely identifies with the culture in place, one will notice "the basest instincts prevail over the better, more humane ones" (*History* 30). No Manichean battle takes place, but we start to realize that the position is occupied by the "worse [hu]man" (30) when it should have gone to the better. Adorno continues to explain the difference between a career advancer in philosophy and a (tongue firmly in cheek) philosophical philosopher: since creative action goes against established opinion, it is already perceived to be inherently oppositional and antagonistic. This established opinion operates as purely a formal principle being defended in spite of its historical sediment, which "conceals the dominant relations and the dominance of the universal" (32).

To bear this out, Adorno talks about a young scholar whose promotion is "up for discussion, as they say": "[I]f he [/she] has opinions of his [/her] own and is not simply a careerist[,] . . . then . . . he [/she] will decline to mince his [/her] words when criticism is warranted, and he [/she] will not shrink from saying that a dull, unintelligent book is dull and unintelligent" (31). The dominant relations and the dominant universal (the concealed historical sediment), cathected as a merely formal principle, dismiss this intellectual independence *by virtue of category alone*. Excepting substantive content, without fundamental engagement, and without textual evidence, "the mere form of his [/her] deviation" prompts a reprimand (31). In lieu of scholarliness, the reproaches are personal and stylistic: "[H]is [/her] polemical tone is improper, that it is incompatible with the academic tradition and God knows what else" (31).

This "deviant" (32) cannot fall back on institutional structures, and the formal principle continues to regulate as though devoid of social material even when challenged. Such imbroglios in committee work on personnel decisions deeply show their social determination, as hegemonic groups historically control ideas. Accompanying this insensibility to (their own) subject matter is the dominant's exploitation of the prejudicial structures that can be dissembled as acute weaknesses of the deviant. This is a crucial point, for it is the universal that makes one's own experience seem ineffable and remote.[22] Even as formal principles perform as though denuded of societal content, hegemony is retained via categorial rhetoric *without tangible involvement in the material itself.* Adorno concludes that "when they [voices of current majority opinion] lean back in their chairs and give vent to what they imagine to be their own ideas, they merely reproduce the bleating of many" (32).

This, too, is philosophical experience.

As mentioned earlier, Adorno's postcoloniality strives for a negativity that is negative enough to bring to bear the heterogeneous. Other than native informancy of philosophy's many untold wrongs, *this* philosopher's perspective is a love for *this* particular philosopher, who did not see what I have to see, but who sounds an uncannily familiar note. This gesture of welcoming to the commonplace of our sorrow amidst missed opportunities is a proleptic extension of a benefit of the doubt, which like contemporaneity is "intelligible only as achievement" (Said, *Reflections* 53).

Chapter Three

Europe as an Other

Subalternity, Postcolonial Theory, and Philosophers of the Future

[N]othing more is given to [philosophy] than fleeting, disappearing traces within the riddle figures of that which exists and their astonishing entwinings. The history of philosophy is nothing other than the history of such entwinings.

—Theodor Adorno, "The Actuality of Philosophy"

It is impossible for contemporary French intellectuals to imagine the kind of Power and Desire that would inhabit the unnamed subject of the Other of Europe . . . supporting or critiquing the constitution of the Subject as Europe. . . . [I]n the constitution of that Other of Europe, great care was taken to obliterate the textual ingredients with which a subject could cathect, could occupy (invest?) its itinerary. . . . This is not to describe "the way things really were." . . . It is, rather, to continue the account of how *one* explanation and narrative of reality was established as the normative one.

—Gayatri Spivak, *A Critique of Postcolonial Reason*

I repeat: the pepper if you please; for if it had not been for peppercorns, then what is ending now in East and West might never have begun. Pepper it was that brought Vasco de Gama's tall ships across the ocean . . . so that in the period called Discovery-of-India . . . we were "not so much sub-continent as sub-condiment," as my distinguished mother had it. "From the beginning, what the world wanted from bloody mother India was daylight-clear," she'd say. "They came for the hot stuff, just like any man calling on a tart."

—Salman Rushdie, *The Moor's Last Sigh*

I. Philosophy→ Postcoloniality→ Subalternity→ Heterogeneity

In the "History" section of *A Critique of Postcolonial Reason: A History of the Vanishing Present* (1999), Gayatri Spivak tends to archival matters. She focuses on the Rani of Sirmur, wife of Raja Karam Prakash, who ruled Sirmur, located in the foothills of the Himalayas in Punjab, India, from 1793–1815.[1] The Gurkhas violate a territorial promissory agreement as their recompense for helping the Raja against the betrayal of his own brother. When they install themselves as the rulers of Sirmur, the Raja flees to Kulathu and then Buria. The Rani of Sirmur contacts Colonel Ochterlony, the political agent at Ludhiana, for help because the British have just declared war on the Gurkhas. Upon the Gurkhas abdicating occupied territory per an 1815 agreement between the British and Nepal governments, the British do not return Sirmur to Karam Prakash. They place his son, Fateh Prakash, on the throne with the Rani serving as his regent until he is no longer a minor. After Fateh Prakash becomes the Raja of Sirmur, the British subject the Rani to a very peculiar domestic arrangement. It is during this time that, as guardian of her minor son, she pronounces her intention to become a *sati* (a widow who self-immolates and ascends her earthly abode as a goddess) while her husband is still alive. (Karam Prakash dies in exile in 1826.)

How the British manage the crisis produced by the Rani's seemingly sudden resolve (they will outlaw *sati* in 1829) is the legacy of violence and dislocation that renders the Rani irretrievably heterogeneous. Spivak excavates the mechanics by which the colonial archive figures the Rani as merely the agent/implement of the changeover of an *episteme*. Her commodious role revamps colonialism into civilizing mission to execute India's progress from tradition to modernity. Spivak limns the techniques that secure subalternity to purvey a glimmer of colonizer and colonized *in* colonialism, in preference to their nominal ventriloquist functions (Europe and Its Others), ossified under the benevolent aegis of Europe, to unearth their utter contingency. Whereas her reader's perspective leads Spivak to experience the crossing of an aporia—the Rani as neither subject nor object—as a relation with the Rani ("*my* Rani"), I suggest that Spivak's staging of the contrivances that manufacture Europe and Its Others (pre)figures our Euro-US epistemological training.

II. Europe as an Other: We Were Not Yet Such a Group

Spivak makes lack of attention to the general frame her opening salvo against postcolonial theory in the Euro-US academy (*Critique* 1). The general frame refers to postcoloniality's geopolitical determination. In Euro-US postcolonialism, cosmopolitan postcolonials are native informants for corporate imperialism and foreign policy.[2] Spivak considers this geopolitical determination in the four sections that comprise her critique: "Philosophy," "Literature," "History," and "Culture." In "History," Spivak inspects the colonial archive to work out *how* the Other of Europe was consolidated as the self-consolidating other (198). Precisely because the colonial archive expunges these mechanisms of constitution to turn colonialism into civilizing mission, Spivak understands her project as reparative, even though fracture and discontinuity are beyond the jurisdiction of any possible return. In her example, as the Rani of Sirmur is lost as sheer instrument of imperialism, Spivak does not violently retrieve full objects from some original scene of objectification and appropriation. Her proceedings emphasize (by way of Melanie Klein) that we must experience the true measure of this loss of history, which possesses an almost material depth.

Spivak begins her attempt to break the general frame of Eurocentrism by revisiting a 1982 conference, which was originally titled "Europe and Its Others." She suggests to the organizers the title "Europe as an Other," but this suggestion incurs three problems: 1. The organizers face a lack of disciplinary preparation and institutional support. They "were not yet such a group" (199). But, this work the organizers undertake to dislocate Eurocentrism will perhaps be part of an archive called "Europe as an Other." 2. Europe self-consolidated as a sovereign subject and constitutes others as "programmed near images" (199) for markets and administration; this is why colonial is inextricable from European. 3. Europe as an Other presumes that we can recover and restore a lost sovereign self against the sovereign self of Europe. This dangerous nostalgia, however, does not reveal *how* the colonized become (nothing but) a serviceable name (200): *before* "Europe" and "Its [Europe's] Others" as cathected spaces were fixed, *who* were the colonizer and the colonized? The excision of their means of formation from the colonial archive transmutes the colonizer and colonized into ghosts (of themselves) given their bromidic prolegomenon in history.

Spivak thereby elicits the workings of a historical itinerary that flouts its utter contingency to seem teleological.[3] To explain what she means, she appends the example of NGO's and UN agencies that (now) describe their projects as Gender and Development and not Women in Development. The latter refers to women who are in development (they are not women until their nations achieve development), and the former adjudicates local gender norms as contrary to development (local gender norms prevent the development that will yield women), but both monikers construe development as (truer or real) gendering, for capital frees gender. Development agencies (from above) squeeze the breathtakingly multifarious lives of the world's poorest women (down below) into the implacable logic of credit baiting without infrastructural support.[4] Just as gender *means* agent/implement of (nascent) development, the Rani *means* agent/implement of (nascent) imperialism; the Rani of Sirmur becomes an earlier incarnation of us: the class-privileged woman *means* agent/implement of finance capital.

In the mid-80s, to disarticulate this inexorable trajectory of being a (truer or real) woman *comme il faut* instrument of finance capital, Spivak suggests that postcolonial theorists read "a handful of archival material, bits of the unprocessed historical record" (202). This deliberate and onerous proportionality, which privileges the graspable (handful, bits—the nonconceptual), versus the available (total, logical—system), permits her to later earn *her* Rani (240). For Spivak, these handfuls allow the Rani to become meaningful (in place of abstract) *for* postcolonialism (still to come), but at that time, Dominick LaCapra questions whether archival work on colonial history will lead to all the facts (LaCapra 1987; Spivak, *Critique* 202). Spivak answers LaCapra's concerns with general and narrow claims. The general claims: as literature, the archive selectively preserves the changeover of the *epistemé* from tradition to modernity. The archive is a story with a predetermined end composed by loss, which constructs an object of representation and gives names to functions: India and Britain. The narrow claims: disciplinary differentiation of genres dissimulates the archive as a record of all the facts. We name this literature "the archive" to fulfill a purpose that stipulates antithetical entities: fact versus fiction. But, Spivak cautions that "the colonizer constructs himself as he constructs the colony" (203).

The archive produces the fictional/functional names of India and Britain, whose collective effects retroactively establish the reality of these names to uproot heterogeneity—as if they were facts. *Here* (is where) the archive obliterates textual ingredients: *how* did the self self-constitute by appointing a self-consolidating other? Spivak reminds us that historical work *necessarily* depends on tropes and engages in troping (203). Following Paul de Man, she explains: something that claims to be truth is mere trope; what positions itself as that something's corrective, however, is obliged to act out the lie in marking the corrected version. We have to lie to correct a lie by prodding this trope's ramifications when it is deployed as truth (de Man 1979; Spivak, *Critique* 18). Spivak affirms her obligation to lie *for* postcolonialism: only by lying does she rejoin LaCapra's judgment that literary criticism has no general implications. LaCapra asserts that the archive cannot be a substitute for the past; in reply, Spivak deters us from thinking of the past ontologically (204). An archive's formation involves a "crosshatching of condensations, a traffic in telescoped symbols" (205), which give texture to what is selectively preserved, while their density remains significant across time: these ciphers (stereotypes, dog whistles, acronyms, ideograms, autographs, etc.) when hawked still get the job done.

Spivak grants the critical usefulness of an archive that can "answer back," but the archive does not embody the past. If the past is quite other (to us), then this useful fiction (of the past as quite other) might empower us to trace how the self-consolidating other was crafted. Insofar as LaCapra looks to change his mind about *what really happened* in the past (by learning the facts), Spivak looks for the *mechanics* that arrange the past (by *un*learning the facts). LaCapra's pedantic claim that the past "as is" is beyond repossession further elides the methods that devise the useful fiction that the archive is a repository of facts. Defending the past as quite other (against bits of historical material—no less) keeps *this* past (in place) as *the* past—that is, as history. Spivak treats LaCapra's apprehensions, therefore, as a Euro-US investment in maintaining *this* postcolonialism (as a useful fiction): postcolonialism aspires to recoup *the* past, but there are no facts that can show the past "as is." Contra LaCapra's portrayal, Spivak's postcoloniality entrusts something else (entirely): "I pray to be haunted by her [the Rani's] slight ghost" (207). We do not know to whom Spivak's prayers are directed. The Rani's ghost is slighter than other ghosts; there is not even a handful of material to be found (here). Desire and genealogy coincide in Spivak's pursuit of the Rani explicitly because there is not much in the archive "in her [the Rani's] name": after all, "[s]he was only the instrumental agent of the settlement" (207).

The Rani can be figured only as a radical but disjointed sequence of interruptions, which call into question the specious uniformity of the historical narrative of civilizing mission (208). If the colonial Rani is the agent/imple-ment of imperialism, and the postcolonial Spivak is the agent/implement of globalization, then a second couplet emerges as the story of the Rani and the story of imperialism also happen (to be) the same: both are ghost stories whose "repeated tearing of time . . . cannot be sutured" (208). In other words, they are hauntings. The Rani metamorphoses into a ghost story (India) that mirrors the ghost story of imperialism (Europe); both are useful *fictions*. In Spivak's recitation, the story of postcolonialism (still to come) mimes the Rani's slight ghost, which substitutes for the Rani *in* imperialism. By rehears-ing the epistemic violation that determines the Rani, Spivak will enter the archive to make these ghosts real—even though this making real is not (a) fact. Her delineation of the feints of European exceptionalism do not show the past "as is"—as if the past were already *there*. Instead of the denouement of an antonymic categorial discharge that eclipses its utter contingency, the contrivances that consolidate the Rani's subalternity augur that Europe and Its Others is not the only ghost story in town.

III. Proceedings

In the archive are "dispatches, letters, consultations moving at the slow pace of horse, foot, ships laboriously rounding the Cape, and the quill pens of writers and copyists" (209), which record the painstakingly slow and hodge-podge nature of empire building.[5] After referring to the quotidian aspects of colonialism, Spivak provides a geographical description of Sirmur, a movement between texts and terrain that underscores how earth is being (re)inscribed—then, as now. Her description of Sirmur takes place above a footnote chronicling the contemporary Hindu communalist incarnation of the Rani: *this* electioneering Rani in independent India joins the ranks as the agent/implement of Hindu communalism, and seems to sprout almost naturally as a reaction against the cultural dilution imposed by imperialism (the Rani) and globalization (Spivak). *Her* figuration *for* a Hindu nation obliges her to support *sati* as an exalted free choice that demonstrates the superiority of traditional Hindu women in comparison to her Muslim and western-ized Indian counterparts (not to mention western women). Spivak remarks that her own palimpsestic markings on this terrain are also complicit in (re)inscribing earth as if anew, no matter her objection to the steady traffic in telescoped symbols that engineer the changeover of the *episteme* by treating women as efficient ciphers of a nation's sovereign selfhood (210).

According to the archive, Sirmur has a population that lives together in a precarious balance. The Sikhs of Punjab, the Gurkhas of Nepal, the Mughal Emperor, and the Pathan of Delhi, through his proxy the Nazim of Sirhind, are all interested in Sirmur. On August 2, 1784, David Ochterlony writes to the governor general of the East India Company that "Goorkha" [*sic*] encroach-ment allows the East India Company to claim entitlement. (Recall that the Rani asks Ochterlony for help when the Gurkhas violate their promissory agreement with the Raja and seize the land they were to repossess from the Raja's brother.) In the opinion of Ochterlony, the company must "*vindicate [their] insulted honour*" (211) through settlements. This trope of empire—vin-dication of honor—calls itself truth: Sirmur is feminized and reclaimed by Europe from improper men. Spivak must lie to correct Ochterlony's lie. What is *her* claim to vindication of insulted honor and settlement of the territories? She answers: "My Rani" (240). Subsequent to this coupling of a chivalrous and manly Europe (empire) with a timorous and effeminate India (colony), Spivak introduces us to the chain of command that takes place thirty-one years later in 1815: from Geoffrey Birch to Charles Metcalfe to John Adam.

When she introduces us to Geoffrey Birch, another pairing emerges, as he proceeds on horseback through the territories with a "single native escort" (211). Birch gallivants about Sirmur to conduct the prosaic labor of consolidating the self of Europe. To Spivak, he comes across as a "slight romantic figure" (211). (Recall the other slight ghost in this story.) Born just before the French Revolution into a petty merchant's family from Middlesex, Birch is twenty-nine when we meet him (in the archives). Tumbling into Birch obliges the native to "cathect the space of the Other on his home ground" (211); when persuaded by Birch that he is not yet properly (a) man, the native adopts the alien as master. Domesticating this world with aplomb, the golden Birch travels with his dark escort[6]: he *is* the Company's honor. As Birch writes the self of Europe (romantic, authoritative, honorable), Spivak says that he exceeds his skeletal slot in passing off colonialism as civilizing mission (211).

The *violence* of fracture, interruption, and discontinuity is appreciable owing to Birch's *intimacy* with his opponents when he personally addresses the natives as the Company's subjects. Spivak stresses that this scene shows the colonizer *in* colonization (recall Women in Development) and not the already primed colonizer *and* colonized (recall Gender and Development). The notion of a rift ("in") mislays the coolly connotative sense of a gap ("and"), as the former expresses a mutual happening, which results from Birch's sudden insertion into Sirmur, but the latter transmits a mutual distance, which results from Birch pulling off a prefabricated dichotomy. Since Birch does not pass through unresisting elements when he encroaches upon native turf as the epitome of manhood vindicating the Company's honor, Spivak looks (out) for *in-between* spaces that can prompt *place* to appear and *not* the fiction(s)/function(s) of colonizer and colonized (212).

In the colonial archive, Birch comes across as a site/sight to behold. His figuration as a European emissary mapping newly acquired spheres registers as his proceeding backward in time to encompass ungraven earth in the folds of a benevolent and sacrificing personage. Where Birch appears as agent/implement of capital, an actual place is conjured into being. The Company (rumored, unseen, omnipotent) acquires the *quality* of being real because the natives *see* Birch. But, Spivak reminds us, lowly, insignificant people like Geoffrey Birch realize the conversion of cartography into empire in the narrow sense. (I would add, however, the awe-inspiring, anonymous technology of capital jolts these new-fangled subjects, for Birch as trope is *simultaneously* real and ghost, authoritative and romantic, solo and escorted.) *While* he logs palimpsestic land to inaugurate a domain, he generates the vivid, living *force* imperative to make the native *see* himself as other (212).

Birch's betrayal of intimacies, fostered with the natives specifically to lodge the Company's dominion, is compounded by the ridiculousness of the only qualifications the Company requires: cadets must be "well-grounded in Vulgar Fractions, . . . [have] a good Hand, and [have] gone through the Latin Grammar" (213). *This* is Birch's preparedness as he ruthlessly slides

native discourse under the discourse of another (213). In a letter to the
Board, Birch says,

> [I have undertaken this journey] to acquaint the people who they
> are subject to, for as I suspected they were not properly informed
> of it and seem only to have heard of our existence from conquering
> the Goorkah [sic] and from having seen a few Europeans passing
> thro' [sic] the country. (213)[7]

Spivak does not note how these quintessential *understatements* bypass the
outright cruelty of the rift Birch creates because the "inform[ation]" (facts?) he
kindly disperses to those "not properly informed" glosses over what colonization *actually* takes. As written, these descriptors enact what was happening
on the ground as benign sketching and apprising rather than the plunder of
a people. Yet, Birch's passing through is the passage into history for these
"wild regions" (213).

Spivak concludes that Birch sees himself as an archetypal figure of
Empire. *He* replaces rumor with information; the European transmogrifies from
stranger to master, and the protean population of Sirmur collapses into the
self-consolidating other of Europe. Birch becomes the point of reference for
Sirmur per se: his injection (conquest *as* vindication) is History. But, Spivak
exhorts when we meet him: "Let Captain Birch as agent of determination
remain a reminder that the 'Colonizing Power' is far from monolithic—that
its class-composition and social positionality are necessarily *heterogeneous*"
(213, emphasis added). *Here*, any hope for history lies.

Let us docket Birch for the moment as a young man (with knowledge of
Vulgar Fractions) for whom consolidating the self of Europe *felt* like making
history. Were this absurdity not so unbearably tragic, we could laugh at our
Euro-US epistemological training.

IV. *Avant La Lettre*

Spivak's next example of the maneuvers needed to concoct Europe's self-
consolidating other is a letter written by David Ochterlony to John Adam.
Spivak does not describe Ochterlony as a romantic figure but as someone who
"cordially hated the hill people": "He is the kind of person one imagines in
the first flush of enthusiasm against Imperialism" (213). So counseling against
the temptation and naïveté of caricatures, Spivak likens Ochterlony to *Jane
Eyre*'s St. John Rivers. What we picture is the prodigious petulance of a Major

General doing God's work (read: impeccable ledgering) of History. In his letter to John Adam, Ochterlony says: "[T]he restoration [of Sirmur] will be received so much as an obligation as a right, and I look forward to . . . any play which does not give back the Territory unalienated, and the revenue undiminished in all its feudal relations" (214).[8]

Oddly enough, these restored feudal relations do *not* include the divine right of kings; the deposed, syphilitic Raja "Kurrum Perkash [*sic*]" cannot claim divine right because he is not *entitled*. In this enlightened judgment, the Raja of Sirmur, who fled into exile, becomes a rationalized object of imperialism: (he is) diseased. Upon the Rani's request for help, the Company invalidates Gurkha encroachment into Sirmur albeit with revenue more than halved. The Raja ought to accept this transformation of right into obligation: *his* right to his kingdom's revenue is his obligation to the Company, which duly requisitions more than half of the revenue without any change to the feudal nature of amassment and exchange. Spivak recognizes a particularly long standing (and insidious) trope: that, in the long run, victims must feel nothing but obligation (214); gratitude *for* imperialism is the (leftover) experience *of* imperialism. (The British, for example, gave India the Railways.)

We can call Ochterlony, then, a racist. He hates the native for what the native *makes* him do, but remains unaware of the native's terror at the affability of this hatred.

Spivak's third example of the pugnacious understatements used to translate colonialism into civilizing mission is a letter to Lord Moira, governor-general-in-council, by the board of control of the East India Company. She states, "This [example] serves to re-emphasize the *heterogeneity* of the 'Colonizing Powers.' We are once again witnessing the production of othering" (214–15, emphasis added). The board of control of the Company corrects the court of directors when it reprimands the governor-general. By distinguishing between native and colonial governments, the board chastises the governor-general for allowing half-pay subalterns to serve with regular troops. Only the Self of Europe can *know* the *épistemé* that will determine *meaning* for the Other: to the Company's board, any science of war used in the interest of government is to be withheld from native troops. Officers directly employed in allied Indian governments may impart limited amounts of this science to half-pay subalterns, a calculus that will guarantee that the Company's intentions are not superseded. Spivak illustrates how a pedagogically manipulated space of lack devises an innate natural difference: European and native become different "human or racial material" (216).

The Company's board of control substitutes discriminatory prudence (down below) with command (from above): "whatever may be your [the governor-general] opinion upon the propriety of these orders, we desire that they may be implicitly obeyed" (216). An excerpt from the passage the court of directors author but the board of control removes:

> The first and main point in which you [the governor-general] have erred has been in permitting Europeans not in the Company's service to remain in India. [This practice] would lead to an implicit improvement of the Discipline of the Troops of Native Powers. . . . The limited degree of science which it may be consistent with good policy to impart to the troops of native powers in alliance with the British government, should be imparted by officers in our own service: because . . . we have a guarantee that our intentions shall not be overstepped. (215–16)[9]

Spivak notes that the stricken passage marks the unequivocal mandatory coincidence of desire and law. The board of control's desire is the governor-general's desire before the former's desire is divulged as law. Indeed, "it must have been known [beforehand] that we [the board of control] should disapprove" (216).[10]

This anonymous agent/implement is unmistakably paternalistic and his desire is adeptly funneled to its cipher to get the job done: the anonymous agent's/implement's duty is to the law, which is revealed only upon violation; nonetheless, the cipher *should* have known better. Reprimand recalibrates the useful fiction of civilizing mission, and, again, the little bits of archival material are breathtakingly understated. But, Spivak prays to refrain from blaming a monolithic Colonial Power because "[o]f course, Freud [as metonym for Europe] never speaks of imperialism" (219). Spivak's project remains to make the Rani of Sirmur meaningful as distinct from reprising the clash of the colonizer and colonized as *finished* agendas.

The provocation to shelter significance transpires within the general frame of ad hoc state formation and economic crisis management. As the Company's interests become territorial, the Company mutates into a monstrosity that behaves like a real state: "The governments of India were the *Company's* governments, the army the *Company's* army, attempts at legal re-inscription the *Company's*" (220). Although British only in name, the settlement tracts of Sirmur are simultaneously the Company's state (thus the installation of the Raja's minor son) and empire (thus the Raja's liability to pay revenue), a paradox that structures the Rani's entry in the colonial archive. Spivak points out that ad hoc state formation is traditionally considered symptomatic of India's lack of modernity, as standard historical approaches ignore desultory and situational forms of empire building to substantiate the other's lack:

> The standard historian . . . assume[s] the growth-pattern in
> Europe . . . as the unquestioned norm, consider[s] the problems
> only in the domestic context [India as lack]. . . . Here what is
> one narrativization of history is seen not only "as it really was,"
> but implicitly "'as it ought to be." (222)

Because desire and genealogy coincide in Spivak's quest for Europe *as* an Other,
she announces: "I am no historian" (222). (Recall she must lie to correct a lie.)

The archive discards everything but the narrative via euphemism and
ellipses: "To lend the name 'transformation' to this tremendous and uneven
clash of discursive formations is to exclude all else in the history of the colony
and postcolony but the itinerary: native informant/colonial subject/postcolo-
nial subject/globalized subject" (223, note 42). So, *how* did these differently
abled discursive formations conflict? *Who* we meet in the colonial archive is
a romantic Birch, a cordially hateful Ochterlony, and a self-righteous board
of control pained to inflict penalties because the cipher should have known
better. If this is the trajectory that miraculates us into being—native infor-
mant→ colonial subject→ postcolonial subject→ globalized subject—we lose
that future where Europe is an Other. Spivak's reader's perspective, haunted
by the Rani's ghost, haunting being a trope for unfinished business, strives
for heterogeneity—that is, for (the possibility of) history.

V. The Good Woman

Spivak remarks, "In order to construct the Rani of Sirmur as an object of
knowledge, then, it should be grasped that she emerges in the archives because
of the commercial/territorial interests of the East India Company" (227).
The Company protects a woman who is protecting a child; the shareholders
(then, as now) are important; for their interests, the Company establishes
its ad hoc state and empire (224). Ochterlony maintains that the native
government "ought to possess all the visible signs of sovereignty . . . which
may give it responsibility in the eyes of subjects" (225).[11] Granting that the
mood is subjunctive, the native's own (lying?) eyes reform (feudal) command as (British) responsibility. John Adam reminds Ochterlony that the
contested land is to be permanently occupied, and a proclamation (to *that*
effect), which can be expeditiously disseminated in the provinces, seems the
appropriate course of action. John Adam insists on free passage for British
merchants in captured areas and the guarantee of a pleasing (profitable)
outcome (226). (He can be reliably docketed as the mouthpiece of free trade
and democracy—to come.)

Nascent in this proclamation is the intransigent imperial versus feudal polarity, but the official reports belie through what design these facts are produced. Any *quid pro quo* of commercial monopoly gained by territorial infraction is oppression, for the authenticating voice denies any exercise of "a local version of *their* [native] so-called entitlement" (226). In fact, in needing to be vindicated, honor becomes the right of the invader to deny legitimacy. Birch uses local stereotypes to impugn the "Mahajens" [*sic*] and "Bunneahs" [*sic*] to this end. Native businessmen along the trade route in Sirmur apparently take advantage of the paucity of Company shelters. By independently inviting British merchants to convalesce in their homes, they infringe on their own privacy for gain (226). (This infringement of privacy is different from what the Rani will face in the absence of her husband.)

Local merchant castes/classes covertly negotiate with the solicited vendor for access to prevailing markets (as they are) written over by the Company's (proclaimed) right to (entitled) acquisition. Made under the *obligation* of hospitality (oppression), individual deals hoodwink British buyers and shut out other regional barons from the ensuant privatized marketplace. This extortion-that-is-hospitality becomes the Company's right to protect their emissaries from shrewd "Mahajens" [*sic*] and "Bunneahs" [*sic*] who find a way to make a buck (*their* free market competitiveness). Supervision of negotiations and "weights and measures" (226) are introduced for "fairness." Spivak observes that the Company initiates exploitation without violence by grafting a so-called industry standard, which debuts as neutral rules of exchange to foil coercion of the Company's representatives *by the people being colonized by that very Company* (227). Exerting the sheer force of rhetoric, the arbitrating voice spins native agency as a cunning populace, untutored in the protocols of a modern marketplace, voiding fair play.

The East India Company cultivates the field for gauging fairness by resorting to a phantasmatical discourse of race, but Spivak diagrams the rationalizations differently: "The usefulness of the Rani-with-prince-separate-from-husband in this feudal capitalist textualizing of the limits of the colony [the rest waiting to be written] is a complex deployment of gender" (227). Smoothing out the ludicrous quality of feudalistic-capitalism-that-is-colonialism archived as civilizing mission, *she* serves as trope *and* object at the colony's edges within a metonymic chain made possible by other useful fictions (of the archive). Race and gender crisscross when a rift perforates the domestic sphere: in the absence of the diseased and exiled Raja, a romantic Birch proxies "husband" to effect the Raja's appropriation and displacement for permanent settlement. Even though the proximity of a strange male in an unattached woman's household riles up formidable opprobrium and ignominy, this is how Birch comes to live in the palace of Sirmur.

We now alight upon Robert Ross who Spivak flags as a "truly a vulgar-fraction lad": "What is important for us is that *this* was the boy who, between the ages of twenty-three and twenty-five, compiled a brief history 'Statistical and Geographical Memoir of the Hill Countries Situated between the Rivers Tamas and Sutlej'" (227). As reported by Ross, the Sikhs, Gurkhas, and Mughals are foreign invaders; motleys of aboriginals inhabit the hills; and, the rightful lords of this sphere are the Hindu chiefs (he is silent about the provenance of this appurtenance). *This* boy produced *this* historical document about *these* people. And: "*This* . . . 'authoritative' document [was] constructed out of *hearsay* and *interpreted conversations*" (228, emphases added) yet gained authorization for adjusting perimeters in Sirmur; the East India Company's court of directors merely suggested that Ross provide some sources.

We will docket Ross, then, as the trope of institutional racism, as he takes for granted the screening curve for mediocre white men. For them: coddling, tradition. For us: hearsay, interpreted conversations.

Ross fabricates a story that is identical overall with the Aryan-centric account of ancient India, which formalizes the pretensions of the Hindu chiefs advocating for Indian nationhood qua Hindu survival of unremitting conquest by outsiders (228). Spivak recalls a sign over the Indian Institute in Oxford: "May the mutual friendship of the land of the Aryans and . . . Anglos constantly increase" (229). The Hindu-Aryan myth obscures the extraction of surplus value such that kinship is metonym for obliged action: imperialism is mutual friendship. With this "race-divisive historiography" (230), Ross is to fix each state to the boundaries of this second (seventeenth- or eighteenth-century) origin. Kinship that begets friendship that begets restoration that begets obligation puts the Rani "in the shadow of shadows" (231), a slight ghost in the company of a slight romantic figure. She is the guardian of her minor son, Fateh Prakash; together they grant Sirmur enough "visible signs of sovereignty" to exculpate permanent rule. In the period that the Company sought to clinch its trade routes and borders against the Gurkhas of Nepal, "the Rani surfaces briefly as an individual" (231). Thanks to her part, Ross and Birch transcribe her (for the record) as "this Ranny" [*sic*]. (Spivak calls Ross "this boy" in another record.)

She is the wife of a king, a relatively benign piece in the "chess-board of the Great Game" (230); she appears once as Rani Gulani and once as Gulari, but, Spivak underlines, she gets more space than the most detailed record of women's names in colonial India: the horrifyingly misspelled names of immolated women belonging to various classes in Bengal (peasant, money-lending, clerical, etc.) (230, 231). The names are sickeningly sweet—Love's Delight, Soft Eye, Dear Heart, Smile, Love-bud—and manifest the danger of using proper names turned common nouns as "sociological evidence" (232).

> [A]s one goes down the grotesquely mistranscribed names of these
> women, the sacrificed widows, in the police reports included in
> the records of the East India Company, one cannot put together a
> "voice." The most one can sense is the immense *heterogeneity* break-
> ing through even such a skeletal and ignorant account (castes, for
> example, are regularly described as tribes). (287, emphasis added)

The names intimate that the burnt widow is always figured as "pretty and
constant"[12] *for* the efficient traffic in telescoped signals of European chivalry
and native brutality. Spivak registers the effrontery because "[b]y this sort of
reckoning, the translated proper names of contemporary French philosophers
[Jacques, Michel, Emmanuel] . . . would give evidence of [an] . . . archangelic
and hagiocentric theocracy" (232–33). On the contrary, baptismal certificates
of every cadet in the Company's service are painstakingly preserved to attest
to proper identity.

For the King of Sirmur's wife there is only a title and a nebulous first
name; this is enough given her limited purpose, and only two specific deeds
are recorded. Spivak describes her as "astute." Knowing her aunt will ask for
more maintenance, the Rani initially allows her less, an action mentioned
because it requires expenditure. Spivak extrapolates that "[w]e imagine her in
her crumbling palace, separated from the authority of her *no doubt* patriarchal
and dissolute husband, suddenly managed by a young white man in her own
household" (233–34, emphases added). In this odd domestic arrangement, the
crumbling palace is the syphilitic Raja while loss of patriarchal protection is
loss of autonomy. The Rani must acquiesce to an alien outsider in her private
quarters, and, for all that Birch is a slight romantic figure, she is not figured
as pretty and constant.

Caught between patriarchy and imperialism, the Rani is in "a representative predicament" (234). The switch from the Raja to Birch dovetails with the
switch from feudal to modern: on her archetypal dilemma rests any passage
into historicity. As a mother who acts in her child's name, *her* heterogeneity
underwrites the smooth transition from agent/implement to subject (234).
Somewhat removed from the clutches of patriarchy by the banishment of her
husband, she is indecorously but quintessentially coupled with Birch—both
domesticities (diseased and romantic, respectively) "no doubt" patriarchal.

VI. The Good Wife

Within her established historicity ("And then . . ."), "the Rani suddenly declares
her intention to be a *Sati*" (234). (It is unclear exactly when this declaration

occurred.) Insofar as she is the hinge or pivot for the changeover of the *epistemé*, Spivak reads her as intending to be an example of (the general proper name) *Sati*; (her) desire and law coincide *as* good wifehood. Birch seeks counsel from the Company's superiors, as, Spivak grievously adds, a royal *sati* in the prelude to its abolition in 1829 would be an embarrassment (238). (Again, the predicament is representative, a double bind: *sati* qua clever foiling of the Company's best-laid plans, *sati* qua fittingly extirpated atrocity.) Birch's affective language in his correspondence to the board of control stands out amid his paltry chronicling of the Rani. In his letter, he uses the word "devoted" because she states, "her life and the Rajah's are one" (234). *Here* in the archive are the scripted (perhaps cynical) interpretations of the Rani that betray intimacies on the ground.

The colonizer *in* colonization (recall the sense of a "rift") writes her as the devoted Hindu wife whose (native, not the Company's) pronouncement is unquestioning servitude (recall the sense of a "gap"). Birch's use of "allude" understates her gendered overdetermination: in the thick of the opposition and antagonism of Indian nationalists contra European colonizers in debates on *sati*, she could not *possibly* choose. Birch informs her of proper patriarchal protocol: "[S]he should . . . devote herself to the love of her son and live for him" (234). (Spivak does not explicitly notice the audacity but Birch tells the Rani how to be a good mother.) Then: Hindu wife means unquestioning servitude (to the Raja); now: Hindu wife means unquestioning servitude (to the child); selfless life (with a stranger) in place of selfless death (with a husband) is proper devotion. The Rani demurs. She states "to the effect, that it was so decreed" (234). (Another coincidence of desire and law is emergent here as she seems to refer to the authority of sacred Hindu texts.) Furthermore, the Rani insists, "she must not attend to [foreign] advice deviating from it [the decree to commit *sati*]" (234).

As mentioned earlier, she is "astute": her desire is decreed, yet also her intention; her intention is law, yet also dissuadable. At this confluence of patriarchies, Hindu Law and British Law coincide: the Rani's allusion (aka ordained choice) should be availed by Birch. When he questions her, he takes her to mean "her intention of burning herself at his death" (234). (The Rani's precipitous resolve happens when the Raja is still alive.) After the Rani rebuffs his solicitous dissuasions, Birch concludes that she is steadfast upon sacrificing herself (234).

This Ranny [*sic*] appears to be completely devoted to her husband, of which you may greatly judge by the following conversation which took place in a conference I had with her sometime ago [*sic*] she observed, that "her life and the Rajah's are one" which

> I consequently concluded to allude to her intention of burning herself at his death, so I replied, she should now relinquish all thoughts of doing so, and devote herself to the love of her son and live for him. She said to the effect, that it was so decreed and she must not attend to advice deviating from it: so I conclude, she has resolved upon sacrificing herself.[13]

Here, Spivak interjects: "*Now* begins the tale of a singular manipulation of her private life" (234, emphasis added). Birch must ensure that the interests of indigenous patriarchy and the colonial government remain unmistakably discrete.

But, the Rani's impromptu profession (of intention) stumps Birch, as her maneuvering of the discourse of honor and sacrifice unseats the Company's own inveigling of said discourse for prima facie incompatible objectives: reverting to tradition (the Rani), or progressing to modernity (the Company). By placing Birch and the Company in a conundrum, the Rani *in* colonialism overreaches her role: as regent, she gives the royal household enough "visible signs of sovereignty" for the Company to usurp revenue unimpeded by native rebellion. Only as guardian of her subject-child can she bequeath imperialism the veneer of respectability needed to mitigate the passage from feudal to modern. *Her* unpredictable resolution (that is also mere wifely devotion) inserts a twist in a contrived narrative of sovereignty and domesticity, which drives her unconventional housemate and his Company to scramble. Birch dresses up this ad hoc crisis management as his gratitude to the Company for his felicitous selection to dissuade the Rani. His self-exaltation as envoy of history lends venerability to the circadian stopgap measures that fade into the staid impermeability of Europe and Its Others.[14]

If *sati* is decreed as lawful honor and sacrifice (for the Rani), then regulation is decreed as lawful honor and sacrifice (for Birch). Birch writes to his superiors,

> I should consider a very grateful office, if Government may think [it] proper to authorize my interference to prevent the Rani from fulfilling her intention. The best mode of effecting it would probably present itself on the occasion, but I should feel great satisfaction by being honored with any regulation from government for my conduct upon it.[15]

Only when rescue fails should statutes be resorted to because the valiant tutelage of women versus what can only be unwitting adulation makes colonialism *look like* civilizing mission. The Rani roils the scripting of good motherhood that produces her obligation as regent to her minor son. Her edict to commit *sati* while her husband is still alive, moreover, may bring the deposed Raja back into the picture, given the cadet who invades her household, but she does not signify good wifehood if she commits *sati*: for the "astute" and purposeful Rani Gulani of Sirmur, *sati* is the possibility of surfacing as Woman; for the "grateful" and slightly romantic Geoffrey Birch of Middlesex, *sati* is the possibility of surfacing as Hero.

Gulani's insinuation of a rift ("in") into a feigned scene of proper family life burnished as good motherhood perturbs the coolly connotative sense of a gap between the Rani and Birch ("and"). *This* is the rationalized nonsense, dispensed under the aegis of reason for ad hoc crisis management, which Spivak forsakes. When she asks *how* it is possible for someone to want to die by ritually burning oneself for the deceased husband as an act of mourning, she does not make the widow ventriloquize (her) free will or (her) coercion (282). Spivak tries to figure out what could have made this (final) sentence—"White men are saving brown women from brown men"—possible *as a sentence*.[16] The widow shuttles between hyperbole and piety, admiration and guilt, as the sentence is met with another sentence, which was formulated by nationalists: "The woman wanted to die." The two sentences are pitted against each other as if they comprise the entirety of viable deliberations (287).[17] Spivak sidesteps, therefore, the not *un*interested formation of free will and coercion, which precipitate the imperialist and nationalist sentences, by oppositional and antagonistic entities.

The British institute the spirit of the law of noninterference in Hindu custom by breaking the letter of the law. Another pairing emerges as British regulation and Hindu law both sanction transgressions. The *Rg-Veda* and the *Dharmasastra* permit a woman to commit suicide on her husband's funeral pyre as an exceptional signifier of her will. The *Sati* Abolition Law (1829) protects a woman from this ritually sanctioned singularity. Because Woman surfaces (or occurs) as (an) *exception* (to the rule of suicide) (235), this crossover from private to public spheres converts ritual into crime (288). *Suttee* (recall the British spelling of the practice) as synecdoche for (radical) cultural difference dissimulates imperialism (now globalization and finance capital) as creating a *good*—not just civil—society. Championing the woman as requiring safekeeping from her own kind (291), this strategy is countered by a trope of woman's consciousness: the good woman's desire (is) to be good (by burning) (235). Spivak terms this abyssal *mise en scène* "a constructed counternarrative of woman's consciousness, thus woman's being, thus woman's being good, thus the good woman's desire, thus woman's desire" (302). The *sati* is either victim or cultural hero (293). (Rani Gulani and Geoffrey Birch are also similarly but respectively placed.)

The sheer force of rhetoric unleashed by the (inverted) coincidence of exceptional interference (regulation) and exceptional prescription (ritual) adumbrates the actual (empty) place of the widow. For nationalists, she has the right to be courageous (295, note 151); for imperialists, she has the right to be dissuaded (296); both identify (exceptional) good wifehood with self-immolation. For imperialists, *suttee* is social mission; for nationalists, *sati* is reward (296); both transcriptions mean the *same* thing: good wife (291).[18] Woman as (empty) signifier is persistently appropriated and displaced (307, note 171): good wife/widow, tradition/modernity, victim/hero, culturalism/development, object of repression/subject of law, etc.[19] For Spivak, to be haunted by slight ghosts and slight romantic figures,

> it is important to acknowledge our complicity in the muting, in order precisely to be more effective in the long run. . . . All speaking . . . entails a distanced decipherment by another, which is, at best, an interception. . . . Yet the moot decipherment by another in an academic institution willy-nilly a knowledge production factory many years later must not be too quickly identified with the "speaking" of the subaltern. It is not a mere tautology to say that the colonial or postcolonial subaltern is defined as the being on the other side of difference, for an epistemic fracture, even from other groupings among the colonized. What is at stake when we insist that the subaltern speaks? (309)

At the edges of the free will versus coercion narrative, subalternity embodies a hopeful despair for that postcolonialism wherein Europe is an Other.[20]

VII. My Rani

Unlike the dissuaded widow at the scene of the crime, saving the Rani would not serve as the work of founding a good society. She is entreated to live for her son because she could not be presented with the choice of freedom (236). For *her* state of exception, pundits (Hindu priests) must come up with some advice to stymie her decisiveness, a *transgression* of the *Rg-Veda* and *Dharmasastra* punishable by prescribed penance. Similarly, the governor's secretary reiterates the official policy of noninterference in native "religious prejudice" (236), which is especially incumbent due to the Rani's high profile. (Strikingly, to choose [to live] or to choose [to die] is still to surface as [an] exception.) Her political importance for the continued administration of the

"Raj of Sirmore [sic]" disqualifies direct impediment, which Birch thought to be the most judicious of options. (Raj is the Hindi word for kingdom.)

Instead, "His Lordship in Council is ardently desirous [that] every means of influence and persuasion should be employed to induce the Ranee [sic] to foregoe [sic] her *supposed* determination" (236, emphasis added). The euphemisms used let slip the intimacy of opponents, as His Lordship in Council divulges his frustration with the Rani (or women) for her mercurial fancies. (We might imagine him as an older, punctilious, toffee-nosed, white-haired male sitting in his lavish chambers.) The prospect of a royal *sati* during the Company's watch compels a *substantive* transaction between the Rani and Birch via the latter's "influence and persuasion." The Company disavows its brute power, for *this* situation (of capricious but faithful desire) requires delicate handling. Its disquiet must be imparted to local pundits with appropriate skill and deference to convince the Rani "as would satisfy her mind."[21]

She cannot accompany her husband on his farther banishment from Kulathu to Buria, and no communication must take place between them, as her supreme duty is to her son. His Lordship does concede that in different circumstances compliance with "*his* [her husband's] wishes [not *her* wishes] [would be] expedient and proper" (237, emphasis added).[22] Remarkably, if the Company were not scheming for permanent settlement to colonize India, *sati* would be apposite (even while the Raja is still alive). These improvisations place the Rani in a (convenient) state of exception (mother) *from* the state of exception (wife) of the state of exception (male) from sanctioned suicide. In this collusion of patriarchies, good Hindus and good Birch remind the Rani (with "every means of influence and persuasion") that she ought *not* to follow through on her exceptional yet proper intention. As cautionary actions (*just in case*), the Company postpones banishing the Raja farther away and Birch does not let the Rani leave Sirmur. It seems they do not want to try the Rani's resolve. And, "*there* the matter is dropped" (237, emphasis added). Spivak asks if Birch had "read the Rani right" (237). There are no textual ingredients to ascertain how the Rani of Sirmur became the object of imperialism, but the erstwhile Company and its surrogate Birch did indeed work overtime to cinch the Rani's eventually uneventful death ("in an academic sense") (238).

In order to accomplish *this* "end of the story" (237)—that is, her uneventful death—the Rani becomes the repository of extreme deprivation of agency *and* extreme manifestation of agency: she is resolute *and* devoted, willful *and* sacrificing. To claim *her* Rani, Spivak searches for disregarded everyday details (238), which uncover how the Rani comes to occupy what the itinerary only names: guardian of subject-child or wife of "Kurrum Perkash [sic]." As the most intimate details are the most inaccessible, the bits and pieces of unprocessed life hold greater promise. Attentiveness to how we put together our "everyday life" (238) is a space clearing gesture since these rough-hewn particulars elude the knowhow of ready-made parts. *For* a reader's perspective, the absurdities that bring about the denouement of identity and difference quash the "chanciness" (Derrida's term) that makes any story (happen). The discontinuities of *how* we cathect the spaces (down below) that the narrative commands (from above), which cannot be archived (as the past), are the history of our vanishing present.

VIII. The End

Spivak briefly mentions the "fadeout points" (239) of the Rani in the unremarkable routine of her death.

> I caught the Rani in an "alternative" record, a minimal thanatography for the priests' convenience. The priests of the House of Sirmur are in Hardwar [a Hindu holy city where the sacred river Ganga enters the Indo-Gangetic plains in northern India]. In the priests' house, the past is not a past of memory. Indeed there is no past. The "books" are long scrolls, each resembling the other, a kind of "living present," released by death as simple punctuation. Where does this stream of parchment begin? You could construct a disciplinary "historical" answer by consulting the right sources, or becoming a source yourself. But in fact it begins nowhere, for the first available scrolls are in media res. The Rani was not a *Sati.* She died in 1837, and the list of ingredients for her funeral indicate that her death was "normal." (243–44)

Spivak's "narrative pathos" (241) evinces the Rani's "fadeout points" to mark (out) what could only be violently cordoned (off) to effectuate a geopolitically determined general frame; this is why "[t]here is no romance to be found here" (234).

She absorbs these "fadeout points" as the rhetorical limits of logic: how far can the logical precept go before it constitutes a margin (239)? Amid efficiently distributed telescoped signals, "[her] account can at best mark rupture, fadeout, colonial discontinuity" (241). Any "groping" (239) for the Rani, of course, will not lead us to the marginal aborigine women of the hills, a remembrance and forgetting that subtends Spivak's reader's perspective. She holds *this* question of meaning at bay because such a jaunt would (she parenthetically notes) "take us too far afield" (239). In the story of imperialism as a social mission, "[m]y Rani . . . can be invoked, for she is Fateh Prakash's mother, and he is in history, when history is understood on the Western model. . . . [S]he cannot be commemorated" (240); there is too little left of her. Even so, she *comes across* as a cheeky precursor who discomfited the Company's efforts towards a seamless theft of revenue. Her subalternity may animate the dreadful yet also prosaic calculus of imperialism, but, in transcending her designation as particular (*this* Ranny), she discloses Europe and Its Others' spurious integrity: *my* Rani.

The Rani as agent/implement (*for* Europe) and as slight ghost (*for* postcolonialism) amounts to the *same* thing: if these proceedings are to be closed, the Rani can be only a depreciated yet also adamantine ghost story. Spivak follows a "route of an un-knowing" (241)—that is, how she does not know—by chipping away between bits of language and mobilizing what logic discards (239): "a revised politics of reading can give sufficient value to the deployment of rhetorical energy in the margins of the texts acknowledged to be central" (13, note 13). Uncertain provisional work shows us that the archive is "a silence filled with nothing but noise" (239) *because it is an other's ghost story*. To be the apocryphal possibility of *this* truthfulness is what postcoloniality defines as a philosopher of the future.

IX. Proceedings 2.0

To recall our docketed figures: the ghosts of Birch, Ross, and Ochterlony haunt us still. For example, is Ochterlony not *that* colleague who smiles amiably but his glinting, pin sharp eyes betray his malice? Is Ross not *that* colleague whose wholesale dismissal of our work is endowed with authority (despite lack of citations) to extol Eurocentric conceptual cultures? And, is Birch not *that* colleague whose race neutral liberalism chastises us for being confrontational and socializes us to be collegial? The Self of Europe cannot hear us because it knows who we are *in spite of what we actually say*. Only by creating scapegoats can we shore up the aspirational loyalties of Eurocentrism's practitioners. Do we not recognize the familiar tropes that still maintain the model Europe and Its Others? If we read Spivak carefully, she (pre)figures a contemporary global epistemology. Will a postcolonial pedagogy be developed within the humanities in the Euro-US academy? Can our anguish be measured into objects of investigation because philosophy is yet to come?

Chapter Four

The Second Sex

Philosophy, Feminism, and the Race for Theory

It is not news that by virtue of our race and gender, black women are not only the "second sex" . . . but we are also the last race, the most oppressed, the most marginalized, the most deviant, the quintessential site of difference. And through the inversionary properties of deconstruction, feminism, cultural studies, multiculturalism, and contemporary commodity culture, the last shall be first. Perhaps.

—Ann DuCille, "Occult of True Womanhood"

[W]here white women are depicted . . . as "objects," black women are depicted as animals. Where white women are depicted at least as human bodies if not beings, black women are depicted as shit.

—Alice Walker, "Coming Apart"

I stood between them,
the one with his travelled intelligence . . .
and another, unshorn and bewildered . . .
Then a cunning middle voice
came out of the field across the road
saying "Be adept and be dialect . . .
Go beyond what's reliable . . .
and recollect how bold you were . . .
with departures you cannot go back on."

—Seamus Heaney, "Making Strange"

I. Introduction

Four years after Spivak suggested "Europe *as* an Other" as a conference title, black feminist literary critic Barbara Christian gave a presentation titled "The Race for Theory" at The Nature and Context of Minority Discourse conference held at the University of California, Berkeley (1986). Organized by Abdul Jan-Mohamed and David Lloyd, the conference assessed the relationship between current theoretical trends and minority scholarship. In her presentation, subsequently published along with others in two special issues of *Cultural Critique* (spring and autumn 1987), Christian stipulates that an impoverished understanding of difference leads hegemonic theories to proscribe minority production a minor political role. Her affirmations of black women's works received widespread derision for passing off her lack of theoretical proficiency as cultural pride and exalting black female victimhood. This chapter revisits this over three decade-old moment to retrieve the critical force of Christian's cautionary tale. It suggests that Christian contests major discourse's cultural competency in offering a meaningful understanding of difference. By virtue of denying black women's works any general implications, the oppositions and antagonisms of major and minor are inadequate for the historical moment at hand. In barring minor discourse from actual significance, *this* race for theory forfeits a philosophical understanding of difference.

II. "ASAP"

The Nature and Context of Minority Discourse conference organized by Abdul JanMohamed and David Lloyd in 1986 at the University of California, Berkeley, had a few specific goals: presenters will detail how marginaliza-tion has detrimental effects for creating collectivities among disenfranchised populations, and they will solicit strategies to withstand such disempowerment ("Toward" 6). In the introduction to the special issues of *Cultural Critique* (1987), JanMohamed and Lloyd describe the NEH (National Endowment for the Humanities) reviewer who rejected their funding proposal for the conference. This reviewer's opinions were apparently so crucial that the NEH solicited them belatedly—"at the last minute" *after* the other five reviewers had delivered favorable judgments. The NEH announced this reviewer's concerns post-haste ("ASAP") and rejected the conference proposal on the basis of this *one* review. The comments of the "ASAP" reviewer bear repeating at length:

> I cannot but feel that a conference that would bring together in
> a few days of papers and discussion specialists on Chicano, Afro-

American, Asian-American, Native-American, Afro-Caribbean, African, Indian, Pacific Island, Aborigine, Maori and other ethnic literature would be anything but diffuse. A conference on ONE [*sic*] of these literatures might be in order; but even with the best of planning, the proposed conference would almost certainly devolve into an academic Tower of Babel. It is not at all clear that a specialist on Native-American literature, for example, will have much to say to someone specializing in African literature. It is also unlikely that the broad generalizations Professor JanMohamed would have them address would bring them any closer. (6)

Multiplicity can only lead to a Tower of Babel, as the participants are per-ilously dispersed. Reasonable academic judgment, therefore, predicts, not copious knowledge production, but a descent into internecine conflict and mutual incomprehensibility.

The "ASAP" reviewer's stress on a single ("ONE") minority literature overlooks the very common ground the conference petitioned to recognize: the nature and context of minority discourse. The dismissal that scholars in diverse literatures will have little or nothing to say to one another sets up the pejorative that follows. By making "broad generalizations" about the nature and context of minority discourse, Professor JanMohamed (David Lloyd is not referenced) disempowers minority discourse. *He* takes the many and turns it into the incomprehensibly diffuse when he should have focused on ONE. The *actual* context that turns the divergent into the marginal is let off the hook. Notably, it did not occur to the "ASAP" reviewer that the nature and context of minority discourse is in fact the nature and context of major discourse. Scholarly standards are disbanded ("cannot but feel") for exaggerated ("not at all clear") and merely asserted ("also unlikely") conclusions: the attendees are "almost certain [. . .]" to "devolve" into a chaotic horde.

This chapter begins *here* at this historical moment, when the threat of the undifferentiated masses (of academics, at an event about their work) needs to be kept out of the University of California, Berkeley—ASAP.

III. Are there black women, really?[1]

Black feminist literary critic Barbara Christian commences her analysis of the nature and context of minority discourse by criticizing the dualism of major and minor: Europe is major, everyone else is minor; furthermore, the rest of the world is obliged to view itself as minor ("Race" 54). Her 1986 presenta-tion and 1987 published essay conceive of major discourse's entitlement as the race for theory. At that time in the Euro-US academy, African-American studies gained visibility (primarily through the intellectual labors of Cornel West and Henry Louis Gates, Jr.); women's studies programs grew; and Afrocentricity ascended as a form of canon formation. Christian points out that black women's works comprise a long standing tradition that precedes deconstruction, French Feminism, postmodernism, and Afrocentricity, but are read (if at all) as (minor) examples of these broader (major) forms of theorizing. Only in deliberations on the (minor) difference of race or gender do black women's works appear to have relevance.

This kind of subsumption leads to another false binary as a direct result of the (major) binary of major and minor: the dualism interprets the *difference* of black women as political *plus*; black women are excess and ground zero at the same time—much too political (radical), which is, really, pre-political (ineffective), yet, not really figuring (significance). Erroneous periodization also perpetuates (major) false genealogies, as appropriation and displacement advance "general ignorance" (55) about black women's works. Upcoming scholars are discouraged from the research required to understand "why that statement—literature is political—is now acceptable [under the major's auspices] when before it was not" (55).[2] What results is a one-directional traffic in intellectual commodities: "I was supposed to know them, while they were not at all interested in knowing me" (56). Christian thereby turns the proverbial accusation of identity politics detrimental to minority scholarship on its head, as "many of us have never conceived of ourselves only as somebody's other" (54).

Contra major discourse's sanctioned ignorance, she foregrounds *how* major discourse attains preeminence "interestingly enough" (55) at a peculiarly felicitous moment, right when (minor) difference makes a qualitative impact in (major) academe. Along with this extremely hard-won historical achievement, demographic changes in student populations and faculty as well as diverse curricula seem imminent (55). Eurocentric scholars, however, express discomfort with salient aspects of "their *own* tradition" (56; emphasis added), but breed indifference towards those Europe colonizes or enslaves. In its extraction, production, marketing, and dissemination, discourse seems to function as (major) patented cultural capital with a guaranteed hearing, "even as it claims many of the ideas that we its historical 'other' have known . . . for so long" (54).

"The Race for Theory" was mocked and admonished by co-participants of the conference and the larger academic community. Indeed, JanMohamed and Lloyd are barely able to conceal their impatience as they simultaneously introduce and undermine ("it *must* be argued") Christian's work via incorrectly reporting on her penchant for an "implicit" critical practice ("Toward" 7, emphasis added).

> Barbara Christian argues forcefully for the priority of close exami-
> nation and an intrinsic articulation of minority texts; minority
> critics, she *feels*, should not succumb to the *glamor* of high theory;
> the theoretical assumptions of minority culture are contained
> within its literary texts. (7, emphases added)

Apart from mischaracterizing her attentiveness to archival work as a rejec-
tion of theory per se, they surprisingly overlook her first book, *Black Women
Novelists: The Development of a Tradition*, 1892–1976 (1980), which is one of
Christian's most enduring contributions to literary criticism.

Her scholarly remedies for trivialization (close reading, genealogical
labor, archival work) and her prioritization of primary texts become facile
validations of black women's distinctiveness (9). As a response to Christian,
JanMohamed and Lloyd propose an essential (masculinist) reading practice
that assumes facility with major theory as "*our* [all minority scholars] formal
training" (7, emphasis added). Minority scholars pursue theoretical reflection
because their discourse is the battleground upon which they must ward off
(major) theoretical encroachments. But, they go even further by suggesting
that Christian does not quite comprehend "the nature of current political
reality" (9).

> [W]hile members of the dominant culture rarely feel obliged to
> assimilate various ethnic cultures, minorities are always obliged,
> in order to survive, to master the hegemonic culture. . . . To
> believe otherwise [as Christian does] is either naïve or self-
> serving . . . [and] den[ies] the fact that cultural struggle contin-
> ues . . . *most importantly at the theoretical level.* For example, to
> argue that one has never considered oneself "minor" and then to
> *complain* that ethnic literatures have traditionally been marginalized
> is to confuse cultural pride with the nature of current political
> reality. (9, second emphasis added)

Christian misdirects her pre-political (political *plus*) energies because "*surely,*
it is the political situation" (9, emphasis added) that renders ethnic literature
of minor repute and not deficient "cultural pride" among its generators.

According to the conference organizers and special issue editors,
asserting the major's failure in persuading the minor of its subsidiary rank
is merely cultural pride; protesting that (minor) difference is not inherently oppositional and antagonistic is naïve; boosting the scholar's life of
the mind and fundamental creative freedom against an enforced peripheral
role is exoticism; and, promulgating archival work to manifest presence

across time is self-serving. JanMohamed and Lloyd belittle what they brand as Christian's *feelings* by ignoring the critical difference that minor gender (race) and minor race (gender) actually makes in combating neutralization and disempowerment.[3]

And yet, it *must* be argued that *surely* Christian recognized "the nature of current political reality" when she presented her paper. At that time in the 80s, the end of formal apartheid in the United States was just over two decades old; President Ronald Reagan's policies dehumanized AIDS victims, impoverished and isolated African-American families, and were environmentally catastrophic. Apartheid South Africa was facing some of its most brutal years. Nelson Mandela was still on Robben Island, and, fittingly, Ronald Reagan and Margaret Thatcher refused aggressive economic sanctions ("Security Council"; Pauw, "Death Squads"; Dugard et al., "Last Years"); their free market fundamentalism, which included an erstwhile mining corporation, ceremoniously titled *Anglo American* (*un*-hyphenated), emblematic perhaps of a colonial/ postcolonial symbiosis, held the line against increasing pressure at home and abroad to confront South Africa ("Compensation Case"). Thatcher proclaimed that anyone who believed that the African National Congress (ANC) would one day create a united South African government lived in "cloud cuckoo land" (Pressly, "Mandela's Triumphant Walk").

Perhaps Christian knew all too well that it was not the United States and Britain that led the way against apartheid but African and Asian Commonwealth nations (South Africa withdrew from the Commonwealth in 1961 at the Bandung Conference because of this dissidence).[4] Hazel Carby notes the discrepancy between the academic language of diversity in the 80's and the regressive conservatism of the Reagan era. In fact, South Africa was a crucial part of African-American consciousness: black communities called the Bronx "New York Johannesburg"; Chicago became "Joberg by the Lake"; and black politicians named the *Minneapolis Star Tribune* the "Johannesburg Times." Students across the United States not only protested apartheid but also demanded that universities divest their economic assets in South Africa (14).[5]

JanMohamed and Lloyd omit the circumstances under which Christian speaks (of which they were obviously aware) to cast "The Race for Theory" as a petulant and anxious outburst. They enact what Ann DuCille terms an "intentional phallacy" ("Occult" 620)[6]: their lack of recognition of Christian's participation in black women's transnational feminist tradition prevents them from understanding her arguments; their lack of understanding of her arguments prevents them from recognition of Christian's participation in black women's transnational feminist tradition. The premise that proficiency in major discourse entails knowledge of "the nature of current political reality" may safeguard free trade between major and minor by allaying (minor) cultural pride, but it risks mistaking dominance for historical adequacy.

IV. Pallid Ephemeras

Michael Awkward also implies that Christian creates illegal trade barriers between major and minor, especially when she places particular emphasis on hitherto unknown black women's works. He presses on Christian's inability to apprehend (major) literary theory (360), even though she purportedly avails of (major) tropes to depict black women's academic status. As per Awkward's critique, Christian blames literary theory for corrupting a previously scrupulous black feminist criticism (disloyal native women fraternize with white men); literary theory compels black women into silence (the subaltern cannot speak); and, black women are under siege by white phallocentric discourse (female slaves fight off white masters) (362). Taking (major) liberties during his assault on Christian's intellectual capacities, he contends that

> Christian's representation of theoretically informed black female (and other noncaucasian and/or male) critics as "co-opted'" *can only be read* as an attack on their personal integrity and recent work. She apparently *cannot even conceive* of the possibility that these critics *choose* to employ theory because . . . [they view] theory . . . as useful in the critical analysis of the literary products of "the other." (362, first two emphases added)

This (major) determination ("can only be read," "cannot even conceive") of Christian's lack of collegiality (towards scholars wielding more power) is followed by the peremptory verdict that she become "clearly informed" (362) about her "villainous post-structuralists" (364).[7]

Awkward censures Christian for addressing only the "best, *blackest* interests of our literary tradition" (366)—the blackest is de facto not complex in the split he sets up—and consummates his appropriative gestures (a play on Zora Neale Hurston's term) with a gentle, paternalistic warning: for black women's work to make "*inroads* in the canon . . . [and garner] the respect it doubtlessly deserves . . . [it must progress] beyond *description* and *master* . . . contemporary literary theory" (367, emphases added). As the "rich" raw material prior to development via active reasoning, black women's texts cannot passively await the thrill of discovery and subsequent ravishment;

evidently, black women must strap on a (minor) dildo and pummel their way through the master's house to display their (hopefully imitation) leather-clad mastery of the master's tools.[8]

Surely black women are not responsible for explaining their texts to their (major) colleagues who may use their impeccable skills to read against the grain of what purports to be "*our* formal training." In Awkward's account, after centuries of experiencing their own impossibility, black women have mustered the pallid ephemera of a (minor) description. Of course, when all women are white, all blacks are men, and all men and women are heterosexual, offering a historically adequate account of the present is a revolutionary act.[9] Underestimating the philosophical problems at hand, Awkward recapitulates the very separation between (major) theory and (minor) description that disavows black women's capacity for substantive insight. Black women's works are also not on equal footing with Eurocentric conceptual cultures in a merit-based altercation wherein the "best, *blackest* interests" confirm their worthiness.

Unsurprisingly, Awkward does not describe the (major) conditions in which black women work, for along with exhaustion, depression, and seclusion, black women suffer hypertension, lupus, cancer, diabetes, and obesity with greater frequency than their white cohorts (DuCille, "Occult" 623). Should we be shocked that Audre Lorde and June Jordan were not granted medical leave for cancer by their institutions (Hunter College and University of California, Berkeley, respectively)? University of California, Berkeley, refused Jordan less than two years after refusing fellow black feminist Barbara Christian. City University of New York (CUNY) refused Lorde when she was poet laureate of New York State. Audre Lorde died. June Jordan died. Barbara Christian died. Alexis Pauline Gumbs avers, "Black feminists are a trouble more useful as dead invocation than as live," as these institutions continue to profit from using black women as symbols of prestige (CUNY held a conference on Lorde to mark the twentieth anniversary of her death); the university is not a place that will spend money to save a black feminist life ("The Shape of My Impact").

Institutional mechanisms of service and accreditation do not acknowledge how black women endure the burden of representation to the detriment of their research. While senior black male scholars often evaluate black women's works without the requisite expertise, white scholars (not just male) feel affronted by the very presence of black women in their departments, and penalize them for the very work they were hired to do (DuCille, "Occult" 596–97). Acclaimed university presses and journals use male intellectuals (black and white) to review book manuscripts of newly minted scholars and not senior black women with relevant expertise (596). Minor disciplines (for example, African-American Studies and Women's Studies) are consistently severely underfunded. When Christian, Jordan, and Lorde were forging a movement as part of a long standing black feminist tradition, the term "multiculturalism" operated as a code word for "race," as do "drugs" or "inner city violence" (8). (We may add "thugs," "urban voters," "sons of bitches," etc.)[10] Hazel Carby reminds us that Ronald Reagan used racist backlash against affirmative action as a presidential platform barely sixteen years after the Civil Rights Act (14), as did his successor, George Bush, Sr., during his single term.

In her 1990 essay, published three years after Christian's essay appeared in *Cultural Critique*, Carby includes a reprint of a *Newsweek* magazine cover (December 24, 1990), which warns its audience to "watch what you say" and features an image of the capitalized words "THOUGHT POLICE" engraved in stone. The disingenuous question posed by *Newsweek* is whether political correctness is a new McCarthyism or a new enlightenment. Reactionary backlash assaults the putative terrorism of political correctness (8), a conservatively coined term that equates requests for civility with McCarthyism or worse. *Newsweek's* epistemograph astoundingly inverts Kant's plea to have the courage to use one's own understanding, made in a Berlin newspaper in 1784, to abnegate basic history: the very *recognition* of diversity sows division and persecutes the white majority.

The expectation of rational and humane public discourse, when experienced as loss of a rightful place in the social order, deflects the nation-state's fraught relationship with its variegated constituencies, who until twenty-five years ago were either living under American apartheid or colonized by European powers. Ultimately modest gains provoke overwrought reactions but the fact that more than 90 percent of faculty members are white is not cause for scandal or headlines (8).[11] Carby also inveighs against institutions that espouse the rhetoric of diversity but do not build diverse faculty bodies and administrative classes. Extreme rhetoric is directed against curricular endeavors, which usually amount only to a few (minor) books added at the end of a (major) syllabus. Like Christian, Carby denounces the waning number of tenure-track positions held by black scholars as well as the declining number of black graduate students, which prohibitively affects institution building, given the often tokenistic presence of minor discourse in (major) disciplines (13–15).

JanMohamed and Lloyd enjoy a particularly masculinist conversation with liberal humanism when remarking on Christian's essay because they ignore *this* "nature of current political reality." They read Christian's criticism of major discourse's impoverished understanding of difference via a standard polarity between individual and system and not as an exposition of economic rationalization ("What" 12). Although systemic and individual alienation "spring as inevitably from . . . capitalist society as do the systemic exploitation of . . . minority groups and the feminization of poverty, the demonization of third world peoples and homophobic hysteria" (12), black women's struggles against these forms of alienation somehow do not produce knowledge. A masculinist understanding of resistance results because they conflate discourse with culture and culture with capitalism: "ethnic or gender *difference* . . . [is] one among . . . [many] residual cultural elements which . . . have to be repressed . . . [so] that the capitalist economic subject may be the more easily produced" ("Toward" 11). To wit: "[I]in rejecting the (premature) avowal of humanist pluralism . . . minority discourse should neither fall back on . . . an a priori essence nor rush into . . . some 'non-humanist' celebration of diversity for its own sake" (10–11). These (major) clichés of minor discourse's penchant for essentialism or approbation of diversity *an sich* disregard the actual history of black feminism.

In Christian's formulation, the proponents of Eurocentrism are not the race for theory; instead, this race is begotten by an apocryphal genealogy of (minor) black women whose words and deeds did not come to pass but will (always) have been.

V. For the Record

JanMohamed and Lloyd suggest that minor cultural forms get their value from their economic and political difference from the major. This economic and political difference is minor culture's mode of existence, which determines its value and establishes disciplinary boundaries. The culture that defines minor culture's economic and political difference, and, hence, determines its value, is a sublimated form with universal validity, which per Spivak, is the "cultural dominant" qua economic system of production and the international division of labor (*Critique* 313). But, this cultural dominant that determines minor culture's value based on the latter's economic and political difference cannot be directly apprehended. This means it cannot be wholly represented; as the abstract, it is disclosed under erasure (315).[12]

Whereas JanMohamed and Lloyd valorize the (allegedly new) discourses that transgress disciplinary boundaries ensuant from the minor's mode of existence vis-à-vis the cultural dominant ("Toward" 11), Spivak warns that interdisciplinary work can allegorize transnational systems of production and divisions of labor. Since

> *we* are imprisoned in and habituated to capitalism, we might try
> to look at the *allegory* of capitalism not in terms of capitalism

as the source of authoritative reference but as the constant small failures in and interruptions to its logic, which help to recode it and produce our unity. ("Teaching" 16)[13]

Spivak asks for "transnational literacy," a keen grasp of the political, economic, and cultural standing of national origin places—that is, of the terms of exchange—in the financialization of the globe (she does not say countries or nation-states to accentuate the transnational recoding of the cultural dominant) ("Talk" 295).[14]

For example, notwithstanding the rhetoric of globalization, direct foreign investment is still concentrated in the North and does not drain capital to the global South (Bartolovich 132–33). Nation-states in the North guard their borders while imposing abjectly medieval systems of production and unmitigated debt-bondage in the poorest nations (Spivak, "Planchette" 243). If transactions between major and minor allegorize transactions between North and South, respectively, then minor discourse runs the risk of being ideologically compensatory. Attributing to minor discourse a privileged aptitude for cultural critique, given its noncompliance with disciplinary confines, deflects attention from how the cultural dominant withholds from minor discourse a claim to the constructive frame. In contrast, JanMohamed and Lloyd insist that minor discourse's interdisciplinarity makes theory and practice isomorphic at the "at least" level of institutional formations ("What?" 9).

This isomorphism can also be read, however, as the surplus value of interdisciplinary work under the aegis of (major) disciplinary patenting. Extracting a celebrated similitude of theory and practice from minor experience contracts the latter's cultural production into an in-built mechanism of opposition and antagonism to recode the cultural dominant as all-embracing. Considering that minor discourse already *exceeds* the (major) terms of exchange, even at the "at least" level of institutional formations, acceding to (major) trade agreements may afford minor discourse effective product placement, but valuing minor discourse is not a "purely cultural" (9) task. It *also* involves figuring out the arithmetic that licenses JanMohamed and Lloyd to engage with (major) liberal humanism and not black women's works when interrogating the nature and context of minority discourse.

For the record, Christian is typecast as emotional because she *personalizes* (distinct from pathos) the effects of systemic and individual alienation. Minority resistance is de facto a transaction between the major and minor liberal humanist—both, "no doubt," male. Consequently, JanMohamed and Lloyd use rather unfortunate language when introducing Christian's concept of the race for theory: "*Unmediated* by a theoretical perspective . . . [Christian's] *mere* affirmation . . . lends itself . . . to selective recuperation . . . [as] a *depo-liticized* 'humanity.' . . . [S]uch *premature* integration is . . . to be avoided" ("Toward" 9, emphases added). A masculinist cliché, dressed up as (patriar-chal) false modesty, supposes the continuity of socially constructed cultural explanations and collectively defined subjects.[15] Yet, minor discourse's mode of existence is *also* a state of exception at the "at least" level of institutional formations.

What this means is that minor discourse's economic and political dif-ference from the collectively defined subject qua cultural dominant reput-edly safeguards this discourse from being a facsimile of socially constructed cultural explanations.

> Herein lies the specific difference between the objective alienation which the minority intellectual seeks to overcome and the pathos of alienation which afflicts the traditional humanist. For the minor-ity intellectual is situationally opposed to that alienation, while the traditional intellectual either seeks to make the characteristics of the alien prefigurative of deferred universality, or in a recent version which is just an insidiously logical development of the former, to accept positivistically as merely the alienated conditions of labor in the glorified form of "professionalism." ("What?" 13)

In this tangle between socially constructed explanations, collectively defined subjects, and minor discourse, we can concede the situational difference of the minority intellectual. We can also concede JanMohamed and Lloyd's qualms about quelling the pathos of alienation through aestheticism and professionalism. But, the minority intellectual's situational difference in itself is not resistance to objective alienation if the situational minor discourse produced repackages (major) disciplinary boundaries via interdisciplinarity without altering the *terms* of exchange.

JanMohamed and Lloyd unlike Christian do not tackle major discourse's accreditation *as* a form of irreducible discontinuity in the present machine despite preventing minor discourse from actually changing the *frame* of knowledge production. Contrary to JanMohamed and Lloyd's characteriza-tions, Christian's concept of the race for theory is not a (minor) property rights dispute, which can be rectified by free trade zones between major and minor. If the capacity to know can be called culture at ground level,[16] then on *this* tax-sheltered (minor) ground, which is also a (major) tax *write-off*, major discourse's *pouvoir-savoir* is sanctioned ignorance trafficked as subli-mated culture with universal validity.

VI. Dialectically Down[17]

Black and white feminists also criticized Christian when she presented and published "The Race for Theory." For example, bell hooks calls into question Christian's undue fear of theory and the (reverse) racist consequences of her claims. She flags Christian's declaration that "people of color have *always* theorized [but not in] . . . Western forms of abstract logic" (52, emphasis added) as simply inaccurate. She emphasizes that we would be disturbed if a white person made that statement (*Talking Back* 39). In hooks's bid to be "dialectically down" and to confront anti-intellectualism (38), she gives the impression of chastising Christian for discarding the common currency of (major) ivory, sugar, coffee, and tobacco by settling for (minor) glass beads, cowries, and cotton cloths. In hooks's estimation, Christian's statement that using abstract logic is *one* way to theorize is a dubious proprietary claim about the authenticity of experience. Admitting that the black community (unspecified) often views postmodernism with suspicion and hostility ("postmodern blackness" being hooks's exemplary intervention), she nonetheless downplays this hesitation as a miscomprehension of postmodernism (*Yearning* 28).

It may be worthwhile to mention Linda Nicholson's acclaimed volume *Feminism/Postmodernism* (1990), published three years after Christian's by then much-anthologized essay, in the same year as hooks's *Yearning*, and one year after *Talking Back* (1989). This volume does not contain a single chapter that addresses the impact of this kind of (major) theorizing for either black women in the United States or women of color globally. A pernicious example of this volume's primary concern with the impact of postmodernism on gender is Susan Bordo's essay. Not only does it claim historical and epistemological priority for second wave feminists, but black women are also notably absent except when (parenthetically) used to underline the gravity of white middle-class women's oppression.[18] Black women seem not to be a race for theory (at all), but trouble gender by troubling the difference in (major) theory that Bordo believes gender in fact "first" made (138, 141). At odds with hooks's assessment of postmodernism, Nicholson's volume could not defy the transnational traffic in (major) knowledge and its consequences for (minor) knowledge emerging from the rest of the planet.[19]

The book does mourn the loss of European grand narratives, as Nicholson and Fraser proclaim that "with philosophy no longer able credibly to ground social criticism, criticism itself must be local, *ad hoc*, and untheoretical" (25). They do not start with the condition of philosophy but with (major) feminism's social object: patriarchy (26). In other words, when confronted with the historical inadequacy of Eurocentrism, scholars turn to minor discourse *not* for its claim to the constructive frame but for the *local, ad hoc,* and *untheoretical*, which consign philosophy to incoherence, disintegration, and chaos (recall the "ASAP" reviewer). In lieu of acquiring cultural competency for a meaningful understanding of difference, philosophy must abandon being theoretical at all. Nicholson and Fraser bear out Christian's charge that western forms of abstract logic erase how she experiences the world ("Race" 56) when an antagonistic understanding of difference *still* grounds social criticism: theoretical versus untheoretical, grand versus local, rational versus *ad hoc.* Since major discourse explicitly uses black feminist *difference* without having to seriously engage black women's lives,[20] such dualisms are inadequate for the historical moment at hand; they confuse an (abstract) logical reversal with an actual (substantive) one.

Christian shares that she abandoned her study of philosophy and pursued literary criticism as literature provided her a sense of wholeness (not conflict and detachment). This integration of feeling and knowledge is qualitatively different from the sameness effectuated by identity and difference (56). She privileges language that can speak to black women's needs and dispositions (52), and clarifies (not mystifies) black women's condition (55).[21] For Christian, major discourse curtails language as a form of pleasure and comes across as an "assault" (52) (perhaps like the increased volume in television advertisements or billboards signposting a landscape), as distinct from communication, play, or affirmation (54).

In a piece on the highs and lows of black feminist literary criticism, Christian tells us, "[we] . . . moved to excavate the past and restore to ourselves the words of many of our foremothers who were buried in . . . distorted history" ("Highs and Lows" 49). Unearthing the diary, the journal, the letter, and other graspable bits and pieces of the historical record, they urge that those "who look high . . . [should] also look low, lest we devalue women . . . even as we define Woman. . . . [Otherwise,] our voices [may] no longer sound like women's voices to anyone. But *who* knew what *we* knew?" (51, emphases added). Black women telling stories could not regard themselves as "artists of the word"; many aware of their genius became "crazy women crying in the wind or silenced scarecrows. *Who* could answer us but *us*?" (47, emphases added).[22]

This begging of the question creates both sender and receiver at the same instant—people of color have *always* theorized—by opening up the future anterior *for* an apocryphal genealogy of "silenced scarecrows" keeping watch. Christian's timely intervention is not an individual instance of sheer audacity in-spite-of-it-all; instead, she transforms present impossibilities of giving and receiving into a proleptic act of attrition. hooks surprisingly sidesteps the disparity between major and minor, highs and lows, "artists of the word" and "silenced scarecrows," and neglects the (major) identity politics that concern Christian the most—that black women's currency is artificially devalued, they are harassed and intimidated into the minor role, and their work is refused actual significance.[23] Thus, there is a race ("first") for theory, but *this* race squanders historical opportunities for a philosophical understanding of difference.

VII. Timeliness

Not a single scholar mentioned above acknowledges another important question Christian raises in "The Race for Theory." Other feminist participants at the 1986 conference who were also published in the special issues of *Cultural Critique* raise this question as well: why now? Nancy Hartsock is suspicious about the timing of postmodernism, poststructuralism, and deconstruction: just as (academic and non-academic) nationalisms were emergent across the globe, the Euro-US academy doubts the status of the subject, notions of historical progress, and the viability of universal social theories (196). Henry Louis Gates, Jr. goes further: "*[F]or the record*, . . . we have been deconstructing . . . since that dreadful day in 1619 . . . in Virginia. Derrida did not invent deconstruction, *we* did!" (34, emphases added). Kumkum Sangari draws attention to how instrumental technologies are disowned precisely when Euro-America continues to extract necessary information and mineral resources from the world's poorest nations. These neoliberal operations of exploitation and extortion uncannily recoil in the first world as an alleged but timely crisis in meaning, representation, and legitimacy.

A postmodern aesthetic raids third world cultural forms to textualize "lost" geographical terrains, which pulsate the west "*eternally*" ("Politics" 183, emphasis added). Economic and cultural domination become homologous when the periphery operates as the "permanent yet desired challenge to (or subversion of) a suffocating Western sovereignty" (184). A self-ironizing subject does not just stay enthralled with itself, but ensures (only) ONE race for theory (no risk of a Tower of Babel) is entitled to free trade. Yet, as Sangari emphasizes, the "crisis of meaning is not everyone's crisis (*even in the West*)" (184, emphases added). In *this* parenthetical insertion, Kumkum Sangari and Barbara Christian coincide when they object that many of us have never conceived of ourselves only as somebody's other.[24] And, the consonance between a feminist in India and a feminist in the United States empowers us to notice *another* actor caught up in the race for theory in the Euro-US academy.

At that time, albeit not mentioned by Christian, certain Eurocentric strands of postcolonial studies were also complicit in the devaluation, appropriation, and displacement of black women's works. Postcolonial theory not only established itself as a model minority discourse in comparison to the knowledge production of older minorities but also postcoloniality became synonymous with South Asian diasporic experience. Sangari's parenthetical insertion cites a transnational feminist practice that refutes the major's crisis as determinative. Christian and Sangari confirm the minor's general implications for theory and activism in the rest of the planet: a transnational feminist practice crosses (out) a geopolitically determined Eurocentric frame by engaging minor discourse *without* pitting it against major discourse and its (diagnostic and/or corrective) postcolonial instantiation.

Within Sangari's parenthetical insertion, therefore, the next chapter places black women's works not as *hegemonic* but as *exemplary* US feminism.

Chapter Five

Hit-Take, Hit-Alliance

Paradigmatically Postcolonial and Exemplarily Western

Simply by being postcolonial or the member of an ethnic minority, we are not "subaltern." That word is reserved for the sheer heterogeneity of decolonized space.

—Gayatri Spivak, *A Critique of Postcolonial Reason*

"Hit-fortune?" Aurora wondered.

"Like hit-take, hit-alliance, hit-conception, hit-terious," Vasco explained. "Opposite of mis-."

—Salman Rushdie, *The Moor's Last Sigh*

'Cause you never can tell
What goes on down below!
. . . From the world's deepest ocean,
. . . From way down below,
. . . From down in the mire and the muck and the murk,
I might catch some fish who are all going, "GLURK!"
. . . If I wait long enough; if I'm patient and cool,
Who knows *what* I'll catch in McElligot's Pool!
. . . Oh, the sea is so full of a number of fish,
If a fellow is patient, he *might* get his wish!

—Theodor Seuss, *McElligot's Pool*

I. We Were Not Yet Such a Group 2.0

In her essay titled "Teaching for the Times" (1992), Gayatri Spivak posits the African-American experience of negotiated independence as the paradigmatic case of postcoloniality in the United States. Published five years after Christian's "The Race for Theory" in *The Journal of the Modern Language Association*'s issue on "oppositional discourse," Spivak's essay divulges the "scandalous secret" (3) of the large-scale immigration of South Asian scholars to the United States: a hope for justice under capitalism.[1]

> We have come to avoid wars, to avoid political oppression, to escape from poverty, to find opportunity for ourselves and, more important, for our children . . . *Only* to discover that the white supremacist culture wants to claim the entire agency of capital-ism—re-coded as the rule of law within a democratic heritage—*only* for itself. (7)[2]

Spivak avers that assimilation in the Euro-US academy necessitates "Anglocen-trism first, and a graduated Euro-centrism next" (10). Metropolitan models of multiculturalism make *this* agency of capitalism available to South Asian scholars who mutate fraught histories of national origin into benign cultures thrown into the United States melting pot.

Such a putatively seamless process of acculturation relies on a precon-ception of latter-day United States' manifest destiny as asylum for everyone ("Foreword" xvi). Selectively self-represented South Asian scholars sustain US exceptionalism by recoding aspirational class advancement as available-to-all US benevolence, even though assimilation involves the continued exploitation of older racialized immigrants and indigenous disenfranchised populations (Anglocentrism first; Eurocentrism next, *for* aspirational class advancement) (*Critique* 360–61).[3] When South Asian scholars abnegate postcoloniality's constitutive conditions, they assume representative status of the postcolonial per se.[4] This claim to speak for marginality on a global scale not only appro-priates and displaces black women's works (as minor and untheoretical) but also substitutes South Asian diasporic experience for actually decolonizing terrain (places of national origin).[5]

At that time, therefore, when Barbara Christian spoke at the University of California, Berkeley, another discourse also makes the scene: postcolonial theory.[6] This related disciplinary development plays a role in aiding and abetting "the multicultural wars" between model minority and (effectively) non-model minority discourses. Spivak's analysis of a particular moment in postcolonial theory's institutionalization targets the multiple retrenchments impelled by diasporic South Asian scholars; this chapter explains *why* the African-American experience of negotiated independence is the paradigmatic case of postcoloniality in the United States. I pick up where Spivak's 1992 essay leaves off to make the following suggestions: 1. Black women's works are paradigmatically postcolonial because they contest the antagonistic understanding of difference that protracts major discourse's hegemony. 2. Their pursuit of the heterogeneity of black women's lives is exemplarily western because *this* difference is underived from the oppositions of major and minor. The heuristic metonymy—black women's works are paradigmatically postcolonial *and* exemplarily western—brings Eurocentric identity politics to crisis: if people of color have *always* theorized, albeit without using western forms of abstract logic (as Barbara Christian prescribes), then the metaphysics of presence is no longer the only knowledge the west has to offer. If the crisis of meaning is not everyone's crisis (even in the west) (as Kumkum Sangari instructs), then black women's works are essential for a philosophical understanding of difference.

II. Postcolonialism and Its Others

Postcolonial theorists claim a common experience of racism with non-model minorities as well as academic prestige as a model minority participating in major discourse; in relation to other minor discourses (African-, Native-, Hispanic-, and Latin-American, etc.), postcolonial theory alleges analogous marginalization, but certain strands strengthen Eurocentrism. Model minority standing, furthermore, abjures the requisite battles non-model minorities (African and Black Diaspora, LGBTQ, and Women's Studies scholars, etc.) already waged to clear a space for minor discourse (Bahri, *Native* 38). Crystal Bartolovich reminds us, postcolonial theory would not exist without decolonization and diaspora; "ditto for identity politics and poststructuralism" (130). Indeed, postcolonial theory's prominence for Ann DuCille stems from the very resistance discourses it threatens to exclude (*Skin* 126) because it did not transpire from the political activism for civil rights and equal treatment that spread to college and university campuses (Sharpe, "Postcolonial" 116).

As the agency of capitalism made available by metropolitan models of multiculturalism, cathecting a laudable stature vis-à-vis older minorities has insidious consequences in an overwhelmingly white academy. bell hooks looks at postcolonial scholars as mediators who mark a middle ground between the homegrown, unruly, and troubling (blackness) and the global, learned, and sober (whiteness); they either explain "bad" black people to their white colleagues, or they help "naïve" blacks understand whiteness (*Yearning* 94). Major discourse's favoring of postcolonial theory further objectifies difference, for a supposedly benevolent hierarchical system diffuses potential alliance-based resistance by passing the stature accorded to a few as respect and due consideration for the field itself (95). DuCille maintains that postcolonial theorists usurp subject matter first articulated by diasporic blacks. By not crediting this extensive genealogy of the study of enslavement and colonization, academe does not just act as though colonial relationships are a new field of inquiry, but legitimizes areas of study hitherto otherwise dismissed. Non-model intellectuals experience these derelictions of duty as a foreign takeover that riles up xenophobic sentiments in their scholarly communities (*Skin* 124–25).

The racist contempt postcolonial migrants too often use to acculturate and assimilate exacerbates mistrust and intolerance (hooks, *Yearning* 93). To challenge this mode of postcoloniality's existence, DuCille creates a binary: postcolonial theory is "dis-course" because academic stratification grants this distant, exotic field (major) prominence; Afrocentricity is "dat course" because this same pecking order brands this field anachronistic and meant to lend (minor) "local color (homeboys and homegirls)" (*Skin* 123). On one hand, the unsettling provocations of African-American studies and Afrocentricity hit close to home. On the other, postcolonial theory disapproves from a (polite) distance (127). African-American studies implicate the United States; via merchandising a different kind of difference, postcolonial theory lets the United States off the "imperialist hook" (134).

According to Carol Davies, black women are retroactively interpellated in cultural ideologies of post-ing or postponing due to postcolonial theory's global discourse, which promulgates postmodernism as a singular narrative of dissent. But, postmodernism refers to post-European modernism, a discourse that ignores internal colonization in western nations as well as decolonizing terrain, and arrogantly allocates itself a quality of always first, a "done-by-Europeaness," or a European already-ness (83, 86). Contra black women's ontological belatedness, an axiological prefix bequeaths postcolonial theory an aura of antipathy to these ideologies of post-ing or postponing. False canonicity and periodization encompass black women's works even as black women are still recuperating and revitalizing their (fractured) genealogies.[7] Patricia Hill Collins details how feminists before her found black women's works as fragments that evoke the fate of untold numbers who "lie buried in unmarked graves" (2). Her scholarship and activism reclaim "thrown away" black women who built a resourceful intellectual tradition whose invisibility is neither propitious nor inadvertent. In these circumstances, the semblance of pliancy does not mean that black women collaborate in their own debasement (2–3).

For evidence, we may return to Barbara Christian's 1987 essay, "The Race for Theory," included in the volume *Contemporary Postcolonial Theory: A Reader* (1996), in a section titled "Disciplining Knowledge." The piece is set alongside works by Gayatri Spivak, Anthony Appiah, and Arun Mukherjee.

Padmini Mongia, the volume's editor, says Christian concentrates on the impact of hegemonic theorizing, in a "related [to postcolonial theory], if albeit different, vein" (9), when she fights against the silencing of black women. Although the only black feminist literary critic included in the collection, the "related, if albeit different, vein" evinces no further elucidation but is chronicled as (contemporarily) postcolonial. In another example, let us contrast how Spivak and Homi Bhabha approach Toni Morrison's *Beloved* (1987). Spivak reads *Beloved* in *A Critique of Postcolonial Reason* (1999) as the figuration of an "Africa" (strictly differentiated from the contemporary continent of Africa) that registers as the pre-history of the Afro-American or New World African. This *figured* place "Africa" tropes what is materially impossible for the Afro-American or New World African: contact with *this* "Africa" as an actual place (431).

In *Outside in the Teaching Machine* (1993), Spivak dedicates a chapter to Morrison wherein she turns to the absence of contemporaneity attributed to the slave: the slave's roar (that haunts the Ohio River and 124 Bluestone Road) does not make it across to the living-as-benign not diabolical humanity. We read:

> Eighteen seventy-four and whitefolks were still on the loose. . . . He smelled skin, skin and hot blood. . . . But none of that had worn out his marrow. It was . . . a red ribbon knotted around a curl of wet woolly hair, clinging still to its bit of scalp. . . . "What *are* these people? You tell me, Jesus. What *are* they?" . . . He kept the ribbon. . . . The people of the broken necks, of fire-cooked blood [in a lynch fire], and black girls who had lost their ribbons. What a roaring. (Morrison 212–13)

Across the Ohio River, the slave must use the master's trademarks (perhaps cooked blood, whipped backs, and broken necks) to cobble together a history (Spivak, *Outside* 200). What remains is not deconstruct-able *because* (it is) impossible (to experience); here, Spivak safeguards the ethical singularity of "a red ribbon knotted around a curl of wet woolly hair, clinging still to its bit of scalp."

When Homi Bhabha discusses *Beloved* in *The Location of Culture* (1994), however, he transcends the specificity of black female slavery to announce the *metaphorical* power of the Middle Passage: "[A]s *with slavery itself*," the Middle Passage emplaces non-totalizing forms of disjunction analogous to the cultural discontinuities and disarticulations of the postcolonial era (5, emphases added). Bhabha broaches American slavery without referencing a single black feminist work but relies on Elizabeth Fox-Genovese's *Within the Plantation Household: Black and White Women of the Old South* (1988).

White feminist scholarship recounts slavery's impact on black women and becomes representative of US feminism. What kind of sanctioned ignorance is entrenched, furthermore, when greater critical currency lies not with black women's intellectual tradition but with Bhabha's exposition of slavery's repercussions on black female experience?[8]

If Spivak reads *Beloved* to be haunted by a murdered, crawling-already baby girl, Paul Gilroy avails of Margaret Garner (whose story inspired *Beloved*) to argue against Patricia Hill Collins and Hegel. Empathizing with Collins's project to counteract "*their* [black women's] experiences" of denigration (*Black Atlantic* 51, 52, emphasis added), Gilroy derives Collins's approach from Foucauldian methodology. In separating himself from Collins's black feminist tradition, he does not notice that *their* exclusion is also *his* exclusion; that the black intellectual history he calls upon for *his* project of destabilizing reactionary forms of black nationalism is also *their* history; and, that Collins's *feminist* tradition is part of the very *black* intellectual history to which he appeals. Despite the opportunity, Gilroy does not forge a trans-Atlantic alliance with US black feminism because the subject and author of black intellectual history—that is, *his* black intellectual history—are irreducibly male. He goes so far as to pillory Collins for creating a cross-dressed sovereign subject (female and black), even as he acquiesces to the paradigm of modernity that undergirds uses of Hegel, as acutely demonstrated in his discussion of Margaret Garner.

In this discussion, Gilroy scrupulously avoids black feminist writers as he ponders what he terms "male" and "female" forms of violence. Frederick Douglass's violence against slave-breaker Edward Covey is directed outward against the oppressor; Margaret Garner channels (not directs) violence inward against her "most precious and intimate object[. . .]": her daughter (66). (He neglects that she was also destroying not her child but Sweet Home's *property.*) Enslavement and rape of black women, moreover, are horrors perpetrated in contempt of black men, for the latter are unable to impart patriarchal protection (64). Upon this confirmation of the power of the patronymic, Gilroy mentions Lucy Stone's visit with Garner in jail. Stone is purportedly able to identify with Garner at least psychologically because of the *idea* of maternity (68). To make this claim, Gilroy must assume a gendered continuity between Garner and Stone that history actually denied because for black women "carefree, motherlove was a killer" (Morrison 155). In fact,

> [it was] very risky. For a used-to-be-slave woman to love anything
> that much was dangerous, especially if it was her children. . . . The
> best thing . . . was to love just a little bit; everything, just a little
> bit, so when they broke its back, or shoved it in a croaker sack,
> well, maybe you'd have a little love left over for the next one. (54)

That was the point (of *Beloved*): the casual brutality meted out to children illuminates infanticide as a special dispensation. To invoke a maternity-based identification between Stone and Garner is to assume too much and too little.

What we notice is that *Beloved* is the paradigmatic postcolonial text *par excellence* for these male scholars, but reading *Beloved* does not necessitate reading black women's works, as *Beloved* becomes shorthand for (and interchangeable with) US female blackness. Bhabha and Gilroy are able to deploy formidable figures as Hegel, Heidegger, and Lacan, yet fail to include black feminist thought in their deliberations on slavery. A peculiar form of colonial–postcolonial–neocolonial symbiosis deems European philosophical paradigms appropriate for understanding black female slave experience, but understanding black female slave experience does not require reference to black women's works. (Can we even imagine an interrogation of the rich tradition of European thought using only black women's works? Or that black women's works might ever yield an understanding of Eurocentrism?)

III. Postcolonialism as an Other

Spivak cautions that postcoloniality qua migration "lets drop the vicissitudes of de-colonization and ignores the question: Who decolonizes?" (*Imaginary* 207). Letting a particular experience of migrancy *stand in* for decolonization leads to postcoloniality's ventriloquizing function in the house of US multiculturalism (*Critique* 18, 33).[9] Largely museumized and culturalist accounts of national origin and its diaspora put postcolonial theorists forward as victims of US knowledge production to obfuscate agency-via-domination ("Transnationality" 75). Any scrutiny of debates regarding intellectual capital would readily show that aspirational class advancement is implicated in US foreign policy. Spivak comments, "for example, that Article 301 and Super 301 in the General Agreement on Tariffs and Trade thwarts social redistribution in our countries of origin" ("Talk" 295). Postcolonial theorists are Americans, irrespective of spectral identitarian collectivities that create culture (*was* nation-state) as a species of "retrospective hallucination"; we migrated to be Americans, but American does not necessarily mean being an Anglo-clone ("Interview" 84, *Critique* 360–61).

Culturalist accounts of places of national origin are handy for postcolonial theorists who portray themselves as privy to that culture after managing to escape this culture's preternatural qualities. Peripheral nation-space, now oversaturated with an excessive but overreached-via-migrancy culture, becomes a space to be read for the production of knowledge under the aegis of first world nation-space as proper culture (liberal humanism) ("Interview"

82). Without examination of postcolonial theory's geopolitical determination, therefore, aspirational class advancement assumes the patina of an oppositional and antagonistic identity *by virtue of category alone*.[10]

Spivak petitions that we defer to the African-American experience as paradigmatic because its history exhibits the vagaries and triumphs of postcoloniality ("Talk" 294). Any attempt at building coalitions with the African-American community dictates an investigation of the institution of a white-supremacist origin for the United States, the African-American experience of negotiated independence, and the failures of decolonization due to racist fury and backlash ("Transnationality" 71). We, too, are US colonialists and *not* postcolonials ("Teaching" 11), for migrancy for aspirational class advancement is not just an endorsement of the American Dream, but a way to further blackens blacks if postcoloniality assimilates all difference. The resultant nonthreatening presence of blackness, DuCille confirms, is not like the disquieting proximity of "Spivak's black blacks" (*Skin* 129). Afrocentricity and postcoloniality are commodities in a "skin trade" that promotes the very alterity it disavows. Race as metonym for blackness may signify irreducible difference, but race itself is depleted to an exchangeable sameness (129).

Following Spivak's instructions, therefore, we can determine that a paradigmatically postcolonial Barbara Christian gives life to a metaphor that has no literal referent: the inclusion of women as women.[11] In so doing, her concept of the race for theory expresses *real* historical conditions through its philosophical significance.

IV. Significant Blackness

Withholding from black women's lives a claim to the constructive frame results in an obverse *fort/da*[12]: refusal of significant presence by overstating difference acts as a destabilizing declaration of black women's works being "gone"; yet, hegemonic conceptual cultures seem also to be repeatedly anticipating and preparing for their works' arrival "there"—or "here." Christian's statement, that people of color have *always* theorized, is not inherently oppositional and antagonistic, but imparts this sensibility of right-*here*ness and *now*-ness (rather than *over-there*ness). As Carol Davies attests, despite these credentials black women are either perpetually in the midst of an identity crisis or are paradoxically unintelligible brute matter (36). She concurs with Christian that black women are not ascribed theoretical contributions (for example, the critique of unitary subjectivity) because of the "politics of citation," which ascertain intellectual bona fides and disciplinary pedigrees (41, 36). Similarly, DuCille challenges any apparatus that posits black women as perennially "othered" matter awaiting deconstruction ("Occult" 591). (Recall Awkward's accusation of passivity.) An impoverished understanding of difference leads to denial of complexity, or complexity is judged as ontological and unbridgeable (12).

Davies's disparagement of major discourse's "strategic deafness" (35) (the metaphor is ableist) demonstrates how authority stems from what I term an inverted form of strategic essentialism.[13] A strategically essentialised culture of concepts fends off phantasmatical black women, "*even as it claims* [Christian reminds us] *many of the ideas that we its 'historical' other, have known, spoken about for so long.*" A dearth of relationships with black people leads to African-American texts standing in for African-American people (Carby 12). Even so, multicultural pedagogy centralizes the responses of an apothegmatic white reader of African-American texts; a presupposed (white) norm refuses the work as an aperture to questions of both a timeless and timely nature. Elizabeth Abel expounds on how major scholars mimic the lived perspective of what is named woman, native, or other[14] instead of patiently engaging the difficulty of a given concept (483, 486, 496).[15] In another inversion, though not mentioned by Abel, this discourse appropriates and displaces mimicry as a tactic of resistance: if the colonial subject uses mimicry to subvert the colonizing subject and become a menace (Bhabha, *Location* 88), then, I suggest, the colonizing subject mimics the mimic to subvert the subversion. DuCille reiterates, "[B]lack culture is more easily intellectualized (and canonized) when transferred . . . to the safety of white metaphor, when you can have that 'signifying black difference' without the difference of significant blackness" ("Occult" 600).[16]

V. Too Much Difference

In keeping with Barbara Christian's exegesis of "the nature of current political reality," we turn now to feminist philosopher Naomi Zack who evaluates why feminism has not succeeded in (theoretical and practical) inclusivity. Zack disapproves of a (major) conceptual accomplishment of black feminist thought: intersectionality. (Three years after Christian's presentation at the University of California, Berkeley, conference on The Nature and Context of Minority Discourse, black feminist legal scholar Kimberlè Crenshaw introduced the concept of intersectionality in 1989.) Unfortunately, *Inclusive Feminism's* (2005) methodology misconstrues logical coherence as inclusivity—that is, what is logical is also inclusive.

Zack mounts a challenge against exclusive feminism, in particular, intersectionality, which centralizes multiple systems of oppression (age, ability, sexuality, etc.) (7). She applauds the historical pause (minor) feminist thought provides to US feminism, but her analytical strategies assist the omission of black women. In her attempt to address glaring, real world issues such as obscene poverty, she is rightly contemptuous of academic practices that forfeit substantive insight for institutional self-validation. But, she depicts black women as divisive in their rejoinder to white women's de facto original feminist contributions.[17] By starting out with an antagonistic understanding of difference, she paradoxically ignores postcolonial, transnational, and nonwestern feminist theory when arguing for a global awareness of injustice.

Zack like Christian runs out of patience with the dominance of French feminism, especially as this tradition is an Anglo-American construction. Under its influence, Anglo-American feminism exercises a symbolic approach to material realities (86–91, 98–99). Zack's subversion of merely symbolic approaches is apposite, but she does not elaborate on the choices she makes concerning audience and citation. She speaks *to* third wave feminists *from* a second wave perspective, and presents this particular narrative of first, second, and third waves as *the* history of US feminism. Ratification of a (major) narrative of history that black women challenge ad nauseam steers Zack to postulate the former's historical adequacy. On this basis, Zack is able to present the historical FMP category as a curative to what she censures as minor feminism's undue hyper-particularity (8).

The historical FMP category is as follows: "Women are those individuals who are designated female [F] from birth or biological mothers [M] or primary [P] sexual choices of men" (8). It is crucial because "*too much* ontological and discursive difference on a *theoretical* level" (8, emphases added) may circumvent essentialism but does not result in inclusive feminism (7). Zack concedes that "too much difference" is more a theoretical feat in contrast to actual diversity in academic feminist movements, but she neglects why the excluded bear "too much difference" and not anyone else. This lapse allows her to confuse the logical problem of infinite regression of difference with the historical conditions that make the FMP category necessary. When making crucial distinctions between essentialism and inclusiveness, Zack cites prominent black feminist thinkers (for example, bell hooks, Patricia Hill Collins, and Barbara Christian), but black feminism garners hyper-particularity not tradition (1–8, 16). To avoid the pitfalls of a difference that seems unbridgeable (because "too much"), Zack pits third world material realities against the symbolic approaches of French feminism. But, to do so, she creates a slippage between "too much difference" on a theoretical level with "too much difference" on a material level.

Since she concentrates on pandemic disparities, she charges French feminism and its Anglo-American inheritors with turning destitute women in the global South into an alternative species. They may eschew worldwide realities because of speciously unbridgeable chasms, but we must use our imaginative capacities, she poignantly stresses, to build relationships with those whose situations or attributes appear very far removed from our own (35). She incurs two problems: first, cross-cultural transnational analyses of economic systems of production have *always* been a pivotal part of black women's works, as they build feminist solidarity against (major) feminism[18]; second, by including nonwestern feminists as *activists* not *theorists*, Zack further ingrains the symbolic methods she argues against. For example, she relates the story of a little girl named Haseena from Andhra Pradesh, India, whose adoption by an American woman gets international attention (35–38). This news item appears after a complex textual analysis of Simone de Beauvoir's Other, as Zack uses Haseena's story (actually, just news) to challenge Beauvoir's ontological impulse.

Beauvoir's analysis fails to fulfill a prerequisite of a system of categories—logical relations—because she depends on categorial circularity to transmit actual relationships between men and women. In order to *have* logical relations—that is, relationships must be logically possible—women must have independent characteristics; all characteristics of women cannot be derivative of men's; otherwise, the category would have no semantic content (meaning) when invoked. In deriving women from men, Beauvoir's phenomenological investigation neglects the *historical* fact that not all women are so Other-ed. Beauvoir's logical failure, however, exposes another manner of being Other-ed, different from being a woman (like her) (35); this other mode is predicated on the absence of (any) relation with a certain category of beings.

Upon delineating the logical consequences of Beauvoir's ontological elisions, we are asked to ponder Haseena, who is the inarticulate, yet over-determined subject of a foreign adoption (35). Haseena's example elucidates how difference supplies "women" with semantic content, and, hence, makes logical relations possible. Haseena's historical condition assigns attributes due to which she is being Other-ed, but differently than Beauvoir. In fact, Beauvoir's description of being Other-ed forecloses logical relations with Haseena because the mechanisms by which Beauvoir is Other-ed are also the mechanisms by which Haseena is Other-ed by her. Having characteristics derived from men, Beauvoir *can* be logically defined, and, has the capacity to testify that "woman" is not recognized to exist (35). At this precise moment, Haseena is trotted out onto the page as a transparent but newsworthy example of the real world to signify the absence of logical relations between the first world Anglo-American French feminist and her third world Other.

Zack conducts an in-depth analysis of Beauvoir and Marilyn Frye, but she does not incorporate a single Indian feminist in this news-called-story about an Indian girl nor does she cite any transnational feminists. She refers to third world women's activism (albeit not in the context of Haseena), primarily via Haleh Afshar's *Women and Politics in the Third World* (1996), a section that is four-and-one-half pages long at the end of her 173-page long book. In duplicating Beauvoir's absence of logical relations, Zack posits a skewed (onto)logic: (major) first world feminism showcases those whose difference is diagnosed as "too much," and, then, subsequently corrects this historical condition with the FMP category.

When Zack says that Haseena is not adoptable in India because of a mild deformity in her feet, she parenthetically adds: "whatever that denotes" (37). Whether said denotation is valid or not, Zack does not procure the local knowledge and language training that *could* tell her whatever that denotes. For example, since *haseena* means "desirable and beautiful" in Hindi and Urdu, perhaps the name disputes that her feet make her unadoptable. If Haseena symbolizes the quest for a feminism that can speak to little girls all over the world, then the continuity of ableism in first and third worlds may avoid the problem of "too much difference." Haseena's deformed feet instead are synecdochal: Indian culture is essentially different, and ableism is essentially Indian culture. They bear the weight of India itself: poverty, disease, over-population, and illiteracy—hardly newsworthy in the first world.

The historical FMP category is meant to implicate the historical conditions that enable logical relations.

> The relation of women to the disjunctive FMP category is that of being assigned to the whole category or identifying with the whole category. . . . [This assignation and/or identification] is a necessary and sufficient condition for being a woman, and there is every reason to view it as an essence . . . [that] does not entail that all . . . are mothers or male sexual choices, or that they have been designated female from birth[,] . . . [or] . . . that female birth designation, heterosexuality, or motherhood are feminist values (or virtues). They are, rather, the *historical conditions* and facts that have made feminism necessary in a dual gender system of men and women. (8–9, emphases added)

If essential relations come from historical conditions, then it is puzzling why Zack does not underscore cultural competency when setting the case of Haseena against symbolic practices.

She does not follow up on Haseena with more research to avert emblematic treatment although she offers in-depth work on Lacan, Kristeva, Witting, Sartre, and Nagel. (For example, the referenced *New York Times* article states that Haseena's orphanage was charged with selling babies to foreigners. Zack does not discuss this part of the article or the exertions by Indian organizations and governmental bodies to stop international trafficking rings that prey upon the poverty-stricken.) The news item gives readers some background to Haseena's story, that her "relinquishment document . . . was 'signed'—with a fingerprint—by a woman who claimed to be Haseena's mother[,] . . . an illiterate, unmarried 20-year-old peasant woman, who said she was putting Haseena for adoption because of the stigma in India of raising a child born out of wedlock" (Bonner 2003). Strikingly, this paltry piece is the crux of Zack's argument against symbolic approaches to global impoverishment,[19] an argument she could make without the pathetic specter of Haseena in (ableist and girl-prejudiced) India and the benevolent specter of a weeping western woman trying to adopt her. She could have chosen a little girl in the United States whose poverty would powerfully bear out Zack's aim of countervailing symbolic practice. Haseena is tagged on, much as third world politics are tagged on, to manufacture the "hyperstatic alterity" (DuCille's term) that is the law of theory's limit: Haseena's irreducible, yet also "too much difference," is where first world feminism stops short.[20]

It remains unclear in Zack's version of inclusive feminism how "too much" material difference resolves the problem of "too much" discursive and/ or ontological difference. She presents Haseena's historical situation as her jejune material condition but creates a culturalist account when she dismisses what mildly deformed feet might denote for a poverty-stricken little girl in India, perhaps abandoned, perhaps sold, or perhaps given up by a desperate, unwed twenty-year-old mother. When Haseena's story is presented as a concrete example made available by a major metropolitan newspaper in the United States, Zack repeats the production of the periphery as a space to be read (in *The New York Times*) at the end of discourse.

Zack formulates the historical FMP category to intervene in discursive excesses:

> [C]ritiques of white feminism have resulted in segregated feminisms. But intellectual segregation is not a solution to inequality, any more than demographic segregation is. The white feminism that once saw itself as universal feminism has not succeeded in reconstructing an inclusive foundation, and as a result a *crisis* underlies *all* feminist efforts at this time. (6, emphases added)

The use of the word "segregated" is obviously unfortunate. Per her logic, excessive difference causes segregation, not that women of color are victims of segregation (hence Zack's criticism of French feminism). The theoretical

preoccupations of particular feminists, moreover, are not inevitably representative: just because white feminism lacks an inclusive foundation does not
mean that "a crisis underlies *all* feminist efforts at this time."

What race for theory, therefore, empowers Zack to stymie an encounter
with difference even during a crisis?

VI. *Synoikismos*

This chapter does not intend to overstate the difference of various schools
of thought from black women's theorizing. Scholars such as Gayatri Spivak,
Cynthia Willett, Tina Chanter, Judith Butler, Hazel Carby, Hortense Spillers,
Mary Rawlinson, and Elizabeth Abel, etc. deconstruct to set to work anti-
imperialist politics, which cannot be conflated with solipsistic reading practices.
I am interested in why a particular historical moment that witnessed the
arrival of difference in the Euro-US academy (minority scholarly traditions,
feminism, poststructuralism, postcolonial studies, deconstruction, etc.) caused
strife rather than affinity-based ("hit-") coalitions. (For example, both Paul de
Man and Homi Bhabha rejected the hostility their fields received by reason
of a commitment to theory incumbent for social change.)

In the wake of these mis-takes, mis-alliances, and mis-conceptions that
overwhelm our actual hit-fortune (à la Rushdie), Barbara Christian's concept
of the race for theory is a fundamentally *imaginative* exercise ("Race" 62).
JanMohamed and Lloyd recognize that black women's works evince how
"domination can destroy the 'human' potential of its victims" and should
be integral to discourse as "utopian exploration[s] of human potentiality"
("What?" 14).[21] Given that whole bodies of knowledge are co-opted or driven
to extinction by conceptual cultures that truncate our imagination, Spivak
similarly presses that an active imagination is exigent to entering the space of
difference ("Cusp" 207). *For* philosophers of the future, therefore, I propose the
following tweak to Spivak's appellation for the gendered subaltern: "Incanting
to [ourselves] all the perils of transforming a 'name' to a referent—making
a catechism, in other words, of catachresis—[we] name (as) [western] that
disenfranchised woman whom we strictly, historically, geopolitically *cannot
imagine*, as literal referent" (*Outside* 139). In *this* alternative citation, black
women's works are *exemplarily* western.

Christian's concept of the race for theory empowers us to ask why works
by black women are not considered western. What makes something western?[22]
Is western precisely what is not black, American, and female? Edward Said
once said that Derrida fudges the deconstruct-ability of the western canon,

which leads his commentators to act as if western culture itself were being undone by the deconstructive exercise (*World* 209, 160). A form of "cultural insiderism" (Gilroy's term) precipitates the presumption of historical adequacy to shirk the risks involved whenever disciplines confront history,[23] simply because major discourse finds itself thrown on *this* side of history, of dark territory, of capitalism, above deck not below, as an active verb rather than a parenthetical qualifier.[24] Christian's proleptic act of attrition—in that people of color have *always* theorized—dockets how Eurocentric conceptual cultures do not have the cultural competency necessary to even *have* a (major) crisis.

What space clearing gesture transpires if we cite works by black women as exemplarily western? This imaginative eponym is not guaranteed via an antagonistic understanding of difference that legitimates by reversal,[25] but may confer variation in a nomenclature's repetition (Butler, *Gender* 145). If black women's works are paradigmatically postcolonial and exemplarily western, then the metaphysics of presence is not the only discourse the west has to offer. To convey and uphold that these works are extremely hard-won historical achievements, Anna Julia Cooper perhaps beckoned *this* race for theory (in 1892): "[W]hen and where I enter, in the quiet, undisputed dignity of my womanhood, without violence and without suing or special patronage, then and there the whole Negro race enters with me" (31). The (then) "nature of current political reality" bears mentioning: in 1892, the United States witnessed its greatest number of lynchings (161 black; 69 white).

I revisit Barbara Christian's presentation and published essay to ask whether our professionalism demands more than compulsory *non*-citationality of black women's works for authority and expertise—that is, a negative reference that in the end turns out to be self-same difference—both, "no doubt," minor. Christian, Spivak, and Butler become fellow travelers in this negotiation of the patronymic to disassemble the specific citation practices that foster a cloistered *beau ideal*.[26] In black women's struggle for readership, representation, and canonicity, Christian inverts Butler's notion of compulsory citationality to show how lack of citation of black women's works has philosophical costs. Insofar as performative expressions aggregate what is to be expressed, Butler questions whether normative gender performance and the performative use of normative discourse converge so that compulsion can create a "more promising deregulation" (*Bodies* 231). Christian already takes up Butler's charge via a "*process of repetition* . . . [that has] substantializing effects" (*Gender* 145): reading the heterogeneity of black women's lives not as the law of theory's limit but for an apocryphal genealogy of lost mothers who shelter significance.

Such a paradigmatically postcolonial *and* exemplarily western understanding of difference brings Eurocentric identity politics to crisis (even in the west).

VII. Conclusion

In Spivak's marvelous reading of Virginia Woolf, she highlights the indeterminacy of collectivities. For all that "including women as women" (*Death* 27) will not have been calculable and predictable, we as readers seem to decide hastily on definitions. Spivak asks us to learn how to "let go" and takes us to an example at the end of *A Room of One's Own* (1929).

> As [Woolf] is winding down her famous exhortation to young Oxbridge women, she says[,] . . . "you should embark upon another stage of your . . . career. A thousand pens . . . suggest what you should do [to] what effect. . . . My own suggestion is a little fantastic, I admit; I prefer, therefore, to put it in the form of fiction." . . . She inaugurates a ghost dance, asking all aspiring women writers in England to be haunted by the ghost of Shakespeare's sister. She quite gives up the "room of one's own and £500 a year" in her closing words: "I maintain that she would come if we worked for her, *and that so to work, even in poverty and obscurity*, is worthwhile." (34–35; quotation ellipses mine, emphases added)

Spivak reorients the conventionally postcolonial diagnostic and/or corrective claim about the imperial source of those five hundred pounds a year to another postcolonialism (to come): the work of letting go to become part of an apocryphal genealogy *for* Shakespeare's sister. If postcoloniality as a historical era and conceptual accomplishment is a space clearing gesture, then "[w]hat does it mean 'to work for her,' especially as a principle for . . . an unintended collectivity?" Spivak declares ("I will call") that this work be called "open-plan fieldwork" (35), as we must struggle to initiate a "ghost dance," make the ghost of Shakespeare's sister appear (to us), by "a prayer to be haunted by her ghost, to be othered by her" (50).

We may ask, therefore, what lecture on women would Virginia Woolf have delivered had she not simply had a room of her own and five hundred pounds but also a different library.

PART TWO

A RESURRECTION OF THE FLESH

Chapter Six

I Am an Animal

Time, Cruelty, and Metaphysics

All critters share a common "flesh," laterally, semiotically, and genealogically.

—Donna Haraway, *Anthropocene*

I was six when I first saw kittens drown. . . .
Soft paws scraping like mad. . . .
. . . [F]or days . . .
the three sogged remains . . .
Turn mealy and crisp as old summer dung
Until I forgot them.

—Seamus Heaney, "The Early Purges"

"I am just going outside and may be some time."
The others nod, pretending not to know. . . .
In fact, for ever . . .

—Derek Mahon, "Antarctica"

As for me, even in justice, all that goes beyond plain death seems to me pure cruelty, and especially for us who ought to have some concern about sending souls away in a good state; which cannot happen when we have tortured them and made them desperate by unbearable tortures.

—Montaigne, "Of Cruelty"

Spellbound, the living have a choice between involuntary ataraxy—an esthetic life due to weakness—and the bestiality of the involved. . . . Once overcome, the culpable self-preservation urge has been confirmed . . . by the threat that has come to be ceaselessly present. The only trouble with self-preservation is that . . . the life to which it attaches us . . . turn[s] [us] into . . . a specter, a piece of the world of ghosts . . . perceive[d] to be nonexistent. *The guilt of a life which purely as a fact will strangle other life* . . .

—Adorno, "Metaphysics After Auschwitz"

I. The Horror, the Horror

In his confessedly ironic and melancholic deliberations, Adorno reverses the direction that metaphysical inquiry presumably takes. His lecture "On Dying Today" (Lecture Seventeen) in *Metaphysics* (2000) reproaches the synonymy between absolute abstraction and transcendence. Although abstraction of human experience is meant to prevent this experience's cultural determination from tarnishing the metaphysical enterprise, this pathway to transcendence bolsters the culture it sought to elude: metaphysics recapitulates what modernity assails as our natural culture—dehumanization and functionalism. Metaphysics privileges what Adorno terms "the side of being turned away from us," but what keeps (the concept of) death alive is its historical inadequacy when pushed up against reality (not tradition). To assess whether (the concept of) death is adequate to the historical moment at hand, Adorno suggests dying *today* as the proper object of metaphysics, as the concept's repeated failure to grasp the manifold ways in which people *actually* die, today, empowers us to resist the nothingness extorted by capitalist culture. (No piece of life can *be* nothing, and, hence, must be *experienced* as nothingness.)

During the course of this particular lecture, however, when he elucidates how the emphatic insistence of death stems from its substantive apprehension, Adorno says that compared with all other species, humans are uniquely aware of our biological floor. Ignoring how we could ever know all other species (and what they are aware of), this casual aside appropriates and displaces *all* species to radically humanize (the experience of) death. This chapter begins *here* with this effortless generalization that posits a species embodying *lack* of self-preservation as somehow exceptionally aware of its biological floor. At this moment, when all other species are present and absent, known and unknown, self-preserving and unaware, we move in further reverse direction to cross the threshold of our naturalized culture. In *this* place, where all other species live, we may resurrect the flesh to figure our species as animals.

This figuration is proportional to the actual predicament of (our) dying today because of the possible impossibility of our self-preservation that is anthropogenic climate change. Our self-preservation as a species, as a (now) metaphysical aim, entails tracking the process of unknowing that turns the heterogeneity of the side of being turned towards us into a signifier of ineluctable human difference. From within the catastrophic frame/arena of anthropogenic climate change, we are able to notice how effortless generalization substitutes this heterogeneity with nothingness *for* human exceptionalism. Seeing as (our) animal life in a humanized world cannot be invoked as a "here" in the regime change from nature to culture, metaphysics in its reverse course must think of something that is not "there." A resurrection of the flesh provides a cosmogonic peek at how gratuitous performance of identity—that is, of the awful singularity of our cruelty as a species—(un)makes the ground upon which we are dying *today*.

II. Dead Zones

A culturally constituted nature and naturally constituted culture install culture as our proper nature to harvest a subject who reifies consumption of an increasingly inhospitable planet. Annexed (now) to this second nature, the nature left "outside" our naturalized culture signifies irreducible human difference. But, if anthropogenic climate change is the potential loss of nature, then it also portends the potential loss of our ability to signify at all. This immediate but impossible-to-imagine threat is compounded by the fact that we have a definite time frame by which we will save (or fail to save) nature as we know it. The paramount metaphysical project of our self-preservation as a species, therefore, obliges a paradoxically philosophical sensibility: insofar as self-preservation is traditionally calculated as the purview of *mere* animal life to initiate (our) historicity, saving nature from ourselves furnishes a qualitative variety of experience. In lieu of dissipating this historical moment to reprise human exceptionalism, it is *this* qualitative variety of experience that is fundamental for (the concept of) dying today to be an essential gesture of negativity.

Howsoever the animal is segregated as that which lives in nature—outside, over *there*—the nonhuman world, which is everything (other than us), in the end augurs the illogic of this segregation. We separate ourselves from nature vis-à-vis a culture that conflates animal-being with being-in-nature even though culture does not, in fact, cannot, take place outside of nature: we are animals, too; we live in nature, having no other place (to go). What does it mean, therefore, to be an animal circumscribed by *lack* of self-preservation? The current ongoing mass extinction event yields a radically humanized world, which means the loss of presence itself, as our future is no longer defined by the real: the radical otherness to which we are utterly tethered.[1] Our future is our new equivalence with absence beyond death itself—that is, with oblivion; notwithstanding culture's abdication of contemporaneity with nature, life that insists (without insisting) on its otherness (from us) haunts, and comes back, for us. As this life is not a history we leave behind "in the beginning," philosophical possibility sprouts from metaphysics' potential to be disturbed by our contemporaneity with nature.

Metaphysics today must effortfully create a relation between itself and what resists appropriation by facing up to the decomposition of meaning that arises from the interchangeability of living and dying.[2] Nature is neither empty nor abstract, nor simply waiting to be saved, being instead a busy, indifferent, and occupied place (if allowed to *be*, every conceivable biological niche would be filled with life). *For* our moral legitimacy as a species via transcendence of animality, the subject's secession metamorphoses nature into a façade; the seemingly natural power of *this* planetary culture of severance and disloca-tion is essentially historical because we die just the same. Contra nature as the nothingness background to a catastrophic fracture, a culture adequate to its historical predicament of our self-preservation as a species upends our individual isolation because I am an animal. Adorno's offhand comment radi-cally humanizes our biological floor but it does acknowledge that we share this biological floor with (all) animal life. From this culturally determined performance of exceptional human identity, in a reproach of metaphysical inquiry's forsworn cultural determinism, we may persist in Adorno's probing of the intrinsic relatedness of philosophy, culture, and history.

Adorno solicits the substantive content of dying today by accentuating how people die because being is derived from its categorial opposite noth-ingness. Whilst metaphysics' reversed course checks the emptiness enshrined within a concept, this moment in Adorno's lecture manifests the unreason-able amount of work (the concept of) the animal does for us. An effortless generalization about our unique ability to be cognizant of our biological floor contracts the actual heterogeneity of nonhuman life to get a metaphysical project off the ground. To establish whether dying today is adequate for *this* historical moment, I extend to animals Adorno's efforts to harbor a particular concentration of understanding that materializes from dying one's own (not the *same*) death. Being and nothingness, as antagonistically complementary, reenact in dialectics a culture wherein (alive) animals are already dead; they might as well not be there, as identity takes center stage; all else recedes into an indistinct backdrop. The *immanence* of dying today roils the uniformity impelled by the abstraction that metaphysics coalesces into transcendence. From within the catastrophic frame/arena of climate change, therefore, saving nature from us entails our self-preservation as animals.

III. $t=0^3$

As metaphysics jockeys for what resides timelessly above the vicissitudes of the actual happening of history, it blocks scrutiny of "what [concepts] mean in terms of their origins, their historical dimension" (Adorno, *Metaphysics* 5). In mistaking its cultural coding for the absolute, metaphysical inquiry does not equip the subject with the elementary structures of being, but consigns it to a cultural niche. The so-commissioned subject aggrandizes its own mediation by taking for granted the transcendence it must endeavor to attain. Thus, metaphysical inquiry truncates the very qualitative variety of experience through which the subject could put being and nothingness to the test via reifying existing things (4).

Adorno lambastes the bathic reduction of life to self-preservation, and the pathic exaltation of this self-preservation as metaphysics. Socio-political realities diminish metaphysical inquiry to the upkeep of inured cultural conditions, a philosophical antinomy that results from the failure of culture; metaphysics colludes in preserving its own prerequisites by sustaining the very culture that inhibits metaphysical inquiry (118–19). To hinder the depersonalization and neglect of concrete experience characteristic of contemporary culture, Adorno scours the "deepest strata of humanity's historical life" (133). *How* people die may vex the sameness culture inflicts, but holding onto human exceptionalism via our unique awareness makes dying today (still) dying a second time.

A reversed metaphysics delves into the concrete example in humanity's "historical dimension," which is the side of being turned towards us (101, 131).[4] Ideological renouncements of metaphysics' historical formation brings Adorno to the structures that inaugurate (our) being at ground level (45, 71): unlike (all) other species, culture is our evolving nature, as we ascend to culture from our biological floor. Being *in* (proper) culture is indispensable for experiencing time continuously (133); unanimity is superimposed on human history as something that happens somewhere else, and the nonhuman world is the elsewhere where nothing essentially happens. Exceptionalism propounds that nature has chosen us to surpass mere survival by ascending to culture, a naturalization which evolves by occluding the immanence of its own disposition through ideological manipulation.

By-products of an objective mode of production, *experience* (timing) and *being* (is-ness) deprive historical experience of its quality of being historical, as if this ipseity were a humanized kind of natural selection (44–45). The pretense that culture qua self-same time and space is not fortuitous (there, but for kismet, go I) unilaterally disarms culture before its own contingency (135); the subject no longer thinks about what it experiences, and no longer experiences what it thinks about, meant only to live out its cultural life. Acquiescing to its own abstraction, "in its social liquidation today[,] the self is only paying the price for what it once did by positing itself" (108). This version of culture, which expunges nature to bring to pass (the semblance of) concordance, voids the self. Owing to culture setting up the circumstances for the question of culture, culturally administered subjectivity hypostatizes its objective—that is, its cultural—make up as neutral.

These socio-political tautologies are the structures that manufacture (our) being today; and "[o]ne might say that the pure identity of all people with their concept is nothing other than their death" (108). In a radically humanized world, the human's categorial antagonist dies the same death, too: it is our culture that kills the animal (first) to sanction that very culture that (then) kills us (second). If cultural habituation is subjectivity's presumed natural origin, then what *can* subjectivity mean? Forged by a sacrifice of the empirical (95) *in* the "historical dimension," this "hellish circle" (125) leads to "an all-ness of thought which actually says nothing at all" (97).[5] Abnegating the subject's qualitative variety of experience by barring death's heterogeneity from bumping up against subjectivity, metaphysics leaves subjects bereft of self-expression.[6] To short circuit the negativity that *is* (made possible by) self-reflection, the (real, not cogitative) law of cultural homogeneity depletes the subject's experience as merely personal. Objectivity, however, expects an entropic counter-pressure despite being relieved of the empirical because nothing actually falls naturally into place (by itself).

What results from the adequation of abstraction with transcendence is a metonymic chain: Culture→ Nature→ Self-Preservation→ History→ Life; culture is nature, nature is self-preservation, and self-preservation is history. The history of our self-preservation, albeit as an exceptional species, *is* culture (at the peak of its evolution), whose discernibly natural power emanates from its sheer immediacy (128): "The . . . thicker the veil under which we hide the face of nature, the more the ideas around which that veil is spun are accepted as the only true experience of this world" ("Why Philosophy?"

43). Overlaid temporal and spatial continuity levels out cultural experience to protect the culture that does the leveling; in other words, the ostracization of the self-reflection culture holds anathema is a constitutive structure of the subject's being. To trigger this immanent negativity *in* the "historical dimension," the subject is obliged to turn away from what resides timelessly above to what is deemed "base, insect-like, filthy, subhuman and all the rest" (*Metaphysics* 123).[7]

In contrast to static ontology's acquisition of a spurious transcendence underived from what it wants to transcend, metaphysics in its reversed course ferrets out the "sedimented history contained in any piece of knowledge" (136). For a qualitative variety of experience, it does not secure validity from the distance it creates between metaphysics and culture, as a sincere philosophical radicalism (or perhaps cultural naïveté) concurs with what amount to fateful and unlawful attempts to dissolve a culture that emboldens power (131).[8] If metaphysical inquiry is the result of doubt (112), then galvanizing discontinuities is the essentially historical condition of possibility for philosophy to *be* philosophical.[9] A system of equivalence instead affirms the ideological as a self-evident claim of reason (88), as "[c]ulture . . . has its truth—if it has any—only within itself" (118–19). Being depersonalized, culture is not subjective enough (108); being neglectful of concrete experience, culture is not objective enough (121). In this barter economy, subjects cling to rhetoric that cajoles via the shrewd but dexterous bucking of reality, "otherwise one could not live" (106). And just like that—how the expanse is disappeared *is* remarkable—"humanity['s] . . . control of nature as control of men far exceeds in horror anything men ever had to fear from nature" (*Minima* 239).

IV. (Ersatz) Animals

For these ill begotten spoils, the culturally fixed subject—the ersatz animal in its cultural niche—deadens all affects "just to be capable of living at all" (*Metaphysics* 112). Dwindled down to a "specimen" and "torturable entity" (108), *this* subject is the placeholder for a stolen transcendence. As the now potentially civilization-destroying domination of nature, such "subjective incapacity" when transmuted into "serene detachment" (119), turns nature inside out—that is, the inside is cast outside—over *there*, not *here*. At the cost of a qualitative variety of experience, which sparks the "vital nerve" (144) of doubt fundamental to any philosophical experience, living's mode of production functions "something like a supernatural nature-category" (*Jargon* 65).[10]

When Adorno suggests that we become mindful of "the base, insect-like, filthy, subhuman, and all the rest," he seeks to mend the false equivalence that clinches the life support system's "total entrapment" (*Metaphysics* 126). To metaphysics is allocated the effort to "extract an essential being from the sensible, empirical world, and hence to save it" (20). Thought brandishes a recuperative intention that tries to quell cultural saturation, which hypostatizes the human as absolute otherness from all there is (125, 126). An immanent culture's abstract definitional prowess becomes the natural alibi for the bloody brutality that actually makes it real:

> Indignation over cruelty diminishes in proportion as the victims are . . . swarthy, "dirty," dago-like. . . . The . . . assertion that savages, blacks, Japanese are like animals . . . is the key to the pogrom . . . decided *in the moment* when the *gaze* of a fatally wounded animal falls on a human being. The defiance with which he repels this gaze—"after all, it's only an animal"—reappears irresistibly in cruelties done to human beings, the perpetrators having again and again to reassure themselves that it is "only an animal," *because they could never fully believe this even of animals.* (*Minima* 105, emphases added)

Animal life is caged, mutilated, starved, dismembered, beaten, skinned alive, exploited, game hunted, and tortured to renege on the truth content of this encounter.

This moment ("when the gaze of a fatally wounded animal falls on a human being") gives the lie to ataraxy because the "key to the pogrom" decided in *that* moment must also be decided *over and over again* for animal life to self-fabricate as being mere self-preservation (96). The animal is altogether humanized, despite the fatal wounding—the animal asked for it: what the human does to the animal, the animal does to itself (by being itself). Nothing remains except "naked affirmation of what [culture] *is* anyway—the affirmation of power" (*Negative* 131, emphasis added).[11]

V. Bleating[12]

As a consequence of the "fateful intertwinement" (*Metaphysics* 121) of metaphysics and culture, metaphysics must explain "how the things which have happened were possible" (120). If transcendence yields foundational structures, then why is the world in agony? Even though the subject admits that cultural consciousness is a *sine qua non* of metaphysical inquiry, the absolute somehow stays unmolested by this cultural consciousness. Inasmuch as this philosophical antinomy is "forced upon us by the real course of history" (*Negative* 166), Adorno vitiates the linking of disconnectedness with a predisposition for objective truth.

To assess the self-deceptive state of culture, Adorno espouses that "urns, refuse bins and sand-heaps in which people vegetate between life and death . . . are exactly the things which matter" (*Metaphysics* 118).[13] If a way to the better there be, it exacts a full look at the worst (to use Thomas Hardy's formulation), as etched in these features of suffering is "the deepest strata of humanity's historical life" (133).[14] When differentiation itself is a system of reification, thought must turn to these hieroglyphics and thwart metaphysics from being unmovable by history. What passes for objectivity devours nature, and *this* nature is presented as inchoate and unformed (78); the subject appears to proceed to culture thoughtlessly, as if through a compliant, invisible element.[15] In this "economy of theft" (Saidiya Haartman's phrase), life is (to be) found in what Adorno calls "the zone of the carcass and the knacker" (117): the dead body substitutes for death because the life lived was already objectivity, and the hide of this dead body, sold as commodity, was already subjectivity. So that one may "mak[e] good at least a part of what . . . is otherwise denied" (113), culture's failure is acutely material to conveying and upholding "the *heterogeneousness* of death" (134, emphasis added).

The *philosophical* importance of life insisting on its otherness (from us) at the deepest layer of historical life lies in appreciation of the force of loss, of making death come alive as an intrinsic force. In the midst of the unraveling of the biosphere, a qualitative variety of experience discomfits our false equivalence with oblivion, a self-abrogation for the "hope that animal creation might survive the wrong that [the hu]man has done it, if not [the hu]man [it]self, and give rise to a better *species*, one that finally makes a success of life" (*Minima* 115, emphasis added). (Note the eschatological language.) It is to be dissolved into something else, to positively express a philosophical antinomy, forced upon us by the real course of history, in a *thoughtful* culture of truth telling: I am an animal. As Adorno states, "[C]hange depends on . . . becom[ing] aware of the ultimate negativity . . . not just [of] ephemeral surface phenomena" (*Metaphysics* 126).

Heeding the historical inadequacy of living qua advancing mastery of nature (*Negative* 168),[16] at the impasse where a reference to life must be created (Adorno crosses this impasse via our exceptional awareness of our biological floor), *secular* (not exceptional) thought may harness our "historical dimension" to avert "catastrophe in spite of everything" (323). *Because* I am an animal, being is not derived from nothingness; being some time is a being *in* time (not all [of] time).[17] And so, Lawrence Oates's last words to his three companions on March 16, 1912, as he departed from the tent with just his socks over frostbitten and gangrenous feet, in the midst of a blizzard on the frozen continent of Antarctica, perhaps consecrate a "eulogized undividedness" (119): "I am just going outside and may be some time." (The bodies of his three companions were found eight months later, but Oates's body was never found.)[18]

VI. Clear and Distinct Ideas

Culture's seemingly natural power clarifies metaphysics as "an emergence and a forgetting" (*Metaphysics* 11), a dynamic Adorno represents in the defiance of a human being repelling the "gaze" of a fatally wounded animal. Nature intrudes upon (or "juts into") culture as death (131), death being the ultimate concrete instance, and the ultimate appearance of transcendence. Death's *heterogeneousness* as object of metaphysical inquiry unsettles the history of self-preservation that is culture, a leveling force that dislodges the concrete example. The contingency that becomes appreciable via the concrete example troubles simulated nature: "[I]f [we] . . . investigate how people die, [we] . . . would find as many mediations of culture . . . as in any other phenomena" (131).

To push Adorno's lecture in further reversed direction, human exceptionalism as the gratuitous performance of identity (betraying the "gaze" of a fatally wounded animal) cedes that cruelty is the marrow of the structures that moor (our) being. Death may be an integral part of how a culture understands itself (ceremonies, rituals, rites of mourning), but cruelty efficiently administers our lives at the expense of reasonable living. Adorno refers to the cruelty of war (specifically the Vietnam War) as the "stench" that culture expels because "it itself stinks" (118); we may tender this concretion to animal slavery, *of the same genus* as torture and genocide, which can be disowned only with great difficulty. When a way of living, cruelty as culture's mode of existence in fact hurls us closer to death—to nothingness, as human exceptionalism does not integrate death; it thereby becomes "the gateway . . . into metaphysics" (130). Given the emphatic insistence of nature, however, "in the face of which one cannot cut a powerful figure" (130), the animal abides, today.

In Lecture Seventeen, Adorno concludes that "the heterogeneousness of death" is the object of metaphysical inquiry, but he seems to fall back on straightforward ideology (to forget) at the precise moment when the thought of (our) animal life emerges. The emphatic insistence of death is subjectively deprived of its objective genesis and dialectical function—*as if* this denial has the force of a clear and present idea. He makes an offhand comment: "At any rate, it *is* the case that, in contrast to the other animalia *known to us,* humans are *clearly* the *only* ones which in general have a consciousness of the fact that they must die" (131, emphases added). What do we really know about animals? What *can* we know?[19] In *this* moment of "an emergence and a forgetting," Adorno cordons off the question of dying, today, and demonstrates culture's power.

What we gather in the rhetorical quality of this spontaneous remark is a rather quick settlement of an immense philosophical problem. The hastiness encouraged by the profound infusion of cultural ideologies in metaphysics counts on the hypostatized difference between human and animal. When viewed from within the catastrophic frame/arena of anthropogenic climate change, *this* difference's historical inadequacy undergirds the culture of dying, today. The ideological constitution of human and animal fails to concede a lack that is natural and cultural to propel a terrible uniqueness: *homo sapiens* cannot sever nature, even as, for *homo sapiens,* culture is nature. This (first) cultural constitution of the (first) subject is the (first) form of violence (against nature)—as if this kind of culture were true essential being in itself.

Adorno postulates that we have attained a point of elevation above nature conducive to reflection on our natural origin, but we are "too much in thrall to the biological life" (132).[20] The possible impossibility of our self-preservation as a species suggests that we are not enthralled *enough.* We may understand that the confined animal feeding operation (or what is politely termed the "factory farm") is the paradigm of our relationship to the planet because we are "corpses from the first" (136).[21] The Earth, which provides sustenance for all, is overwritten with an implement of slavery. (We are at the top of the food chain.) Animals are thereby *meant* to die—otherwise one could not live—hence all life must be taken from them; they are *meant* to suffer. There are no animals living and dying *today* because nature is something we leave behind. This evacuation of the rational and humane obliges metaphysics (in reverse) to critically rescue the subject's self-expression and give a voice to suffering.[22]

A rapprochement with death "is to be found in bodily feeling, in identification with unbearable pain" (116)—that is, by living in the "historical dimension" of (our) animal life.[23] This "accorded . . . historic being" (Gilroy's term) apprehends its "life element" (93), whose emphatic insistence is the *only* possibility for a qualitative variety of experience.[24] If exceptionalism prolongs the culture that makes us exceptional, then this *exceptional* self-preservation "in opening its doors to nature, completely absorbs it, and *eliminates with difference* the [first] principle of culture, the possibility of reconciliation" (*Minima* 116, emphases added).

VII. What's There?

Dying today at the cost of our "unsteady floor" (*Metaphysics* 132) compels the imitation of nothingness for self-preservation, as the cultural façade's logic of force renders the natural discontinuous surplus value (*Negative* 205).[25] Bewitched by a system of false equivalences, "just by continuing to live one . . . tak[es] away that possibility from someone else, to whom life has been denied. . . . [O]ne . . . steal[s] that person's life" (*Metaphysics* 113). In this culture, the dialectic between alpha and omega, subjective and objective, subject and object, and concept and history, has no outside; for thought to have substance is to perforce introduce a dogmatic leap. But, nature has come back for us to disorder the self-identical present; history's real course has made the subject's liquidation a useless conceit that makes death seem inaccessible and remote, distant and peripheral, like an encroachment from the outside of life, (133). Attention must be paid to death's heterogeneousness, "its misery and stench . . . [as an] *animalistic* kicking of the bucket" (*Jargon* 158),[26] to catch sight of culture's infusion with evil.[27]

Adorno cautions that metaphysics requires understanding "that [on one hand] it can be quite wrong; and that, on the other, it requires an objective moment . . . *incapable of being assimilated to it*—that these two motifs together form the dialectical figure, the dialectical image" (*Metaphysics* 142, emphases added). From within the catastrophic frame/arena of anthropogenic climate change, a "topography of the void" (136) can express what *mere* nothingness actually contains (135): *in* the brush with the indigestible, flashes of fallible consciousness vindicate (our) philosophical nature. Death is alien and frightening only because life is not lived rightly (136); dying today entails a positive description of a negative antinomy: I am an animal.

I suggest, therefore, that an emphatic experience of the cruelty that hounds what is actually *here*—not outside, over *there*—as the (missing) link between the categorial and the immanent, may bridge the distance between metaphysics and history.

> The physical moment tells our knowledge that suffering ought not
> to be, that things should be different. . . . The job is up solely to

the species, to which the individual belongs even whe[n] . . . objec-
tively thrust into the absolute loneliness of a helpless object. . . . All
activities of the species point to its continued physical existence,
[though] they may be misconceptions of it. . . . Even the steps
which society takes to exterminate itself are at the same time
absurd acts of unleashed self-preservation. They are forms of
unconscious social action against suffering even though an obtuse
view of society's own interest turns their total particularity against
that interest. Confronted with such steps, their purpose—*and this
alone makes society a society*—calls for it to be so organized as
the productive forces would directly permit it here and now, and
as the conditions of production on either side relentlessly prevent
it. (*Negative* 203, emphases added)

Forthright expression of the essentially historical nature that is (the self's)
utter transience leads to that aporetic juncture whereupon a decision must
be made: "to be" (qua animal) or "not to be" (qua human). Adorno observes
that disasters, when serving as nodal points, have the ability to call forth and
take in far-off realities and insulated events from distant pasts (*Metaphysics*
134), which when strung together superficially proffer an explanation for the
present. But, there is no death that is epic or biblical in the calamitous reality
of climate change—only an ego-weakness *at the level of the species* because
for the *rest of the planet* life has been denied.[28]

The "era of procrastination, of half-measures, of soothing and baffling
expedients, of delays" is over; we are now in a "period of consequences" (Gore
100–101). Howsoever we cross the threshold of this age (and not the threshold in Winston Churchill's 1936 warning of the rise of fascism facing Britain
and Europe), we must forego magisterial proclamations of saving the Earth
when the Earth in fact saves us. Our cruelty concedes our (first) philosophical
nature of practicing *for* dying and death (Plato 64a): with an emphatic sense
of actual animals, we may withhold apprehension of (our) purpose, for the
illusion of nature is not for us to live, but for us to die.

VIII. From Little Things Big Things Grow[29]

In the Anthropocene,[30] is it any wonder that when we are voyeuristically
watching the death of the biosphere, we are also voyeuristically watching the
death of what is rational and humane? The symbiosis of these two sadistic
spectacles, at a time when we have the wherewithal to mitigate the hell we have

created, presumes a relation with animals that culture spectacularly rebuffs. Nature may signify our irreducible difference, but cruelty is our exceptional culture. As the limit-experience that cuts too close to the bone, cruelty is that before which thinking flounders[31]; it is impossible to quantify. Culture qua gratuitous performance of identity capitulates precisely when we most need to be philosophical. Only when the relationship between metaphysical categories and empirical reality is taken seriously can we engender the prospect of self-reflection (Adorno, *Metaphysics* 18). Metaphysics is a movement of thought "in thrall to the biological life," which (further reversed) carries us into the openness of Nature's living power.

We return here to Adorno's dictum that what matters most for metaphysics' self-reflective aptitude is that which culture deems base, insectile, filthy, and subhuman, that which is found in "urns, refuse bins and sand heaps." Metaphysics as "a critical and a rescuing intention" (51) conveys and upholds sustainability through complexity:

> More respect is due the little things that run the world. . . . The diversity of insects is the greatest documented among all organisms: the total number of species classified in 2006 is about 900,000. The true number, combining those both known and remaining to be discovered, may exceed 10 million. The bio-mass of insects is immense: about a million trillion are alive at any given moment. Ants alone, of which there may be 10 thousand trillion, weigh roughly as much as all 6.5 billion human beings. (E.O. Wilson, *The Creation* 32)

Humans cannot survive without insects, but insects have no need for humans. The disappearance of insects would bring about the collapse of the terrestrial environment, which when coupled with several decades of decline would precipitate an ecological dark age. Trapped remnants of humanity would cling to survival by offering prayers for weeds and bugs (33–35).

Literally located in the most fundamental layers of humanity's historical life, *this* essential relation may teach normative culture to be afraid of its own perversity (Adorno, *Minima* 97). A proportional footstep amidst heterogeneous fellow inhabitants of planet Earth unleashes why we began to philosophize in the first place: our historical co-implication in the world in which we actually live. The utmost distance from life that is also proximity is perhaps the rational hope of one's own name:

> Utopia goes disguised in the creatures whom Marx even begrudged the surplus value they contribute as workers. In existing without

any purpose recognizable to [humans], animals hold out, as if for expression, their own names, utterly impossible to exchange. . . . I am a rhinoceros, signifies the shape of a rhinoceros." (228)

How do we know that a rhinoceros is really called a rhinoceros?

Chapter Seven

The (M)other of All Posts

Postcolonial Melancholia in the Anthropocene

The challenge of being in the same present, of synchronizing . . . hope
upward from below . . . provides some help in seeing . . . the irreducible
value of diversity within sameness.

—Paul Gilroy, *Postcolonial Melancholia*

We called at some more places . . . where the merry dance of death and
trade goes on . . . all along the formless coast bordered by dangerous
surf, as if Nature herself had tried to ward off intruders.

—Joseph Conrad, *Heart of Darkness*

If we . . . work toward creative possibilities that are too easily dismissed
as utopian [we] . . . might profitably be reset by acts of imagination and
invention *that are adequate to the depth of the postcolonial predicament.*

—Paul Gilroy, *Postcolonial Melancholia*, emphases added

It is this rationality, and the life and death game that takes place in it,
that I'd like to investigate from a historical point of view.

—Michel Foucault, *Power*

[I]t is only when you *lose your mother* that she becomes a myth. . . . Return
is as much about the world to which you no longer belong. . . . It is to
be bound to other promises. It is to lose your mother, always.

—Saidiya Hartman, *Lose Your Mother*

I. Introduction

In 2005, Paul Gilroy's Wellek Library Lectures at the University of California, Irvine, were published as a book titled *Postcolonial Melancholia*. In response to England's resurgent nostalgia for the bygone days of empire, Gilroy mobilizes Theodor Adorno's negative dialectics to appeal for "a vital planetary humanism" (79). The "demotic multiculturalism" (99) of England's urban areas, as arguably one of empire's most unanticipated outgrowths, is a model for "a negative dialectics of conviviality" (121); these nascent spaces exhibit a form of liberal humanism that can be updated to respond to ongoing environmental devastation. While Gilroy recodes liberal humanism as planetary humanism by extrapolating the planetary from urbanity, this permutation appropriates and displaces the planet itself: the planet is radically humanized, but this humanized planet is radically urban. The naturalized evolution set in motion progressively expands the scale of liberal humanism's alleged provenance: human→ urban→ planetary. A de facto teleology reenacts the very fissure between nature and culture that obliges "a vital planetary humanism" in the first place. In making the planetary synonymous with urban culture, Gilroy rectifies a modern racial logic via urban civic life categorically marked by the *absence* of nature.

A city's concrete bespeaks the threshold that buoys human exceptionalism, as the urban presumes the planet's continued (albeit calculably sustainable) instrumentalization. By making a pitch for the culture that puts (all of) nature *somewhere else*, Gilroy radically humanizes ongoing ecological disaster. At the aporetic juncture where the planetary is urbane and natural, city and earth, concrete and galactic, a melancholia adequate to our historical predicament admits the "*universality* of our elemental vulnerability" (4, emphasis added): "a vital planetary humanism" *today* understands that empire's first victim is the animal. Gilroy proceeds from (racially deterministic) nature to the (demotic multicultural) urban setting; postcolonial melancholia, however, defers to our "deep cultural biology" (6) by moving in the *opposite* direction.

II. Heterogeneity

Gilroy tries to formulate an "agonistic, planetary humanism" (4) that can provide the cultural competency necessary for accountability in postcolonial England. In his estimation, urban multiculturalism upsets the convergent deterministic logics of nature and culture, as organic and unruly forms of conviviality unsettle the "iron laws of mechanical culture" (6) to unnerve our "trancelike moods" (3). He targets the "above all power of race" (6), which prevents his project from accepting responsibility for those colonial cultures that *we* also helped to create. He avoids this postcoloniality's historical failure in two ways.

First, Gilroy uses postcolonial cosmopolitanism as a means to establish his cultural difference from Adorno, who belongs to a bygone colonial world, the Europe of old. (We will leave aside the colonial genealogy of contemporary metropolitan multiculturalism.) Even though Gilroy inherits this old Europe's present possibility, an a priori sense of cultural difference from Adorno qua Europe misses a peculiarly felicitous historical opportunity to concede that the injurious dualism of nature and culture can no longer simply be called western culture. Second, negative dialectics lead Adorno to the conquest of nature and the question of the animal, but Gilroy goes to metropolitan domains to "detonate the historic lore that brings the virtual realities of 'race' to dismal and destructive life" (32). (In this place conventionally *devoid* of nature, note the warlike task of postcolonial melancholia.) He rightly counters human-rights discourses that reiterate western benevolence when ameliorating environmental calamities (5); but, if we are seriously facing suffering on a planetary scale (36), then where is everything else that lives?[1] Since Gilroy relies on human exceptionalism, in lieu of *secularizing* suffering, he overlooks *how* colonial history opens out into the "multicultural promise of the postcolonial world" (143).

Refusing the coincidence of postcolonialism and modern nationhood, Gilroy regards postcoloniality to be a fragile, yet substantive, realization, which is concerned primarily with the de-naturing of race (57). *For* a global multicultural reality, he turns to the ordinary hope found in urban spaces wherein values such as hospitality, tolerance, justice, and mutual care can remake the world (96, 99). In keeping with Gilroy's interest in "a vital planetary humanism," we may turn the understatement evident in his reference to environmental catastrophe into the emphatic insistence of anthropogenic climate change: climate change is not only the singular crisis putting at risk the very possibility of human culture as we have known it,[2] but also will disproportionately affect the global poor.[3] Upon *this* ground, a new understanding of multicultural reality and anti-racist theory must be developed to empower a radical revision of our primarily cultural formation as a species.

From within the catastrophic frame/arena of anthropogenic climate change, we notice that urbanity's camaraderie and vivaciousness are not historically adequate models, as boosting traditional humanism as planetary neglects how humanism is complicit with the conquest of nature. The idealized version of humanity that is the celebrated outcome of a violent fissure makes sense only on the basis of the denigrated animal. We cannot grant this kind of cultural constitution planetary proportions to resist racism's "alchemic power" (32) because precisely the overdetermined nature of *our* animalization betrays the precariousness of cultural saturation.

III. Cultural Biology

Gilroy dismantles notions of race that work as an ingrained "cultural biology": cultural determinism masquerades as biological destiny to doom us to identitarian lives (6). Decrying the conflation of the cultural and the biological, Gilroy prolongs the "historic lore" (32) that turns nature into the signifier of irreducible human difference, even as he attempts to shatter the power of race that furnishes a delusional and ultimately palliative sense of human uniqueness. Our "accorded . . . historic being" (32) as animals, however, relays a cosmic sensibility not predicated on calculable notions of sustainability; it cherishes planet Earth as that which it is—a "pale blue dot" in the black void of space.[4] Encompassing cosmopolitan zones, we can attend to "the nation-defining ramparts of the white cliffs of Dover" (14), whose reimagining is the prospect for an alternative "ecology of belonging" (76).

Here, the ultimate colonial fantasy is the conquest of nature in a supposedly just and "clean war" (43), despite *this* world actually dismissing the demand for (not entitlement to) power and recognition. Gilroy requisitions a different history of cultural relationship, one that does not hinge on the surmised natural basis for racial differences; but such an alternative history also implicates our cultural relationship to nature. Refusing "state-centeredness" and valorizing "vernacular style[s]" purvey creditable capabilities for "'vulgar' or 'demotic' cosmopolitanism" because urban cultures value commonplace encounters with otherness (67). The city is replete with relationships that undermine the hubris of our "geo-piety" (72), which when enclosed within illusory walls, stymie substantive (not abstract) politics. All the same, a planetary geography deduced from selective invocations of urban life recasts humanity as "a legion of clones" (63) whose cultural habits inevitably steer away from nature.[5] Sealed up inside culture, humanity affixes identity to its derived negation (63) instead of sustaining a palpable sense of urgency, given the profound changes in "perception and representation of space and matter" involved (75): if anthropogenic climate change is the (impossible-to-imagine) loss of nature, then this (impossible-to-imagine) loss of nature is a potential loss of our ability to signify at all.

To offset ataraxy, Gilroy uses a (perennially) concrete example of suffering beyond the cloistered realm of overdevelopment. In part one of *Postcolonial Melancholia* dubbed "The Planet," chapter 2 is titled "Cosmopolitanism Contested." This chapter has a section called "From Ali G to Multicultural Democracy." Here, Gilroy says,

[A]ntipathy to destructive global workings of "turbo-capitalism" . . .
promotes a novel sense of our relationship with the biosphere. It
supports an appreciation of nature as a common condition of
our imperiled existence, resistant to commodification and, on
some level, deeply incompatible with the institution of private
property that made land into a commodity and legitimized chat-
tel slavery. (75)

In recognizing that a culture adequate to our present quandary, induced by the
wanton deprivation of most of the planet's inhabitants, demands a "planetary
consciousness" (75), Gilroy nevertheless adopts the specter of dead nature (not
concern *for* nature) to solicit a "hopeful despair" (75), which may instigate
movements for a global multiculture.[6]

The planet is at the heart of postcolonial melancholia by virtue of
a liberal apologia that services the poor management of nature for anti-
capitalist critique. Gilroy does not follow through on *how* nature confounds
and limits the farcical empire of the human erected across already inhabited
ground because he remains caught in the very mechanistic understanding
of culture that he inveighs against. Enfeebling the convergent deterministic
logics of nature and culture by centralizing race (he ignores gender) to
imbricate the (entire) planet only stokes our fantasies of sequestration from
the "tragedy, fragility, and brevity of indivisible human existence" (75). A
planetary consciousness cannot be cultivated via a gratuitous performance
of identity predicated on the naturalness of the schism between nature and
culture; depending upon cultural rationalizations of cruelty for a sense of
collectivity imperils our survival as a species. Underestimating the actual
implications of using nature to inflame grievance-based, culture war angst
cannot account for the "cultural biology" that thwarts apprehension of our
basic vulnerability to each other.

IV. Demotic Multiculturalism

Inimical to the fragmented stupor of consumerism in militarized globalization, a cosmopolitan ethos calls for dwelling at ease alongside the unfamiliar
(3). In light of the profound failures of the political imagination that provoke
proprietary relationships with colonial history, Gilroy's postcoloniality overreaches the seeming insouciance of the nation-state as the authoritative basis
for creating political culture. For sure, the practitioners of realpolitik scoff
at the possibility of a political culture fundamentally intertwined with an
image of planetary humanism, but these failures of the political imagination

are too often the result of trivial understandings of culture (let alone nature); obdurate in its Manichean fantasy, culture dissembles our imperial, yet also precarious identities (4–5).

To suggest that a "historical ontology of race [. . .]" (7) may glean how naturalized prejudice applauds geopolitical power, Gilroy (following Agamben) posits the concentration camp as the embodiment of the institutionalized exception (8). Yet, going forward, I contend that the factory farm ought to be seen as the prime political institution of our anxiety-ridden postcoloniality, which turns the Earth—the heterogeneously inhabited planet is yet to be conjured—into the industrial scale abbatoir's killing floor or the expansive dead zone of the monoculture.[7] The massive scale of living bodies easily abjected, tortured, humiliated, caged, starved, and torn to shreds, just as Gilroy describes the "calculus" (10) of racial difference—too often while still alive—through the innovative use of technology ensures a naturalized identity for other forms of socio-political exploitation.

If we demand that systems of exclusion that we *call* "culture," "nation," or "history" should be historically adequate, then postcoloniality must grapple with the (impossible-to-imagine) loss of nature, for the border fence of a pathological, deep-seated investment in race has caused a genocidal fracturing of species (15). At *this* level, Gilroy implies that we are one planetary race, but his sense of the political imagination stops short at a curiously unpopulated nature and a multiculturally overpopulated culture. The urban myth of proper cultural progress (nature→ culture→ urban), an itinerary that begets global multicultural reality, falls back on itself: radical humanization of the planet is proposed as a panacea for the disproportional stranglehold we already have on our planet.

A secularized understanding of suffering concurs that the animal is ritually reenacted *for* liberal humanism: the animal is condemned for the humanization of the human (77). The ethnic absolutism that (first) lodges the oppositional and antagonistic disparity between human and animal subsists in Gilroy's account under the guise of a sustainability that is eminently calculable and technologically dependent: *our* culture still destines *their* lives. As an example of cultures indifferent to suffering, Gilroy wrangles with the apprehensive, melancholy mood in post-imperial England (12). Like its imperial inheritor the United States, England historically requires war for a sense of national belonging (64, 88); this postcolonial melancholia of the nation-state, however, ought also to extend to those white cliffs of Dover that (now) signify the planet.

In Matthew Arnold's famous 1867 poem "Dover Beach," the speaker ruminates on his view of the Dover cliffs, the English Channel, and on the "tremulous cadence slow" (1101) of the waves interminably striking the stony beach and then being drawn back out to sea. Within this familiar rhythm, the poet hears other patterns subsumed amid what he calls "the eternal note of sadness" at the varieties of human loss, "the turbid ebb and flow / Of human misery" (1101). The poem concludes by emphasizing the exquisite vulnerability of the human community positioned ominously at the edge of time and space perceived as "a darkling plain / Swept with confused alarms of struggle and flight, / Where ignorant armies clash by night" (1101). With, quite literally, everything at stake, this melancholy and fretful position might be reimagined not through the antagonistic fancy of an us opposed to a hostile world writ-large but rather through a sense of identification with the deep time elided in those fossil-filled limestone cliffs.

V. Nation as Narration (Revisited)[8]

Gilroy turns to urban spaces to contravene the equivalence of the modern nation-state to nature as its ontologically intransigent mirror image (14). The urban as the site of "demotic multiculturalism" is the resource *par excellence* for concrete examples of multicultural conviviality. People already dwelling convivially with difference offer the potential for reimagining those white cliffs of Dover beyond their use as a trope for national belonging. Nature can no longer be figured as a historical anomaly owing to its chimerical immovability, and nationhood is no longer capable (if it ever was) of resolving our historical predicament. Taking for granted the already planetary hypostatization of human exceptionalism professes the animal as the conjured object of our hatred and indifference, notwithstanding how we speak about the animal in an abstract or ultra-theoretical manner, just as we do, Gilroy notes, about "multiculture, toleration, and otherness" (16). Conceding that postcolonial melancholia when deracinated may undo biologically deterministic effects of the real (30), we may add that these efforts must include a radical reconstruction of the relationship between nature and culture, otherwise the modern history of race, when unreconciled to the historical moment at hand, deters us from imagining "what it is like to be somebody else" (63).

Taking Gilroy's beseeching lectures at their word, therefore, for an alternative "somatic economy in which *all* lives are seen to be *equally* precious and worth caring for" (81, emphases added), postcolonial antiracist work cannot bring forth a planetary vision somehow bereft of animals. Animal life is present in *Postcolonial Melancholia* only during Gilroy's reading of George Orwell's essays, "Shooting an Elephant," "Some Thoughts on the Common Toad," and "The Hanging" (76–78). We can broaden the scope of Gilroy's contention that race is principally "an impersonal, discursive arrangement" that results from a "raciological ordering" (39) because mechanistic conceptions of race emulate humanistic conceptions of the animal—both produce lives that live out a "cultural biology." Postcolonial anti-racist theorizing can no longer afford to use nature for an intrinsic relatedness (42) that paradoxically still keeps the human race segregated from our fellow planetary inhabitants.

By intensifying indifference, this exclusionary form of inclusion sustains social death: as animals constituted by *lack* of self-preservation, we unquestioningly occupy a fungible niche. If anthropogenic climate change is the wound of our dominance (to invoke Fanon) (53), then this cultural exigency obliges a historical innovativeness that restores moral legitimacy to (our) animal lives. In keeping with Gilroy's attempt to truly historicize race (53), contra its seemingly natural power, an affective "ecology of belonging" permits a qualitative variety of experience; what is dissonant, divergent, and negative can thereby initiate "a new geometry of dependency" that actually disturbs "over-integrated culture" (83). When *homo sapiens* no longer hog the *entire* history of suffering, postcoloniality can repudiate the militarism, cruelty, and compulsion (56) that normalize a paucity of empathy, mutual respect, and fellow feeling (54). To transform *this* colonial culture that we also helped to fashion, postcolonial anti-racism undoes the "telling blockage" (57) of planetary belonging.

Nature's curtailment of our ability to self-preserve as a species is the "cosmic angle" (74), which empowers us to not simply preserve our civilization, as if we were the end of history, but to find pathways for a pivotal transformation. Manifesting these historical opportunities to grasp the imperial history of the conquest of nature is not reducible to sustainable lifestyle choices or facile celebrations of difference. The secularization of suffering facilitates an estrangement from culture for a planetary consciousness that effectuates nature's incontestability *as if for the first time*. (For example, the BBC series *Planet Earth* introduces us to our planet.) This irretrievable archetype of planetary belonging engenders the utopian ethos of (our) animal life to ground the contemporary moment of critique.

Planetary liberal humanism evinces an urban cosmopolitanism whose ramparts are assembled by identitarian efforts to take flight from the actual planet.

> It is telling that the power of the landscape emerges as the dominant element here [in books that seek to either diagnose or remedy the national pathology]. This outcome is troubling because it excludes all urban and metropolitan spaces from the forms of moral and aesthetic rearmament that are necessary if the country is to be reinvigorated and restored. (115)

On account of the relatively greater presence of people of color in England's metropolitan areas, Gilroy's worry about the exclusion of urban spaces is unquestionably important; exactly the (impossible-to-imagine) loss of the power of the landscape, however, tells us of the potential loss of our ability to signify at all. Here, Gilroy appears to challenge even the landscape's signifying force, considering that what arises is a reactive cultural project, which memorializes human exceptionalism as postcolonial melancholia.[9]

VI. The Elephant in the Room

The impetus for planetary humanism and a vital humanity starts from "the '*bestial* floor' of human being in the body" (78, emphasis added). (Recall that Adorno uses the term "biological floor.") Even so, Gilroy's version of a global multicultural reality races humanism by depicting the congruence of the urban and planetary in a way that ignores the immanent, entropic counter-pressure exerted by this "bestial floor." His call for active witnessing[10] (like Adorno's attention to dying today), albeit limited to race, can embrace the loss of our contemporaneity with nature. If the concentration camp figures the absent and the mutilated, then the factory farm in a radically humanized world figures the emphatic force of a *planetary* suffering.[11] In this "somatic economy," all lives are seen as worthwhile—even when we eat them. (One could also suggest that the agricapitalist system of production that ruthlessly enforces devastating monocultures turns the planet into a confined animal feeding operation in which we are the animals.)

If urbanity betokens a "cosmopolitan . . . obligation [. . .]" (97), then the factory farm induces a species obligation. Insofar as the fecklessness manufactured by consumerism *au fait* passes for global camaraderie, "nature enforces limits on . . . [how we] remake and transform the world" (72). For all that nature's hypostatization is an unmitigated "catalogue of horror" (93), we are habituated to the elastic rationality that squeamishly equivocates wanton destruction. The factory farm institutionalizes the terror and torture imperative for the animal to occupy its (designated) cultural niche; *this* loss of our moral legitimacy as a species may break our cultural narcissism because a "morbid culture" (107) prohibits the kinds of "moral and aesthetic rearmament" critical for nature to be "reinvigorated and restored" (115).[12] In the metropolis, ordinary, everyday, and organic forms of admixture turn racial difference into something utterly mundane (119, 124). Spontaneous interactions with otherness not mutilated by fear and violence create a playful cosmopolitan energy rife with democratic possibility. Be that as it may, when Gilroy articulates the "feral beauty of postcolonial culture" (142), he speaks almost exclusively about the politically fortified denomination of (urban) human life.[13]

Attempting to comprehend the Anthropocene, the ethicist Clive Hamilton, in a 2013 interview with Ari Phillips, notes:

> We've reached an event [that] . . . causes us to rethink pretty much everything[, especially] . . . what is a human being. The . . . modern conception . . . is an isolated ego existing inside a body. . . . But in fact that's a very recent and culturally specific understanding. . . . And it's the conception . . . that's consistent with an advanced consumer society. / Collectively though, we are the kind of creatures, like certain types of microbes, that can completely transform the nature of the planet. . . . Something very profound has happened. Human history, which we think of as only being a few thousand years old and is the history of human actions, has converged with geologic history [that is not] . . . operating in a very distinct domain having nothing to do with us . . . [W]e find that our history affects the history of the earth. / If there is no more human history distinct from earth history, then what does that mean?[14]

The confluence of human history and Earth history may prompt an anthropocentrism that is not irreducibly a form of mastery. The impossibility (ultimately) of knowing our ecology does reveal our singularity in annihilating a biosphere we cannot recreate; except, what *is* exceptional about the human relationship to nature and other species is our cruelty.

Cruelty is the mark of the human, not the animal. Cruelty is not extractive; it is gratuitous, the greed of a humanity that enshrines itself as the implement of our estrangement, a superabundance predicated on supererogatory depletion and extreme impoverishment. Cruelty at the individual scale becomes unsustainability at the planetary scale. Gilroy's use of the term "bestial floor" (rather than biological, or animal, or earthly, for example) grants to life that insists (without insisting) on its otherness from us a quality of terror and menace. In a progressive understanding of human history wherein urbanity is teleological, the nature and culture dualism turns beasts into the threat behind us. Without cultural edification (now of the cosmopolitan variety), these beasts are simultaneously the inner threat that can escape from inside us; both cultural genealogies by immuring humans cede (our) animal life.

VII. Culture Talk: Or Else

This reading brings the intricate nexus of nature, culture, and history to bear on Paul Gilroy's rendition of a living postcoloniality. Our elementally enmeshed life manifests how the world *as it is* disallows the entrenchment of rigid categories: nature refuses our historic demand for planetary exceptionalism, and is coming back for us. A continuation of the reified consumption of an increasingly inhospitable planet serves as a historical alibi for the "virtual realities" (32) of postcolonial anti-racist progress. As colonialism and slavery were justified by desecrating the vanquished as indistinguishable from nature, *we* are the memory of *how* culture appears as an impregnable constraint, which boxes "in" and cuts nature "off"; we the other of nature left out/side of history must go back to an/other time frame—where it all began, "in the beginning," to dismantle our genesis machine for an apocryphal genealogy of our cultural relationship to nature. In a globalized world, therefore, using nature to signify irreducible human difference is perhaps one tradition we all have in ourselves, and we can all hate it properly (Adorno, *Minima* 52).[15]

E.O. Wilson warns, "Overall, humanity has altered this planet as profoundly as our considerable powers permit" (*The Creation* 17). Existing as though it were a force of nature, culture's cloying, self-same ipseity may be disturbed by the mass extinction event currently taking place. Culture talk for the sake of a *species* obligation demands that we find it within ourselves to think the threshold of our historical era, the "historical extreme," "the ultimate, the absolutely unthinkable" (Adorno, *Metaphysics* 98, 115).[16] To carry out this responsibility, a planetary postcoloniality asks how we can respect somebody else's life when we deprive ourselves of all yearning for it (in order to live).[17] But, functionality's nothingness can be crossed (out) by self-preservation's beingness; and so, I end with a respectful note to Professor Gilroy that the elephant in the room is an animal.

Chapter Eight

Compulsory Rationality in the Economics of Empire

Sati, Always *Sati*

If . . . the unity and self-sufficiency of th[e] subject is possible only at the expense of the racial, ethnic, and feminine object, why has this perception not produced the emancipation and self-acceptance of the object?

—Asha Varadharajan, *Exotic Parodies*

everything can be used
except what is wasteful
(you will need
to remember this when you are accused of destruction.)

—Audre Lorde, "For Each of You"

The transition to a new age requires a change in our . . . conception of *space-time*, the *inhabiting of places*, and of *containers*, or *envelopes of identity*. It assumes and entails . . . a transformation of . . . the relations of *matter* and *form*.

—Luce Irigaray, *An Ethics of Sexual Difference*

"The groans of this sick person," he said, "distract my attention. And without that it is extremely difficult to guard against clerical errors in this climate."

—Joseph Conrad, *Heart of Darkness*

As we strive for a non-antagonistic understanding of difference to unleash philosophy, feminism, and postcolonial theory's historical co-implication in understanding the world in which we live, we return in this chapter to the widow's irretrievable heterogeneity. By enabling the experience of crossing an aporetic juncture as the resurrection of the flesh, postcoloniality as a historical era and conceptual accomplishment rejuvenates heterogeneity as an ideal and implement in response to a historical moment characterized by a devastating *loss* of heterogeneity, and, hence, of our ability to signify at all. In so doing, we may embolden an anomalous species venerated for its *lack* of self-preservation to forego the antagonistic cultural scripts that turn what is alive into what is ancillary. Such a secularization of suffering may allow us to recognize that the bloody brutality by which we damn nature condemns us all—not just the subaltern—to an illimitable silence.

I. Litmus Tests

Whereas Asha Varadharjan's criticisms of Gayatri Spivak's concept of subalternity may hastily grant the subaltern a transparent subjectivity to impugn the metropolitan feminist's silencing of the subaltern, she correctly implies that *sati* is the Indian feminist's litmus test in the Euro-US academy.[1] By prolonging the colonial seizure of this ritual to establish empire's historical alibi, postcolonial feminism's Euro-US institutionalization tends to oblige practitioners to explain themselves by analyzing this synecdochal phenomenon. Many immigrants like myself cathected the space of the postcolonial feminist on newly acquired "home" ground by responding to stereotypes and cultural theft, obstructing the sameness attributed to Indian women, and augmenting our sense of the practice. The 1829 banning of *sati* by Lord William Bentinck is a watershed moment in colonial history, and, decidedly, women are the ground upon which the imperial and nationalist battles are waged, but the hypervisibility of *sati* as the quintessential object of study spawns much unease in postcolonial feminist quarters.

When writing my dissertation on the 1987 *sati* of nineteen-year-old Roop Kanwar, I even visited Deorala, Rajasthan, spoke with her father-in-law and other villagers, saw the *sati sthal* (*sati* site qua sacred ground), went to a huge *sati* temple, and met a "living" *sati*—that is, an elderly woman whose *sati* was foiled by the police. In spite of this additional research, what affects me most is that Roop Kanwar died at the age of many of my students (in the early aughts these students were closer in age). Her murder becomes real in its abject perversity because of the seeming ease with which the sight of a person burning alive turns into a *darshan* of the serene goddess-imbued wife engulfed in flames. (*Darshan* is a reciprocal viewing or beholding of god and devotee to elicit receipt of a divine blessing.) *How* is it that the former can be *made* into the latter? As this is a qualitatively different question from an immigrant's negotiation of categorial Indian femaleness, Spivak's "Can the Subaltern Speak?" (1988), published just a year after Roop Kanwar's *sati*, registers differently. Unlike many of her critics at the time, it is difficult for me to consider her "groping" for Bhuvaneswari Bhaduri as a self-interested deployment of identity politics.[2]

In my reading, Spivak's protracted sojourn to encounter the subject of *sati* discloses *how* the utter contingency of a singular experience provides a cosmogonic peek at the (un)making of a world. Although Spivak calls her culminating lament that the subaltern cannot speak ill advised, her concept of subalternity bares the grief that no "laundry list[. . .]" ("Subaltern" 308) of women's emancipation or rights-based platforms can capture. As discussed earlier, what remains for Spivak is the proverbial ledger of horribly mistranscribed names that still teem with life notwithstanding our attempts to read them: by Marxist revolutionary discourses, Eurocentric deconstruction, poststructuralist abdications of representative responsibility, neocolonial legitimations by reversal, and postcolonial appropriations and displacements of decolonizing space. Bhuvaneswari's heterogeneity is irretrievable, and, while this dismal conclusion might lead to self-indulgent musings on theory's inevitable groundlessness, which Varadharajan rightly disputes because of the actual suffering of others, it turns knowledge into the *experience* of the impossible.

II. Proceedings 3.0

This chapter returns to "Can the Subaltern Speak?" via a revision of this perhaps most canonical of postcolonial feminist texts: it substitutes the sections on Marx, Foucault, and Deleuze, which precede Spivak's discussion of the archive of antiquity (the ancient Hindu texts of the *Dharmasastra* and *Rg-Veda*) and Bhuvaneswari Bhaduri's *sati*/suicide, with various contemporaneous postcolonial feminist accounts of *sati* (with the caveat that feminists in India do not refer to themselves as postcolonial, as this is a Euro-US appellation). Regardless of whether Spivak specifically addresses these variegated analyses, replacing Marx, Foucault, and Deleuze is a heuristic device used not only to underscore the fecundity of these approaches to *sati* (Spivak's included) but also to change the dynamic of postcolonial theory's Euro-US instutionalization. Marx, Foucault, and Deleuze coming "first" in Spivak's essay runs the risk of depreciating what follows as the product of a diagnostic and/or corrective standpoint. One is demonstrably incorrect if ascribing merely this standpoint to Spivak's work, but the non-antagonistic difference created by the switch dockets the *heterogeneity* of postcolonial feminist inquiry.

Even so, the critical edge of this juxtaposition of what is divergent and diverse emerges methodologically. In terms of this project's concern with reinvigorating heterogeneity as a value and tool from within the catastrophic frame/arena of anthropogenic climate change, what is of interest is the status of particularity in these discrepant investigations. Broadly construed, the epistemic strategy of particularization confronts the allegedly universal subject of liberal individualism through essentially historical categories of identity (race, class, gender, sexuality, ability, etc.). This strategy persists in delivering a better representation of the widow's situation, as this situation's general implications cannot be garnered without studying the knotted dynamics at hand. The chapter marshals Spivak's worry about the widow's readability not to critique culturalist accounts per se but to question the antagonistic understanding of difference that grounds culturalist explanations.

The widow's shuttle between subject- and object-status divulges the heterogeneity that an antagonistic understanding of difference automatically disavows to execute an *authoritative* cultural account, whose truth content is obtained from the compulsory rationality that makes the account possible. She can then (be made to) imbibe several cultural narratives at once: as a sign of history, bearer of sanctified culture, exemplar of good wifehood, manifestation of the goddess, an individual free will, an honorable family woman, etc. In place of deciding whether these authoritative cultural expositions are "right" or "wrong," Spivak decrees the intellectual's project as *intellectual* not identity-based: we are to conceive (of) radical alterity. Once we arrive at the aporetic juncture where the widow possesses *and* is devoid of an authentic voice and free will, utter contingency can be appreciably felt.

In keeping with this intellectual labor of making a culture's utter contingency tangible (what Adorno figures as "felt contact with the object," and Christian as "crazy women crying in the wind"), I suggest the following: allowing that an antagonistic understanding of difference renders knowing and unknowing equivalent—that is, a culture's compulsory rationality exerts a leveling force to make us all (at odds with) themselves—postcoloniality is the striving for a non-antagonistic understanding of difference. As both a historical era and conceptual accomplishment, this kind of postcoloniality's cultural *naïveté* impedes the naturalized itineraries that mutate actual heterogeneity into undifferentiated nothingness via an exegetically created encounter with the subaltern. What Adorno terms "a genuine philosophical radicalism," Spivak terms "tracking a process of unknowing," and Christian terms "the race for theory," might find a way out.

Forasmuch as cultural naïveté is not conducive to authoritative reportage, a deliberated *un*-self-consolidation by refusing hegemonic socialization is not dogmatic or arbitrary but uses the ingredients of the future anterior to (re)inscribe inevitably palimpsestic terrain. While it is clear that the feminist investigations included in this chapter do not pretend that the historical is the ontological—that is, they do not fall prey to the inadvertent ontologizing of essentially historical identity-based categories—we run the common risk of reprising the *functionality* of the cultural by albeit a more tortuous route. Along with providing some context for Spivak's reading of Bhuvaneswari Bhaduri's *sati*/suicide (detailed in the following chapter), the chapter's principal conceit is that etched in this tradition are my own cultural explanations; since we are all products of our time, this tradition becomes (officiates as) my historical alibi. What apocryphal genealogy, catching reality beyond particular identity and radical alterity, will (always) have been writing the history of (our) vanishing present, as we speak?

Here, we begin.

The following sections provide examples of various cultural scripts that too often predetermine the general frame of discussion about *sati*. As these cultural scripts motivate overdetermined identitarian itineraries as dialectics between opposing forces, they turn even emancipatory projects into the widow's ventriloquism. Being heedful that the postcolonial self-implicates as the continuation of a particular logic, these cultural vignettes object to the serviceable positioning of women's victimization for the furtherance of other agendas. For the purposes of *this* postcolonial project, I further interpret these feminist inquiries as delineations of how an antagonistic understanding of difference devises a terrible prepossession: an (un)made world that does not *have* to be this way. These intellectual precursors register the general implications of postcolonial feminist work for alternative understandings of subjectivity and agency.

III. The Sign of History Woman

In *The Nation and Its Fragments* (1993), Partha Chatterjee tackles how Hindu nationalism in nineteenth-century middle-class Bengal appropriates and displaces the subversive force of gender norms unleashed during the struggle for independence. Indigenous patriarchal precepts instrumental to masculinist nationalist aims are amended to seal this neutralization. The kinds of rationalized crisis management put into play effectively contain potential remonstrations against civil society. Given that the domestic realm traditionally establishes women's space, it becomes the arena for imperialists and nationalists to battle for cultural supremacy. A successful reworking of public and private domains in nineteenth-century Hindu middle-class Bengal can be imputed to four primary processes: 1. The categories of male/female become racially coded (also as synecdoche for caste, class, religion, etc.); 2. public/private are (re)inscribed per the colonial project; 3. Victorian feminism gains a public presence and coherence through "colonial difference" (19); 4. and, the "women's question" (116) becomes a story of betrayal by exclusion and abeyance.

To advance imperial interests, the British colonial project in India concocts a diverse range of tactics for social, political, and economic intervention. Anglicists such as Sir Thomas Macaulay, Member of the Council of

India, create the narrative that the civilizing mission is a pedagogical quest to transform natives into respectable scholars. These scholars will comprise a peculiar class that may be "Indian in blood and color," but are English "in taste, in opinions, in morals and in intellect." The mission does not extend to all Indians, as this civilizing pedagogy is only meant to enable an intermediary class that can serve as "interpreters between us and the millions we govern" (1835 "Minute on Indian Education"). Uma Narayan highlights that Orientalists presume to return to Hindu elites the mysteries of their own ancient traditions: Brahmin priesthood keeps a caste-based stranglehold on the Sanskritic tradition; Orientalists represent their task as reintroducing to the people an unsullied form of their own history; and, this historic Golden Age instigates nostalgia for an idealized past to supplant the India of "barbarous customs, snakes, dust, and heat" in the British imagination (67).

Lata Mani describes another tactic to feign colonialism as civilizing mission as "we came, we saw, we were horrified, we intervened" (*Contentious* 55). Colonizers isolate practices such as *sati*, arranged marriages, and *purdah* (veiling) to turn nineteenth-century Indian women into symbols of India's repressive culture. These contentious traditions become the ground upon which colonizers and nationalists wage war. As Chatterjee points out in his discussion of nineteenth-century Bengal, British political concessions to Indian nationalists become provisional pending the quid pro quo of social reform. In response to British accusations of excessive patriarchal violence, Indian nationalists boost an anti-colonial identity by rearranging women's role in the nationalist imaginary; they restructure indigenous patriarchy by adopting the independence struggle as an ideological defense to only selectively adopt certain mores of western modernity, which entails converting public and private realms into the material and spiritual realms, respectively (118).

Such a mutation of public and private space makes the material world of colonial rule the arena of inescapable acquiescence by Hindu middle-class Bengali men for the transition to modernity. But the spiritual realm of domesticity becomes the domain where Indian culture continues to preside, an inner sanctum that persists in deterring the complete destruction of Indian society (121). Maintaining the private realm is women's purview, as the (now) modernized Hindu middle-class Bengali woman is duty-bound to safeguard Indian culture. She can receive an education in classical literature, but she also needs to be homely through "orderliness, thrift, cleanliness . . . literacy, accounting, [and] hygiene" (130). Social, economic, and political alteration aside, she carries on managing the household, yet entry into the material world (for education, public transportation, work in industries, entertainment, etc.) is sanctioned only if she shields her femininity. When kept intact, her femininity acts as a visible insignia of women's superior Indian culture, which keeps them pristine in the crass material world, unlike their western counterparts, who use educational prospects to compete against men.

In comparison to previous generations of women and the lower classes, Hindu middle-class Bengali women do benefit from restructured patriarchal norms; opportunistic portrayals of lower-class women as preternaturally incapable of appreciating freedom, however, naturalize these advantages (129). Now invested with the sanctity of Indian cultural difference by a modified indigenous patriarchy, Hindu middle-class Bengali women are to teach their children the preeminent facets of Indian culture for a suitable cultural lineage. Chatterjee declares, "This [reinstatement of indigenous patriarchy] was the central ideological strength of the nationalist resolution of the women's question" (127–28). Tensions between women's public participation in virtually all parts of the nationalist movement and their divinely ordained allegiances as wives and mothers (*pativrata* and *stridharma*) are curbed *as a very part of the nationalist vocabulary of resistance.*[3]

Women's highly scripted status in nationalist activism can also be spotted in Mrinalini Sinha's description of the Ilbert Bill controversy of 1883–1884 in Bengal. Law Member of the Government of India, C.P. Ilbert, introduced the Ilbert Bill, which proposes to amend the Code of Criminal Procedure of the Indian Penal Code (IPC). In accordance with then Viceroy Lord Ripon's goal to allow Indian civil servants to preside over court cases affecting British subjects, this bill gives native officials limited jurisdiction in the *mofussil* or country towns. Revolt against the Ilbert Bill is severe not only in England but also in Bengal among British plantation owners who are accustomed to the perks they receive from British judges (for example, ignoring the abuse they mete out to Indian workers). According to Sinha, British women visibly mobilize a "logic of colonial masculinity" (1) to deprive native officials of the right to oversee the trials of British subjects, which involves raising the specter of Indian judges using the Sessions Court to replenish their harems *and* effeminizing Hindu middle-class Bengali men as unsuitable for public life. The protests are successful in ensuring that a severely compromised version of the Bill passes in 1884. (That Indian men incur humiliations thanks to the Ilbert Bill controversy is an impetus for the formation of the Indian National Congress in 1885.)

Stereotypes like the "manly Englishman" and the "effeminate Bengali *babu*" (pejorative for a chit of a man suited to be a clerk) smooth the way for the *ignis fatuus* of the hapless British female at risk of rape (33). Effeminate Bengali *babus*' improper manhood requires them to burn, *purdah* (veil), and segregate their women, but manly Englishmen's proper manhood coaxes a natural division of the sexes, as British women clearly quite happily fall in line. Indeed, British men like Lepel Griffin, a senior Anglo-Indian official, retort that Bengali men should anticipate the contempt of the "stronger and braver races" (35) that fought for liberty. British women's increased presence in the public sphere expedites the recalibration of Victorian norms; as with "new" Hindu middle-class Bengali women, white women in India symbolize nationalist pride and the nobility of British culture (45). Alongside this increased representative burden, white women are also held to account for exacerbating racial conflict; for example, Lord Stanley of the East India Association states that "prejudices were more accentuated and more strongly felt and shown by the women than by the men" (47).

British women (arriving in India since the eighteenth century) are confined principally to the auxiliary work of "the enlightenment and amelioration of . . . Native sisters" (48). Those who have greater influence in public life viciously oppose the Ilbert Bill. One of their rallying cries is that the Bill itself (when initially proposed in 1883) is a slight to their honor. Letters, boycotts, petitions, organizations, committees, and associations defeat the Bill, but the imperial project preempts any detrimental effects the "New Woman" can have on the racial politics of empire (54), including insurgent feminist movements for education and professional development in England. For example, the Ladies' Committee in Calcutta drafts an independent petition to block the Ilbert Bill with the aid of the Defense Association, which is denied because the women sign as Miss or Mrs. rather than with their proper names. A popular newspaper, the *Englishman*, scolds, "Mrs. Smith or Miss Smith, as we should have thought every educated person knew, is not a signature but a description" (58). Women at the time, of course, cannot legally sign the petition otherwise.

Public belittlement does not dissuade British women from fobbing off their deep-seated sense of prestige as benevolence towards their native sisters. The Bihar Ladies' Petition to Viceroy Ripon announces:

> [W]e see that in the social systems of India women are ignorant and enslaved . . . [W]e see the men of their races insensible to their degradation, if not contented with it. Therefore, we assert that men born or bred on such a system are unfit to become the judges of women of a totally different type of society. (59)

Besides the neglect of Hindu middle-class Bengali women's active support of the Ilbert Bill, for example, by the teachers at the Bethune School in Calcutta and the Bengali Ladies' Association (62–63), the allegation overlooks that the University of Calcutta admitted women to degree programs in 1878 before any English universities opened their doors for women (62).[4] Sinha terms this form of self-positioning by British women "maternal imperialism" (60) whose legacy still influences western feminist scholarship on nonwestern women.

IV. The Cultural Woman

The outlawing of *sati* in 1829 by Lord William Bentinck is one of the first major legislative acts of the British that intervenes in Hindu practices. Prevalent among particular castes in India, specifically the Brahmins in Bengal and the Rajputs of Rajasthan, *sati* is a primary justification for the British civilizing mission. In the eighteenth and nineteenth centuries, for the British and a handful of Hindu reformers, *sati* and its abolition become the marker for two different kinds of patriarchy: Hindu men burn their women; European men rescue them; European forms of patriarchy thereby remain invisible. Framing colonial occupation in terms of the chivalrous defense of Indian womanhood enables colonizers to attribute a natural, rational, and universal basis for their usurpation of power over indigenous communities.

V.N. Dutta and Romila Thapar question whether *sati* has scriptural sanction as a ritual in Hindu sacred texts. A significant aspect of their analyses is how Hinduism is conglomerated as a tradition by enactments of its texts over millennia. Over and above consistency, they focus on how ancient texts are ritually passed on across generations, together with regional enactments by god- or goddess-cults, caste-based interpretations, local dramatic conventions, linguistic vernaculars, etc. For example, in some of these renditions, *sati* is an enactment of wifely devotion or the symbolic death of an identity.[5] Aside from these arguably indigenous perceptions of *sati*, Orientalist and neo-Orientalist slants on the practice, in the manner of Max Meuller, Katherine Mayo, and Mary Daly, center the Occident as history's protagonist; this Occident happens upon the Orient and its oddities only to self-vindicate as the blessed bearer of universal spirit yet also cursed with the anxieties and perils concomitant with reason qua freedom.[6]

In Uma Narayan's refutation of Occident-centered history, she disputes the depiction of *sati* in Mary Daly's second wave canonical text, *Gyn/Ecology: The Metaethics of Radical Feminism* (1978). To establish the universal oppression of women as a category through their ritual murder at the hands of patriarchal religions, Daly centralizes hypervisible practices that emblematize third world women—clitoridectomy, foot binding, dowry, child marriage, etc. Narayan criticizes what she terms Daly's prototypical "death by culture" (81) argument. Expressing chagrin at her adherence to colonial interpretations (and spelling) of *sati*, Narayan also faults Daly's almost exclusive dependence on Katherine Mayo's demonstrably problematic Orientalist text, *Mother India* (1927). By oddly valorizing western women as victims, Daly discounts their endorsement of colonialism and assistance in building empire.

While Narayan looks at western feminist texts that anchor their sweeping claims in stereotypes about nonwestern culture, Lata Mani shows how the collaboration between colonial and indigenous Brahmanical discourses inculcate a *sati* tradition to condone British incursion as social reform (*Contentious* 14–15). The British calculate the political price of the prohibition of *sati* but officials nonetheless solicit avowedly authentic interpretations of Hindu scriptures. Characterizing religion as the structuring principle of Indian society sets up British officials to showcase their reasonableness contra Indian zealotry (20–21). Undeterred by their pretensions about women's liberation, colonial and Brahmanical discourses benefit caste hierarchy and patriarchal power (194–95). As Lata Mani urges, women "provided the ground for the development of other agendas" ("Multiple" 35).

Jenny Sharpe's examination in *Allegories of Empire* (1993) looks at how this civilizing mission hinges on the nationalist and racialized splitting of femininity (47). Similar to Mrinalini Sinha's research, Sharpe clarifies the development of a dominant feminist rhetoric that harnesses *sati* for its own ends and aids the reconfiguration of threatened indigenous patriarchies (109). Her concern is not so much the ritual of *sati* itself but how white women use *sati* as a foil to articulate their feminist individualism (*Jane Eyre* is the quintessential example), which is then contingent on the absolute renunciation of the self by the devoted Hindu widow (28, 32). As a colonial discourse, feminist individualism fashions what it sets out to repudiate: the native's savagery in burning women alive warrants the need for civilization; but, the native woman *has* to die for white women's self-realization, which leaves her with a baffling form of subjectivity and agency: she is naturally submissive but makes a "decision" to commit *sati* (49–51).

Felicity A. Nussbaum in *Torrid Zones* (1995) especially addresses British and Indian women's mutually reinforcing fates in the fortification of British rule (191). On one hand, India licenses British women to flaunt their natural beauty, as they are heavenly and pure in a sea of dirty "coolies" (178). On the other hand, fragile Englishwomen are sure to find India's torrid climate expressly fatal (177). When the first official conference on *sati* takes place in 1789, the delusion of the primitive native at home in a savage climate raping Englishwomen sanctions the East India Company's deflection of its own rapacity (180, 182). Colonial iconography of *sati* consequently excessively theatricalizes and darkens the menacing indigenous horde to measure them against British devotion to rational observation and recording of facts (184, 185). The proverbial British ledger's tidy log puts the throng's supposedly unintelligible, triumphant, and sadistic clamor to shame.

Nussbaum provides context for later debates on *sati* that result in abolition by referring to the commentary on *sati* by Eliza Fay who comes to India in 1779 with her husband. Disregarding their denunciations of the patriarchal nature of the practice, British women's responses to *sati* become the standard to judge their loyalty to empire. In Fay's assessment, *sati* is a political arrangement that entitles Indian men to exert their control and not an indicator of Indian women's virtuous qualities. Women's devotion to their husbands cannot be the cause of the practice because dedication will also be felt for her children. Fay goes further to argue that *sati* is not the epitome of ardor but is evidence of the dignity of British religiosity: the widow may commit *sati* to escape starvation, sexual abuse, prostitution, shunning, etc., but it is far better to endure horrendous circumstances than to fall back on superstition. Fay concludes that *sati* can also be construed as an irrational response to gendered oppression (185–87).

Fear of potential rape by Indian men assures British women's fidelity and exculpates repressive forms of colonial law and order; the rape of Indian women by British men is ignored. Assigned to a complicitous role in the imperial mission, British women must renounce their own ambitions in the newly expanded colonial frontier (189). For example, in the aftermath of Cornwallis's (Governor-General in India) reforms, which end private pursuits of imperial enrichment, the British army champions Englishwomen's domesticity by forcibly prohibiting miscegenation. Nussbaum warns that despite noticing similar circumstances for British and Indian women, we must "avoid mistaking mutual goals for identity, *especially by recognizing difference without dominance* over other women" (191, emphases added); these differences are ferreted out to found British rule.

V. The Goddess Woman

Since *sati* is the actual burning of a woman alive, postcolonial rationalizations of the practice manage its awful sublimity by both under- and over-representing the event. One manner of manufacturing intelligibility is the narrative of the widow's empirically accessible motive will. An emphasis on the widow's consent confines any debate to determining whether the *sati* is "authentic" or "inauthentic"; it also disappears the fact that a woman burns to death in front of spectators. (Significantly, Mughal emperors and not the British introduced the will of the widow as a factor within initial debates on the ritual.) This either/or framing institutes a dualistic discourse—tradition versus modernity, ritual versus crime, and goddess versus victim, etc.—that puts detractors in a bind.

> To repudiate ancient scripture as a basis for modern practice is to
> invite the charge of alienation; to designate *sati* as a crime rather
> than ritual . . . is merely to replicate the move of the colonial ruler;

> to highlight the plight of the woman is not only to be insensitive
> to the identity of the . . . community . . . but also to be selec-
> tive and hypocritical in the woman's issues that one champions.
> (Sunder Rajan, *Real* 17)

Indigenous elites in post-independence India extend colonial mechanisms of judicial, military, and administrative governance. As a result, the state keeps its patriarchal stance towards women. Notions such as the protection of women's honor turn women's public participation in nation building into extensions of familial duty (5). Postcolonial India's ambivalent commitment to secularism facilitates this mitigation: contrary to secular government, the state must pledge "fair" representation to religious communities, which guarantees that the de facto "true" surrogates are the fundamentalists who can mobilize a communally identified electoral base (Kumar 178).

For example, nineteen-year-old Roop Kanwar's *sati* in 1987 in Deorala, Rajasthan, was followed by The Prevention of *Sati* Ordinance passed by the Rajasthan Assembly and the Central Government (October and November 1987, respectively).[7] Zeroing in almost entirely on the widow's will to preempt communalist backlash, the Ordinance is rather ambiguous about its status. The widow's actions are either voluntary or involuntary suicide, but abetment and glorification prompt either voluntary or involuntary *sati*. If *sati* and suicide are the same, then "[w]here a *sati* has been foiled, the woman will be tried for 'the offence of attempt to commit *sati*.' Here her motivation is considered ascertainable and assessable by the same criteria as suicides. . . . [W]here a *sati* has been successful, those involved will be charged for abetment and not murder" (Sunder Rajan, *Real* 24).

Vasudha Dhagamwar likewise demonstrates tensions in the wording and provisions of the Commission of *Sati* (Prevention) Act of 1987:

> Both the 1987 Acts [October and November] particularly men-
> tion that the offence is "irrespective" of whether the Act is "vol-
> untary." . . . The two Sections 3 . . . differ only in the quantum
> of punishment [for] . . . the woman. . . . Sections 3 and 4 . . . in
> effect . . . treat all *sati*s as voluntary. . . . Had the law used the
> words "burning or burying a woman" the woman could not
> [be] . . . anything but the victim. The only grammatical construc-
> tion . . . possible is "she committed *sati*." This then leads to the
> fiction that she is the actor or principal offender; the others only
> abet her. (38)

Existing laws against murder and suicide in the Indian Penal Code (IPC) have sufficient provisions to prevent *sati*. The government sought only to appease communalists who want *sati* to be recognized as distinct from murder and suicide (Kishwar and Vanita 23–24).

In challenging the widow's dislocation by the ambiguous yet also mythical status of her motive will, Kumkum Sangari and Sudesh Vaid call *sati* a form of violence against women. Institutions, ideologies, and beliefs normalize this violence by portraying *sati* as both a private family matter (qua suicide) and an exceptional communal event (qua *sati*) ("Institutions, Ideologies" 241). Sangari and Vaid pit the widow and the *sati* against one another to determine how murder (conventionally hidden like suicide) becomes a public spectacle for both "colonial spectators and their contemporary progeny" (240). They lay out *sati*'s standard plot (245), which somehow metamorphoses a mob that tortures and murders a woman into the recipients of mass benediction and dispersal of boons (eradication of sickness, birth of a boy, material wealth, a good match for a son or daughter, passing of school exams, etc.): the husband dies, the widow's grief quickly turns into a dispassionate resolve, which leaves all those around her in awe, preparations are made while word by unknown means rapidly spreads, and people from surrounding areas arrive to bask in the goddess's glow of purity and blessedness.

One of the motors of this script is the idea of *satt* (truth), which as divine manifestation via a mortal vehicle exists alongside the widow's volition (279). Quite conveniently, *satt* becomes the legal alibi for rural participants while volition becomes the legal alibi for urban participants (279, 250): neither can prevent the *sati*, as they will incur the goddess's curses. Once *satt* is put into play, any dissuasion is construed as evil elements testing the widow's *satt*; the divine chooses only those who fulfill *pativrata* and *stridharma* (289). *Satt* can *only* be demonstrative, therefore, of the widow's consent. Perpetrators testify to *satt*-miraculated events: pyres lighting themselves; the light of *satt* emanating from the widow; her feeling no pain; the woman's ability to lock and unlock doors without touching them; her raising her hand to bestow blessings while sitting atop the lit pyre, etc. (251). *Satt* allows culprits to disown their active role in the murder, which can include dressing the widow in her bridal finery, burying her in wood, drugging her, or holding her down, if she struggles to escape (248–49, 256), chanting prayers, standing on rooftops, sloganeering, shooting bullets in the air, guarding the cremation ground, etc. (I add these details I learned from my own visit to Deorala to underline that a screaming mob engulfs the widow. *Sati* is not a peaceful and sober ritual.)

For Roop Kanwar's case, the Rajput community uses this "established formula" (255) to fashion an exceptional Rajput ethos of militant masculinity and protect their interests as landowners against the government's redistribution schemes (261); Brahmins propagate ideas of Rajput valor to secure their role in regulating clan and caste superiority through matrimonial alliances

(258); the *bania* caste, made of businessmen, leading industrialists, and traders, provide the (black money) funds to build temples for the adulation of *sati* (258–59, 261). Many Rajputs, Brahmins, and *bania*s believe the post-independence government to be worse than the Mughal and British regimes, as the former interferes in their "right" to worship and commemorate *sati* (263). Rajput *veerta* (valor) commutes a woman burning alive into a beatific, bejeweled, and radiant goddess sitting atop a funeral pyre with her husband's head on her lap.

VI. The Woman (To Be)

The colonial and postcolonial cultural scripts discussed thus far concentrate on Hindu women's entrapment in gendered ideologies that victimize them. In the *History of Doing* (1993), Radha Kumar describes her 1983 encounter in New Delhi with women at a pro-*sati* procession organized by the Marwari-funded *Rani Sati Sarva Sangh* (RSSS). Kumar herself put together a protest rally against the central government, which recently granted the RSSS a plot of land to build a *sati* temple in New Delhi. She admits that she feels unprepared when faced with the hostility of women who vociferously demand their "right" to commit, venerate, and promulgate *sati* (174). Tanika Sarkar observes that women's religious devotion traditionally authorizes them to carve out autonomous spaces, but custodianship of their culture instills a greater sense of esteem. Their militant activism in fundamentalist right-wing movements, furthermore, contradicts their platitudinous identity as self-sacrificing and pacifistic (181).

Women's active role in right-wing politics in India must be dealt with as a "uniquely experimental semi-fascistic formation" (182) that weaponizes gender ideologies to ignite communalistic fervor. Hindu fundamentalists can wield the phantasmic abuse of Hindu women ("through the ages") by Muslim men because Hindu women's work in *sanghs* (alliances) and *samitis* (committees) is domestic service that does not violate family honor (184, 185). Clichés of women as all-powerful mothers embodying a sacred authority are bandied about to infantilize Hindu men for "allowing" the defilement of Hindu women; men are taunted to elicit their reverence and compliance (188–89, 191, 193). The ossification of faith-based norms lets women "establish [. . .] themselves as political subjects through . . . brutality against a besieged minority" (190).

Amrita Basu shares Sarkar's alarm especially because women are accorded greater distinction in post-independence fundamentalism in relation to previous nationalist movements. When Basu conducts her research in the 1990s, the female leadership of the *Hindutva* (Hindu fundamentalist) movement comprises of Vijayraje Scindia, Uma Bharati, and Sadhvi Rithambra. As three of the larger-than-life mouthpieces for Hindu nationalism, they openly use their celibacy to fuel violence against Muslim men to save Hindu women's chastity (159, 153). Per *Hindutva* mythologies, the virile Muslim male consumes huge quantities of meat (unlike vegetarian Hindus), wages a demographic war by fathering many children, and has tremendous physical abilities. The perennial rape of Hindu women by brutish Muslim men stands in for Hindu victimization per se (165).

Hindutva movements couple notions of patriarchal protection with a goddess tradition to normalize aggression, which becomes part of Hinduism's veneration of women's strength (Agnes 139). Embodiments of their faith, Hindu women are able to sidestep western forms of femininity (revealing clothes, lack of family values, rejection of motherhood, etc.) for economic advances, property rights, and legal protections (Sarkar 206). Irrespective of the approbation meted out for holding onto Indianness, Vijayraje Scindia, Uma Bharati, and Sadhvi Rithambra reap political success by breaking normative gender roles. Hand in hand with their economic independence from men (fathers, husbands, sons), their political ambitions forestall any expectations of submissive wifehood or saintly motherhood. Their so-called benevolence towards Muslim women succeeds in ingraining the fantasy that both Hindu and Muslim women are victims of Muslim barbarism (Basu 167, 172). But, in the *Hindutva* nationalist imaginary, Hindu men do not rape Muslim women: "Hindus are victims . . . by virtue of being Hindu, they can be neither communal nor aggressive" (179).

In the face of this perilous landscape, Rajeswari Sunder Rajan articulates feminists' indubitably no-win plight: "[I]t is difficult for women to refuse their communities' demands of loyalty or to relinquish their affiliation . . . for the often dubious benefits of legal rights—nor do they always have this option, where the state's laws are themselves religious" ("Postcolonial Feminism" 63). The formidable and fervent support for *sati* that Radha Kumar runs into rattles feminist rebuttals that chronicle "faith [as] inseparable from instrumentality" (Sangari and Vaid, "Institutions, Ideologies" 287). When Hindu right-wing factions hypostatize what a woman ought to be, they engineer structures that abuse and exploit women. Rajputs cementing their identity in secular India after the 1987 *sati* of Roop Kanwar legitimize this ritual for its material payoff: any disagreement is tantamount to a wholesale invalidation of Rajput culture. Betokening the vehicle for a community's relationship with the divine, women's incoherent yet also rationalized intelligibility forsakes the utter contingency of their cultural significance.

VII. The Family Woman

Lord William Bentinck's 1829 outlawing of *sati* takes place almost a hundred years prior to seventeen-year-old Bhuvaneswari Bhaduri's *sati*/suicide, which occurs in 1916 (her letter is found in 1926—uncannily almost a centennial domestic rather than official decree). At the time of Bhuvaneswari's death, nationalist struggles for independence are gaining traction. For example: Muslim leader Muhammad Ali Jinnah joins the Indian National Congress (INC) in 1916; the British pass the Defense of India Act against nationalist movements the year before (1915); Mahatma Gandhi returns from South Africa in 1915; a transnational alliance between Sikh expatriates in the United States and Canada and revolutionaries in Bengal transpires, which includes a failed assassination attempt of Charles Hardinge, Viceroy of India, in 1912; Mahatma Gandhi launches his first *Satyagraha* (path of truth) movement in 1917; and, the All-India Home Rule League forms with the cooperation of both the INC and the All-India Muslim League after the Lucknow Pact of 1916.

What is curious about Spivak's excurses into Bhuvaneswari's *sati*/suicide is that she mentions the cause of Bhuvaneswari's deliberated act almost parenthetically: participating in contemporaneous nationalist movements, she hangs herself when she cannot bring herself to commit a political assassination. Together with the interior and domestic scene of her death "in her father's modest apartment" (*Critique* 306), over time we become privy to Spivak's familial relationship with Bhuvaneswari, who is her grandmother's sister.[8] When describing her 1988 essay "Can the Subaltern Speak?" in 2010, Spivak reveals, "I inserted the singular suicide of my foremother into that gap between the reasonableness of theory and the urgency of the revolutionary moment. . . . She taught me . . . [to] read situations where no response happens" ("In Response" 235). (Spivak also explains that she did not include this family tie in the original essay to avoid cathecting the space of a native informant who hands over information on Bhuvaneswari's "authentic" experience.) She not only calls Bhuvaneswari "my foremother," but in the speech "If Only" (2006), Spivak invokes her genealogically: "These are the women who bred me. I am nobody's mother." (In this speech, she invokes her mother, great grandmother, paternal grandmother, and her mother's aunts.)

Spivak brings up her own *lack* of motherhood matter-of-factly right after the affective invocation of her family women. A statement that stipulates this very genealogy's end—"I am no one's mother"—follows a call to mark futurity via a women's genealogy. The recent loss of her mother is the loss of a very specific ("that") archive, of women *in* life, at the peripheries of reproductive heteronormativity. She hails life as singular: "Singularity is—repetition of difference, repetition and difference, repetition with difference." She goes further: "That is my relationship with these women. I am their repetition, with a difference."[9] (Repetition of difference is the reiteration of a cultural logic that defines all difference; repetition and difference is difference considered oppositional and antagonistic to a cultural logic's coherence as dogmatic and arbitrary; repetition with difference is the appropriation and displacement of a culture's logic by a glimpse of radical alterity.)

The pathos of this exquisite grief—that she is their repetition, with a difference—is underscored by Spivak's concern with writing her own biography. She bemoans (citing Assia Djebar): "[I]f only one could occupy with desire that single spectator body that remains, and circle it more and more tightly in order to forget the defeat. The defeat that is life." *She* is the spectator left on the edge of death that looks back at her life, and wishes she could tightly hold onto herself to forget her defeat. The doubled self—that is, a spectator body looking back at her singular life—collapses into a self-encircling self-embrace of, and, with difference, to honor an unforgettable defeat that although inevitable cannot be desired. When Spivak halts at her own lack of motherhood, therefore, in an abrupt declarative statement of gendered identity, right after she instances a women's genealogy (that bred her), she is not mourning a past (as is).

As *her* repetition, with a difference, of motherhood, is *in* classroom teaching (as performative), she asks her reader, who follows her along to herself, to abruptly change direction and return to the future anterior.[10] Here, we find the *only* source of the potential for repetition of, and, with difference: heterogeneity; we go back to what was not (hence no response happens) but will (always) have been. *This* is the actual (true and real) ingredient, which the defeat that is life double crosses *for* culture, (to be) perennially bred by an apocryphal genealogy. Summoning an irretrievable women's history, Spivak's subsequent "gesture of mourning" (Sunder Rajan, "Death" 127) dislocates the very terms of making history.

Retreating to the archive of antiquity is Spivak's rejoinder to the emplacement of culture via putting (all) in a double bind.[11] In the realm of family women, even those who are not mothers write genealogies with whatever life can be squeezed (out) from our cultural saturation. Since *that* difference exudes from heterogeneity, the next chapter joins Spivak in her stronghold. As we follow the trace left behind by Bhuvaneswari's menstrual blood, to become foremothers who tend an impossible futurity, we arrive at *that* archive of antiquity that rives nature from culture to make itself real. From *this* place, we may bequeath an apocryphal genealogy for *that* singular family woman whose defeat that is (our) life revives the utter contingency of (our) postcoloniality.

Chapter Nine

Sacred Texts, Sacred Deaths

For Family Women

[T]he critic must write the theoretically impossible historical biography of that very self that is no more than an effect of a structural resistance to irreducible heterogeneity.

—Gayatri Spivak, *In Other Worlds*

As body it is a repetition of nature. It is in the rupture with Nature when it is a signifier of immediacy for the staging of the self. As a text, the inside of the body (imbricated with the outside) is mysterious and unreadable except by way of thinking of the systematicity of the body, value coding of the body.

—Gayatri Spivak, *Outside in the Teaching Machine*

[M]yth is already enlightenment . . .

—Theodor Adorno and Max Horkheimer, *Dialectic of Enlightenment*

The postcolonial woman intellectual asks the question of simple semio-sis—What does this mean?—and begins to plot a history.

—Gayatri Spivak, "Can the Subaltern Speak?"

I. Archive's Fever: A Global Warming

In "Postcolonialism's Archive Fever" (2000), Sandhya Shetty and Elizabeth Bellamy return to what they accurately characterize as the "scandalously underread" (42) portion of Gayatri Spivak's "Can the Subaltern Speak?," which is the section on the *Dharmasastra* and *Rg-Veda*. They regard the inattention to Spivak's reading of ancient Hindu texts as synecdochic; in its Euro-US instantiation, postcolonial discourse centers colonial modernity, although the academic archive, of which Spivak's essay is representative, suggests otherwise. "Can the Subaltern Speak?" reorients postcolonial desire, interest, and subjectivity: in lieu of a precolonial past that colonial modernity retroactively inaugurates, what "we cannot *not* want" (44) is India's (archive of) antiquity. By further elongation of postcoloniality's ironic and melancholic retreat into the past, Shetty and Bellamy foreground the critical force of Spivak's arguably "first" conception of postcoloniality; Bhuvaneswari did not simply negate scripturally sanctioned reproductive heteronormativity as pronounced by the *Dharmasastra* and *Rg-Veda* (aka Indian culture), for Spivak's movement *from* the archive of antiquity *to* Bhuvaneswari's *sati*/suicide demonstrates *how* (the) law commands (a) silence into place to order all (else) that follows.[1]

In other words, *before* the widow shuttles between subject- and object-status in the Manichean battle between imperialists and nationalists, women are (first) written-in into the archive *as* an exception—to the general rule of suicide and place of pilgrimage. *This* difference (*of* the widow), anointing her *as* an exception (*to* the husband), backdates postcoloniality's purview from modernity to antiquity. Contra a reversal of colonial logic figured by an axiological prefix (post), a revised postcoloniality is the resurrection of the widow's heterogeneity *at* the archaic origin for its own possibility. Insofar as the former allows for the cultural logic that justifies the civilizing mission and its nationalist opposition, the latter breathes life into postcoloniality as difference that actually violates (the law of) identity.

By anachronizing postcoloniality's route of unknowing from colonial modernity to the archaic origin, Shetty and Bellamy register the widow's heterogeneity in/as the crypt-ic secret that founds the discipline of postcolonial studies. The underread portions of Spivak's authoritative text manifest postcolonialism's archive fever: postcoloniality (re)inscribes that loss vis-à-vis (the law of) negative interpellation *at* the archaic origin that is the constitutive condition of possibility for (a) culture. As Shetty and Bellamy take postcoloniality to the widow's heterogeneity in antiquity's archive, this chapter suggests that their archaic origin is neither origin-al nor archaic—that is, postcolonial—enough, as they cede the widow's singularity to sexual difference. To understand the widow's heterogeneity as inherently irretrievable yet also marked off via an antagonistic understanding of difference is to reprise (a) cultural logic—women *as* good wifehood—that obfuscates utter contingency as ontology. Women are written-in into the archive, *by virtue of category alone*, as (a) derived difference from the male, which construes women as *lack* even when exceptional. As Spivak attests, "The paradox of knowing the limits of knowledge is that the strongest assertion of agency, to negate the possibility of agency, cannot be an example of itself" (*Critique* 292).

Keeping this contingent yet also ontological decipherability intact, Shetty and Bellamy relinquish good wifehood as women's being qua culture and forego affirmation of the general implications of the widow's tribulations qua her postcoloniality. The *philosophical* import of heterogeneity does not erupt from the widow's safeguarding of the spirit of the law via transgression of the general rule, but from the telltale sign that Bhuvaneswari's carefully orchestrated *sati*/suicide leaves behind—her menstrual blood; *her* breach of scriptural injunction on multiple registers leaves heterogeneity (to) be. Menstrual blood left behind *as* her self is squeezed (out) from the culturally saturated body that *is* her self to figure how heterogeneity's living potential becomes (a) living death *for* culture. Bhuvaneswari doubles herself by unplugging her selfsame self *from* culture to interpolate her singular self *into* culture by letting (her) blood gush forth: "she" is (now) under erasure, but (her) heterogeneity persists. In *this* (re)inscribing of the law's commanded silence—that is, in *this* looking back to resurrect (our) utter contingency—a piece of life endures despite its inevitable defeat.

In expunging her symbolic integrity, Bhuvaneswari bred life as no one's mother *in* women's time to collapse culture: it is not sexual difference that is life's (first) relationship, but (our) impossible singularity that is (our) relationship *in* life. Taking us in reversed direction, not to the god-inhabited lighted heavens but to the bloody nether regions, she appropriates and displaces culture to spurn the myth of autochthony, which equates culture with sexual difference only by bloody sacrifice. While her cultural iconography of *sati* is the site/sight of multiple reversals—her cold yet also bloody corpse hangs by a rope alone inside the home with a still-to-be-found letter—she directs the gaze of those who come upon her from the blood at the dead center to the empty space down below. By inverting the reciprocal viewing of *darshan* with a beholder who encounters nothingness, her framing of *sati's* cultural formation takes us to the ground beneath her feet[2] and not to the broken neck up above. By following the trail of her menstrual blood, we may roil the seeming seamlessness of this cultural logic: she is the exception (menstruating) to the exception (good wifehood) to the exception (the male) to the general rule (of suicide and place of pilgrimage). The rationalizations required to maintain sexual difference (as addendums to addendums to the law at the archaic origin) call into question the very ground of culture that hinges on the widow's silence. If her heterogeneity is voided by sexual difference to inaugurate culture, then where does Bhuvaneswari's left-behind trace lead? I suggest that Bhuvaneswari's iconography (perhaps pentimento) not only flips *sati*'s principal conceit of good wifehood but also resurrects the dislocated place of women's time—that is, of nature—*at* the archaic origin.

Bhuvaneswari's (re)inscription of the light of *satt,* which emanates from the blessing-giving palm of the astral goddess to set the widow aglow, into a rope that hangs from a ceiling and strangles (out) her life can be read as a figuration of *how* nature must be immured to blot (out) culture's utter contingency. The bloody stain that tarries repeats one metonymic chain—sexual difference→ women→ good wifehood→ culture→ transcendence—as another, with a difference: heterogeneity→ menstrual blood→ women's time→ nature→ immanence. Bhuvaneswari's sati/suicide as an exegetically created encounter with heterogeneity at the archaic origin relates how nature is cut (out) and left "there" to encrypt the desiccated human in culture via sexual difference; nature's heterogeneity must (first) be made irretrievable in the archive of antiquity for culture predicated on the widow's written-in silence (to be). Bhuvaneswari erases the widow's outline by filling in what *is* "here": the remainder of culture. Menstrual blood figures the heterogeneity that *lives* in women's time, for nature is actually no *one*'s mother, but the horizon of all (that) life (can be). *She* is the one who circles more and more tightly the single spectator body that stays emplaced by the contraction of heterogeneity for the location of culture. Bhuvaneswari returns to women's time for an apocryphal genealogy of family women written in blood whose inevitable defeat cannot be forgotten, as we are their repetition, with a difference.

II. Same Difference

Feminist scholars Chandra Mohanty and Uma Narayan dismantle cultural prejudices that define western scholarship on third world customs (such as *sati,* clitoridectomy, and foot binding). They challenge tropes that render the female body the hypervisible yet also transparent textual effect of socio-political realities. In her canonical essay, "Under Western Eyes: Feminist Scholarship and Colonial Discourses" (1991), Mohanty explains "third world difference" (53) as difference that is the third world's stable and ahistorical difference from the first world; due to this difference, third world culture subjugates its women. Feminisms that rely on third world difference for a transnational outlook display a consistent array of effects that appropriate and displace third world women's actual lives to produce a composite image. As Mohanty reminds us, the perpetually oppressed third world woman is a signature feature of liberal humanism.

Feminist works based on western humanist ideals repeat "third world difference" via certain analytical presuppositions and discursive methods. For example, an exclusive focus on women as a pre-formed global class results in impoverished understandings of power that presume and reinstate first world privilege (52). Notwithstanding universal models of women's oppression, however, first world privilege sustains a North/South divide wherein the extremities faced by nonwestern women allow western women to become the true feminist subject (71, 74). Third world difference-based stereotypes consolidate a monolithic third world woman who is ontologically bound to absence and disfigurement. As trope of sheer victimhood, she is the recipient of first world women's benevolence: *her* persecution is the pretext to reenact the innate superiority of western culture, which permits first world women to be socially progressive and politically astute.

Similar to Mohanty, Uma Narayan in *Dislocating Cultures* (1997) criticizes first world feminists' "colonialist stance" (41) towards third world realities to buttress the inherent supremacy of western culture (48).[3] Narayan identifies a number of analytical frames and discursive conventions that result in a "colonialist stance": 1. Due to the absence of historical context, variegated problems are strung together as problems that affect Indian women. 2. The third world is a homogeneous and static space. 3. Issues that encumber women in the third world are primarily the result of their Tradition/Religion/Culture. 4. Third world culture is scapegoated for third world afflictions while first world miseries receive non-culturalist accounts; social issues are presented as individual problems. 5. The third world is thoroughly suffused by timeless and unchanging religious worldviews. 6. Third world women are victims of indigenous patriarchal practices or are objects of western compassion. 7. Reproaching western patriarchy bars denunciations of western feminists' approbation of problematic aspects of western culture.[4] Narayan also rejects the chauvinistic belief that feminism is indigenous to western culture because first and third world feminist histories are indelibly co-implicated.

To hypostatize the third world's cultural difference from the first world, western methodologies use "third world difference" and a "colonialist stance" to typify this difference as natural. It would be impossible to overstate the importance of Mohanty's and Narayan's disputation of western humanism in the 1990s for the postcolonial feminist tradition. This chapter picks up where they leave off precisely because of the canonicity of their critiques, which recoup the *heterogeneity* of third world lives from prevailing feminist frameworks. If we take their objections to first world portrayals of third world women's circumstances a little further, we recognize that "third world difference" and a "colonialist stance" already presume that "nature has no history" (Spivak, "Harlem" 134). Only by fixing nature as a stable signifier of degradation and animality can the third world be demeaned and exploited.

This (first) debasement of our relationship to nature and other species occludes its contingency by constricting nature's heterogeneity to set into motion (a) cultural logic via negative interpellation (we are *not* [. . .]) *at* the archaic origin. If we demand that the archive of antiquity be adequate to the historical moment at hand, then postcoloniality must also call into question how culture consolidates the past-ness of the past, for nature cannot actually go "away,"[5] through an antagonistic understanding of difference. To think (the law) of culture ontologically, given a peculiarly felicitous concurrence of archive fever—that is, a global warming—we (all), gathered together,[6] may unplug the female body by calling a *bluff*: the question of nature must be begged to use nature historically (Spivak, "Righting" 527).[7] (This is how the lying begins, and, as we know, we must lie to correct a lie.)

III. Undoing Culture

Although Judith Butler is right that gender is a performance of cultural norms, it is important to point out that these cultural performances, put into play by negative interpellation, are normative because they are *hegemonic*. Repetition, with a difference, entails looking (out) for slips of the tongue in the cultural propaganda that is "the original mother tongue of history" (Spivak, *Other* 211). As ideology's "first lesson . . . is that a 'popular prejudice' mistakes itself for 'human nature' " (211), the chapter suggests that the dualism of nature and culture, which grounds human nature qua exceptional, is (a) cultural prejudice. To think (the law of) culture ontologically, this is the addendum we may make to Shetty and Bellamy's analysis of Spivak's text, as we (re)inscribe heterogeneity *at* the archaic origin. Owing to the general implications of Spivak's tracking of dislocated heterogeneity, we may ask *how* (the) human is written-in into the archive of antiquity *as* (an) exception.

When Shetty and Bellamy return to "Can the Subaltern Speak?," they emphasize in particular that Spivak is "highly motivated" (25) in her usage of the term "archive," as she recuperates lost texts not lost voices. This decided interest in the archive is the impetus for their salient reading of the generally ignored passages of Spivak's essay: the parts where she reads the *Dharmasastra* and the *Rg-Veda*. Spivak initially turns to the *Dharmasastra*, which is comprised of scripts written by multiple authors from 600–100 BCE. Their codification of Hindu custom was "legally speaking, by far the most important of the post-Vedic *smriti* tradition, or 'that which is remembered' " (36). The *Dharmasastra* gains the authority to codify Hindu custom from earlier texts like the *Brahmanas* and the *Dharma Sutras*, which are sectarian-based compendiums that use aphorisms to decree appropriate behavior as received from earlier Vedic literature privileging the symbolism of sacrifice (orally created and issued circa 900 BCE). In the Hindu archive of antiquity, the *Vedas* are the oldest religious texts, with the *Brahmanas* as auxiliary addendums. Among the *Vedas*, the *Rg-Veda*, regarded as the first text of the *sruti* literature (that which is heard), is a prodigious compilation of sacred hymns only chronicled in the 1780s (36–40).

Spivak takes postcoloniality further back from the widow's shuttle between subject- and object-status to the *smriti* (that which is remembered) and *sruti* (that which is heard) canons, a movement to the archive of antiquity that makes "Can the Subaltern Speak?" a foundational text. Shetty and Bellamy ameliorate Spivak's brand of feminism from its crude identification with deconstruction's political failure as the latter's (twice-removed) diagnostic and/or corrective to major tradition's self-referential auto-critique. To follow through on this doubled charge of reclamation and canonicity, they elicit *how* the subaltern woman is textually produced in the archive of antiquity *at* the archaic origin. Spivak's (re)inscription of the feminist intellectual's undertaking as *intellectual* (and, hence, postcolonial) verifies that the silence of the widow is a distinctly textual (and, hence, canonical) moment (26, 28).

Contravening antiquity as an "unnegotiated nonfactor" (28) in postcolonial studies, Spivak " 'think[s]' of the law . . . ontologically" (27) as a loss of memory to exhibit what lives beyond (the widow's) written-in silence. An eternally "lost" antiquity propagates "a foreshortened history of female victimhood," which dispenses the subaltern's generation as a diachronically invested palimpsest (28): the archive is *that* place at the archaic origin that (already) narrates imperialism and nationalism (and now postcolonial studies) as the widow's *legendary* silence. When read in this way, (the interested formation of) the archive becomes the bridging structure between Hinduism and Britain; the widow's silence is *that* place from which two seeming opposites are granted semantic content by their respective *archons* to turn ritual into crime. The impasse effectuates a repeated (traumatic) loss of antiquity, as a fatal dialectic arrests postcoloniality's immanent negativity.

For (the interested formation of) this postcolonial archive, Spivak laments that postcoloniality's methodology of legitimation by reversal desists in articulating radical questions by devaluing classical learning.[8] A (titular) radical question (can the subaltern speak?), however, spurs Spivak to figure out how Sanskrit as a specific *language* becomes susceptible to strategic moments of misinterpretation, which date back to antiquity and repurpose *sati* as *suttee* (29, 30). Her excavation discloses the violence of the archive, which pivots *smriti* (that which is remembered) and *sruti* (that which is heard) from polymorphous polyvalence into the strict letter of the law. In order for the *smriti* and *sruti* traditions to do real political work, in the altercation between Hinduism and Britain, the *Dharmasastra*'s and *Rg-Veda*'s structural damage transmogrifies heterogeneity into cultural logic so that ritual can become crime

(30, note 5). Upon an experience of the impossible, an encounter with (a) widow whose silence is (already) written-in into the archive, Spivak decides that Sanskritic (re)inscription at the archaic origin backdates colonial subject formation from modernity to antiquity (32).

To Derrida's list of European prejudices—theological, Chinese, and hieroglyphist—Spivak adds a fourth, which removes postcolonial criticism of imperialism from the western "science of writing" to preserve the vitality of textuality as a type of political activity; the imperialist prejudice (35) (already) writes us (all) into the archive as geopolitically determined and (consequently) silent. In the relay between Derrida and Spivak, politically pragmatic cartographic specificity may find places on a map, but it can also help apprehend how the widow's written-in silence commands all (of us) that follow(s). At the aporetic juncture, where prejudice is written-in to command (the) all, writing *for* difference opens up domestic and civil society (35), as it (re)inscribes what being in (a) domestic outline *looks* like. If the postcolonial archive is *this* place from which (*that*) order is given,[9] then postcoloniality's backdated provenance revises *how* we are conjured into being (*there*).

As a result of a (Sanskritic) reframing of our being written-in *into* the world (36), we (now postcolonials) may look (out) for a (sexually) subaltern subject lost in "an institutionally sanctioned archaic origin" (32).[10] The relay begins: if *that* word (subaltern) is set aside for the heterogeneity of decolonizing space (Spivak, *Critique* 270), and the subaltern as subject is irretrievably heterogeneous (310), then *this* postcolonial archive writes (us) into the world as *archons* who tend an impossible because foreclosed genealogy—*at* the archaic origin. The sanctioned suicide (*sati*) that is truth-knowledge of the insubstantiality of the self (*tatvajnana*) and piety of (first) place (*agré*) becomes our passage in/to antiquity. *For* the postcolonial archive, *sati* becomes our proper ancestral rite for the dead: we must give ourselves over to *her* place—that is, to *that* place, lost at the institutionally sanctioned archaic origin—as written-in into the archive.

Just the same, (our) acting out of (her) acting out of (the husband's) truth-knowledge (*tatvajnana*) and piety of (first) place (*agré*) is what (*this*) woman is allowed. A performative dislocation of a performative dislocation violates *smriti* and *sruti* injunctions (Shetty and Bellamy 38), but this transgression of a general rule of conduct disengages the dubious place of (a) legendary postcolonialism. In other words, the repetition, with a difference, of prescribed disciplinary boundaries signals that structural violence that remarkably *understates* the heterogeneity at the archaic origin that *can* be remembered and heard (*smriti* and *sruti*, respectively). When reorienting (our) desire, interest, and subjectivity, we cannot *not* mime the loss of heterogeneity, but according to *this* transposition of (our) geopolitical location, (to want) antiquity is (to want) heterogeneity at the site of that violence where postcoloniality is an encounter with nothing.

In Spivak's relay, deconstruction and postcolonialism are (being) commanded from a *place* of mutual untranslatability and irreconciliation, which is the widow's (written-in) silence. The widow's appropriation and displacement as "female subject *in life*" turns any attempt at her recuperation qua lost voice into an "appropriation of a role in gendering"—yet again (*Critique* 235, 227). To make the widow cathect the space of a fully intending subject (who wanted to die; *sati* qua suicide) so that her status as sheer victim (who was forced to die; *suttee* qua murder) *can* be refuted (211, 214) is to leave "her" cultural lineaments (or the domestic outline) intact. But, thinking (the law of) culture ontologically requires extrapolating from the memory of (another) time/frame: the possibilities for antiquity are "nothing short of vertiginous" (Shetty and Bellamy 42) because the subaltern's heterogeneity (*in life*) is irretrievable.

The widow's (written-in) silence in antiquity's archive commands: *for* postcolonialism "in the beginning" is *sati* (43). Postcoloniality is furthered beyond its narrow sense by the remarkable discovery that the (sexually) subaltern subject at the archaic origin is textually unlocatable. And, this opening (out) of the hermeneutic horizon of inquiry vindicates postcoloniality in the general sense by bringing the palimpsestic layers of antiquity into view (42). Shetty and Bellamy describe how Spivak looks for the mechanisms that establish the history of *sati* by mistranslations and disingenuous phrasings of Sanskrit texts, to fix the woman's being as being a good wife (by burning). *Satt* means the True, the Good, and the Right; *sati* is the feminine form of *satt* (truth); the British called widow self-immolation *suttee*; but, for all that, *sati* and *suttee* both mean "good wife." These cunning slippages, under the auspices of an antagonistic understanding of difference, squelch the volatile space of the widow's *non*agency (43). The female's agency is appropriated and displaced on three fronts: she acts out the husband's truth-knowledge of the insubstantiality of the self (*tatvajnana*); her husband's funeral pyre is *the* piety of (first) place (*agré*); and, her insubstantial self can be cast off only where her husband is burning (37–38).

A long-term understanding of the movement between Hinduism and Britain reveals a history of repression that Spivak terms "women's time" (*Critique* 295), and which Shetty and Bellamy term an ultimately "pregendered time" (43, note 15). This kind of postcoloniality takes us to Bhuvaneswari's *sati*/suicide via a temporality that reaches (back) in/to antiquity to track the actual (not willed) revision of the text of *sati*. Bhuvaneswari (re)inscribes a (re)inscription of heterogeneity; she uses her blood to disclose *how* she is (written-in) as silence at the archaic origin. This is a far cry from saying she wanted to die.

IV. For Robert Ross

Since (now) "we cannot *not* want antiquity" (44), Shetty and Bellamy understand postcoloniality as a form of cultural melancholia, for the archaic is what we must dissociate from and what we must call upon. The postscript of Shetty and Bellamy's essay curiously embodies this *fort/da*. They interject a reply ("But we are not finished yet") to the one they regard as the mother/founder of postcolonial studies: Gayatri Spivak—en famille (45). This conversation among family women took place during a conference where the authors presented their work (46). Spivak was present on the occasion. She asks whether Shetty and Bellamy can relate the "riddling story" (45) of Bhuvaneswari's *sati*/suicide to the founding of a discipline; what would Bhuvaneswari's death mean for disciplinary identity?

Shetty and Bellamy feature this legendary family *sati*/suicide as the real payoff of Spivak's canonical essay (33, note 8). Bhuvaneswari's deliberate timing is (a) history not (to be) passed on by family women[11]; she becomes a family secret that is both crypt-ic and crypt-like, as Spivak's "scandalously underread" passages epitomize the failure of family memory. These passages are a gift, however, to postcolonial studies because Bhuvaneswari's (re)writing of the *shastric* prohibition of *sati* during menstruation serves as a reminder: *this* (cryptically) dislocated place of the (sexually) subaltern subject makes the discipline possible (46). And *here*, perhaps mistaking what I remembered and heard (*smriti* and *sruti*, respectively), I pick up this (public) moment of relay to respectfully add to the (now postcolonial) archive a fifth prejudice, which commands (us) *into* the world—at the archaic origin, en famille: the cultural prejudice. If it is remembered that Bhuvaneswari is a foremother who bred us, then repetition, with a difference, ought to signal the prospects of what is actually *there*: (her) menstrual blood.

Far from being merely psychological, a young woman *waits* for the onset of menstruation; she *times* her act of truth-knowledge of the insubstantiality of the self (*tatvajnana*) and piety of (first) place (*agré*) *in* women's time to defer (the promise of) *Time*—the nation/state—through killing (one's) kin. Her *tatvajnana* (*sati*/suicide) and *agré* (menstrual blood) engender a futurity that makes impossible the (genealogical) transmutation between colonizer and nationalist (Britain and Hinduism, respectively)—as if such passages were history. Menstrual blood signals *that* place in view of which Bhuvaneswari breaks temporal and spatial continuity by violations of cultural law, as written-in into the archaic origin, by unleashing her free-flowing menstrual blood, which simply *is*. She cuts herself "out" of a reproductive teleology (and cuts bleed) to leave behind (a) *satt* that refutes the oddity between "[w]hite men are saving brown women from brown men" or "[t]he woman wanted to die" because *both* lexicons command: (to be) woman is (to be) The Good Wife.

When Spivak moves the example of Bhuvaneswari's *sati*/suicide outside the domestic enclosure as a miring movement from private family to public discipline, she changes what being in (a) domestic outline looks like. Her text-that-is-a-classically-learned-radical-question (can the subaltern speak?) asks the general question of founding a discipline by questioning disciplinary identity. Menstruation signifies the lack of an illicit pregnancy in a young woman who is "*no doubt* looking forward to good wifehood" (*Critique* 307, emphases added); Spivak reads Bhuvaneswari's waiting for menstruation, therefore, as a protest against her physiological destiny to serve the passions of a single male. Other family women wave away this not-an-unsanctioned-mother's death by referring either to her brother-in-law's taunts that she is "not-yet-a-wife" (307) or to her failed mourning for her dead father. A letter found ten years after her suicide in 1926 reveals that male nationalists call upon Bhuvaneswari qua incarnation of the fiercely warlike and maternal goddess Durga to commit a political assassination.[12] The public rationale of Bhuvaneswari-as-Durga's death is the pathos of not carrying out the mission but keeping this secret.

Spivak learns of Bhuvaneswari's death through family rumors; she presses a female relative who is a philosopher and Sanskritist for more details because of the similarity in their early scholarly production. This scholar expresses incredulity at Spivak's desire to learn more about the "hapless" (308) Bhuvaneswari. Spivak does not elaborate on what she means, but it appears as though Spivak should inquire after a more empowering example. Indeed, unlike Bhuvaneswari, her two sisters lead fulfilling lives. This scholar's chagrin is "*no doubt*" due to her distrust of *that* (first world) place of postcolonial reason that renders Bhuvaneswari a stand-in for Indian culture. She does learn, however, that Bhuvaneswari's *sati*/suicide was actually a situation involving a forbidden love.

Spivak's imprudent remark that the subaltern cannot speak is made in anguish after her receipt of these legible scripts from family women. Bhuvaneswari transforms her own body into women's writing *in* women's time *at* the archaic origin. Yet, some fifty years after the independence of India, her attempt at writing is silenced (308–9).

> Bhuvaneswari had fought for national liberation. Her great grand-niece works for the New Empire [she has an executive position in a United States-based transnational]. This too is a historical silencing of the subaltern. When the news of this young woman's promotion was broadcast in the family amidst general jubilation I

> could not help remarking to the eldest surviving female member:
> "Bhuvaneswari"—her nickname had been Talu—"hanged herself in
> vain," but not too loudly. Is it any wonder that this young woman
> is a staunch multiculturalist, believes in natural childbirth, and
> wears only cotton? (311)

Spivak is right. She died in vain. If Bhuvaneswari figures "hapless" women of India's past, then her great grandniece figures "empowered" women of India's future. For us, Bhuvaneswari is (a) crypt-ic secret. For her great grandniece, she is (a) scapegoat. Both lies, "no doubt," canonize family shame.

As this great grandniece helps her US-based transnational plug into the emerging South Asian market, she uses her position as an Indian diasporic with the appropriate cultural alibis: for *her*, heterogeneity becomes multiculturalism, menstrual blood becomes natural childbirth, and body-as-women's writing becomes body-as-Indian-lifestyle. Bhuvaneswari refuses ("but not too loudly") to be The Good Wife and forfeits her symbolic potential (or surplus value) to trope an impossible life. By mentioning her affectionate nickname (Talu), Spivak holds on to her bond with the women who bred her, but her heterogeneity is irretrievably lost. As *their* repetition, with a difference, Spivak seeks contact with the anonymously addressed dead letter of antiquity, which seems never to end up in the proper place.

V. *My* Bhuvaneswari

Transcribing Bhuvaneswari's menstrual blood as only a dissent against reproductive heteronormativity makes her *timing* null and void. Forasmuch as menstrual blood denotes unrealized reproductive capacity, womanhood is teleologically intact: she is not-yet a mother simply because she is not-yet a wife. In *this* postscript to Spivak's imperialist prejudice, Bhuvaneswari updates our list of prejudices by (further) backdating the archive of antiquity. Her *sati*/suicide as *tatvajnana* and menstrual blood as *agré* dissolve her to emplace pregendered time and signal the first sacred place: the place without the body. *This* repetition of *that* law, with a difference, leaves (for us) what can be remembered (*smriti*) and heard (*sruti*) in the empty place of the widow's *non*agency. By violating a prohibition against menstruating widows ascending the funeral pyre, Bhuvaneswari fills in what was missing from the husband's truth-knowledge (*tatvajnana*) and piety of (first) place (*agré*) to make *sati*/suicide real: she is not the (ethereal) goddess who blesses but a (bloody) legend.

The anguished passages in "Can the Subaltern Speak?" commemorate the female as subaltern who *is* the possibility of the discipline. But, regardless of this payoff, Shetty and Bellamy note that Spivak refuses the "gift" of death that names her the founder of postcolonial studies, as she does not "see anything called postcolonial*ism*" (Spivak, "Interview" 95, 47).[13] Her demurral, repeats, with a difference, how someone rejects ("but not too loudly") an unwanted gift *for* the heterogeneous. Bhuvaneswari's refusal takes place *in* the decidedly women's time of menstruation whereupon for *these* family women she is the "arena" of judging or testing our explanations of culture—that is, of "thinking the undetermined wholly-other" (*Outside* 214)—when we attribute meanings to this act.

Bhuvaneswari naïvely leaves behind her blood, as a textual ingredient from the "great, pure, unlivable, inappropriable outside" (99), for a counter sentence that can abide the "proper language of our life" (Derrida's phrase). From our destined misremembering and mishearing, heterogeneity breaks loose to sanction a highly motivated return to antiquity—en famille, for (an) ancestral (re)inscription of what we understand as our genealogy.[14] At the threshold between nature and culture, Bhuvaneswari mimes the (first) cut that disclaims heterogeneity for the sake of (a) legendary silence, for culture, as written-in into the archive of antiquity, dislocates the female subject *in life*. Under this rule of identity, ideological power becomes stable nature for culture to signify human exceptionalism via "third world difference." But, at the archaic origin, the burning *satt* that is a strangling rope puts Bhuvaneswari in a vertiginous place: from here she commands that utopian understanding of the project of culture in which cuts actually bleed. Alongside calculations of the bases for our survival (*Imaginary* 202), our archive fever—a decidedly *global* warming—backdates the postcolonial archive *from* antiquity *to* the blood that makes any archive (real).

VI. Resurrected Blood

In the preface of *A Critique of Postcolonial Reason* (1999), Spivak begins her project by citing UNESCO's *Encyclopedia of Life Support Systems*. Per this report by the United Nations, the Aboriginal period is the "timescale of the *far past* . . . associated with *inactive* approaches in which there is no concern for environmental degradation and sustainability" (ix). (As Spivak wryly notes, it is not like Aristotle could glean the undisclosed expression of "value.") According to this enlightened imagination, the aboriginals are obscure and passive even when something can be learned *from* them. For the facile maintenance of this (now fourth world) difference between the sustainable present and unsustainable past, as figured by history and its prehistoric past, respectively, UNESCO misses the opportunity to assemble coalitions. The obliteration of textual ingredients left behind by the "inactive" aboriginals to retain the active self of Europe—that is, to nurture *this* past as *the* past— prevents us from recognizing that we are the monoculture that beholds its (written-in) exceptionalism as history.

At this moment of inaugurating a culturally scaled critique, Spivak proposes a different kind of postcoloniality, "when freedom from oppression turns around, one hopes, to the freedom to be responsible" ("Harlem" 128). In our miring movements, therefore, we avouch that the (sexually) subaltern subject is neither the residue of a *better* cultured woman nor a logical by-product to be rhetorically crossed (out) for a cultural false positive.[15] Nature as trope for "third world difference," which must be restored to proper cultural lineaments when read via a "colonialist stance," in this version of the past-ness of the past, becomes the historical alibi for colonialism *and* postcolonialism. If nature no longer signifies those who skipped being exceptional, then antiquity's archive passes on to us, as (a) notorious female blood right/rite, the vertiginous possibilities of culture.

A study by James Hansen, et al., published in September 2013 concludes, "burning all fossil fuels would produce a different . . . planet" (24). Hansen continues: "Our calculated global warming in this case is 16°C, with warming at the poles approximately 30°C. . . . [G]lobal warming of that magnitude would make most of the planet uninhabitable by humans" based on the temperature requirements for the human body's metabolic functioning alone.[16] Because we are on a trajectory to create an unfamiliar and deleterious planet, (the concept of) a postcolonial archive cannot leave the rupture with nature intact. By profoundly humanizing the Earth, cultural prejudice evacuates the very archive fever that may (re)inscribe our passage to an essentially historical ground. Thus, third world *difference* may convey and uphold the most sophisticated understanding yet of the archive of antiquity, from where we (all) came (to be).

Chapter Ten

Wagging Fingers and Missing Dicks

An Updated Grammar Book (Race, Gender, and the Animal in the Age of Global Warming)

To *lexicalize* is to separate a linguistic item from its appropriate grammatical system into conventions of another grammar.

—Gayatri Spivak, "Harlem"

To read the archive is to enter a mortuary; it permits one final viewing . . . of persons about to disappear into the slave hold.

—Saidiya Hartman, *Lose Your Mother*

When one has got to make correct entries one comes to hate those savages—hate them to death. . . . [He] bent . . . [to] . . . mak[e] correct entries of perfectly correct transactions; and fifty feet below . . . the grove of death.

—Joseph Conrad, *Heart of Darkness*

Here . . . in this here place, we flesh.

—Toni Morrison, *Beloved*

Why not? Anything—anything can be done in this country. . . . [N]obody, here, you understand *here*, can endanger your position. And why? You stand the climate—you outlast them all. The danger is in Europe.

—Joseph Conrad, *Heart of Darkness*

I. American, Not Anglo-Clone

In "Mama's Baby, Papa's Maybe: An American Grammar Book" (1987), published a year before Spivak's "Can the Subaltern Speak?," Hortense Spillers
observes that New World domesticity needs an *un*gendered legend: black
women. At the institutionally sanctioned archaic origin of the New World
scene, black women are commanded into being via mythical names (Mammy,
Jezebel, Aunt Jemima, etc.) to institute what being in (a) domestic outline looks
like; black women as written-in into the archive of antiquity breed property
not children. Taking into account that the slave-holding civil codes make a
person an object of property (401–2), the peculiar compatibility of "black
women" and "it" ("even the quotation marks do not *matter*") (388) confutes
the generalizability of major feminism. Spillers backdates the patriarchal register of public and private, therefore, to revise the historical record, as during
The Middle Passage, tools of the trade—whips, chains, knives, etc.—(first)
make black women into flesh and blood entities to (then) turn them into
unsanctioned mothers. In Spillers's emphatically American feminism, the
slave ship is a cultural vestibule that offers a glimpse of *how* black women
are so *un*gendered. *This* exception to the general rule of domesticity compels
us to move in *reverse* direction from major feminist inquiry to rescind the
law that mislays black women.

When a peculiar Grammar fills in this empty space of *non*agency by
convenient shorthand (Peaches, Brown Sugar, Welfare Queen, etc.), African-
American persons "register [. . .] the wounding" (387). Spillers's search for
missing persons steers her to The Middle Passage; here, the wayward hieroglyphics left by tools of the trade order all (else) that follows, as docketed in
the commercial logs of maritime cargo. This chapter follows Spillers in her
travails against a misdirected history of female victimhood that purports to
make a slave. It suggests that in seeking the rectitude of the black family,
Spillers teleologically preserves the gendered rule of domesticity—sanctioned
motherhood. As the vertiginous potential of what is available for "pre-view"
(387) on board the slave ship is *already* restricted by sexual difference, Spillers
misses the *other* flesh and blood entity also listed in the ledger as property:
livestock. This (oxymoronic) encryption signals a profound humanization of
the Earth; in other words, we do not even notice that to have bodies ripped
apart, torn open, seared, mutilated, divided, is what it *means* to be (an) animal.
Having (now) pre-viewed (all) resurrected flesh and blood entities, situated in
the interstices of nature and culture, our updated Grammar Book can convey and uphold *that* unsanctioned Mother who is the (only) possibility for
(a) culture.

II. Not the Good Wife

Hortense Spillers begins with names: Sapphire, Earth Mother, Aunty, Black Woman at the Podium, etc., which are *how* black women are summoned into public culture. A fallout of white feminists' cultural investment in a prior ordering of gender, declined to the black community by the "national treasury of rhetorical wealth" (384), is an inept grasp of the resident shorthand that writes the place of black women. *Within* a "historic outline of dominance" (385), an eccentric discourse endows male and female no "symbolic integrity" (385).

> The problem before us is deceptively simple: the terms enclosed in quotation marks [Mammy, Peaches, Jezebel, Aunt Jemima, Earth Mother, Welfare Queen, Sapphire, etc.] . . . isolate overdetermined nominative properties. . . . [T]here is no easy way for the agents buried beneath them to come clean. (384)[1]

This curious axiological ground beckons black women in the New World, whenever her country needs her to be *these* things, via an etymological script that heightens and separates (off) properties to name whatever "it" denotes (384). (Recall Zack's discussion of Haseena.)

Manifesting a telegraphically invested coding, Spillers is mythic before she has her "self"; indeed, marvelously (speaking), she *has* properties that signify, but apparently signify in *plus*. As the spectacular example of "zero degree" (386), she *is* the pathological place of black culture—that is, of the Negro Family. The *archon* of this particular useful fiction (at that time) is Daniel Patrick Moynihan, the author of *The Negro Family: The Case For National Action* (March 1965). Moynihan's report proclaims: "Those persons living according to the perceived 'matriarchal' pattern are . . . caught in a state of social 'pathology' " (386).[2] He writes the absence of the female bastard in patriarchal rites and laws of inheritance as the culpability of the Daughter: *she* astonishingly reverses the castration thematic to expel the Father from the "essential [that is, ethical] life of the black community" (385), a willful violation of natural law that usurps the Name and Law of the Father and dislocates it onto the Territory of the Mother and Daughter. At the archaic origin of the New World scene, therefore, black men (there are no bastard daughters, only unsanctioned transgressions of the Law) are commanded into being on the basis of their debilitating oddity from *"the rest of American society"* (384).

In *this* place, where the child's identity is ascertained through the mother's line, we find fathers and daughters who are indistinguishable from one another in their *"prescribed* internecine degradation" (385). Indeed, one could say that

Sapphire and Old Man actually mean the *same* thing: Sapphire acts out her Old Man in drag and her Old Man is Sapphire in extreme caricature. They are a common manifestation of the absence and denial (of the Father) that is the naturally pathological structure of the matriarchal Negro Family. In this (minor) domestic imbroglio, gender integrity (not gender *un*decidability) is the paradoxically figurative possibility of restoring Power to the Female (Maternity) and the Male (Paternity) (385). The "double and contrastive agencies" (385) of Sapphire and Old Man—I suggest that *her* wagging finger is *his* missing dick—comprise a startling inversion of the *cultural* direction of major feminism. Spillers's American feminist inquiry (not Anglo-clone) centers on the *potential for* rather than *actuality of* gender differentiation, as it may be mapped along an array of pressure points or points of crises. These include the crosscurrents between human biology and the project of culture in the ubiquitous patriarchal business of making humans (385).

The preordained failures of this project in African-American communities elucidate how "ethnicity" can be understood only as a negation of the White Family. While the White Family and the Negro Family assume the *aura* of historical relatedness, they still transpire as alternative stories of "human and cultural motives" (385) (that is, of life) that move through culture almost impeccably. On account of these fixations, ethnicity as a cultural descriptor "for the living" (385), under the weight of this historical order, becomes merely appreciative: it is a "signifier that has no movement in the field of signification" (385). Ethnicity takes on the status of myth by virtue of seeming *sui generis* (and, hence, Moynihan's pained but benevolent tone), but it grounds *either* veneration *or* rape of the "body." Consequently, as an incarnation of social and political structures, the body's "degradation *or* transcendence" (392) makes it a rich resource for metaphor yet also an abstraction even when apprehended in material terms (386).

To search for a "truer word" (384), Spillers drops us on the outskirts of the New World where the human sequence (Father, Daughter, Mother, Son) is written in blood because it represents "*actual* dismemberment, mutilation, and exile" (386). What we find, "[f]irst of all" (386), is a violation of motive will and active desire symbolized by a literal "*theft of the body*" (386). Subtraction of will and desire from the body configures the passage from personhood to being (equated with) something else—"we lose at least *gender* difference *in the outcome*" (386). Male and female bodies become indistinguishable in their transubstantiation as a "territory" to be signified by many things, big and small: the source of a compelling but devastating sensuality; thing-ness; a manifestation of otherness; a trope of powerlessness (386).

Spillers differentiates between flesh and body to describe the fundamental split between captive and liberated subject-positions, respectively: "[B]efore the 'body' there is the 'flesh,' that zero degree of social conceptualization that does not escape concealment under the brush of discourse, or the reflexes of iconography" (386). Whereas enslaved Africans experience the body as a private (separate) and specified (here/there) space—that is, as the confluence of cultural scripts such as biological, psychological, sexual, social, economic, etc.—the literal theft of the body is that loss of culture (symbolized by the subtraction of will and desire) that *regresses* the body into the flesh. Hence, bodies *were* stolen; but from the perspective of the captive community who came (to be) later on, these were "high crimes against the flesh, as the person of African females and African males registered the wounding" (387). On board the slave ship, men and women are reduced to "that zero degree" upon which the cultural project is engraved. The personhood of those spirited away is (to be) found in that which is "seared, divided, ripped-apart [. . .], riveted to the ship's hole, fallen, or 'escaped' overboard" (387).

By dint of this movement between *having* motive will and active desire and *being* a "specimen" and "torturable entity" (recall Adorno's formulation), a "materialized scene of unprotected female flesh—of female flesh 'ungendered' " (387) is palpable.[3] Spillers resurrects (wounded) flesh as the protrusive property of the body to ask whether *this* occurrence of "marking and branding" (387) portents future generations for whom "*symbolic substitutions* in an efficacy of meanings . . . repeat the initiating moments" (387). Splitting open the logical principle of "cultural seeing by skin color" (387) to amass wealth and fortune, she gains *at least* flesh "*in the outcome*," for the subtraction of motive will and active desire (body) and patriarchal protection (culture) leaves (behind) female flesh ungendered (flesh & blood entity). This equation is as follows: Body – [Motive Will + Active Desire] = Flesh & Blood Entity = 0 = Ungendered. Spillers catalogs what we find when we glance at this ubiquitous cultural project:

> The anatomical specifications of rupture, of altered human tissue, take on the objective description of laboratory prose—eyes beaten out, arms, backs, skulls branded, a left jaw, a right ankle, punctured; teeth missing, as the calculated work of iron, whips, chains, knives, the canine patrol, the bullet. (387)

The substantializing effects of this prose write the stolen body into the record only as the surface territory (not persons) upon which these tools of the trade (not persons) acted, which emboss upon the flesh cryptic markings (to be) written over by skin color.

If skin color comprises at most a personalization of the cultural project because of this appreciable ethnicity's negating function, then these "lacerations, woundings, fissures, tears, scars, openings, ruptures, lesions, rendings, punctures" (387) are at least remarkable in the depersonalization of their sanctioned protocol. Within those disjunctures of sliced and riven flesh, Spillers identifies an in-between space, a "cultural *vestibularity*" (387) wherein we find *that* body "*whose* flesh carries the female and the male" (387) indistinguishably to the brink of survival. "It" endures (our) cultural markings and brandings "whose inside has been turned outside" (387) for all (of us) to see: this is how "he" and "she" are written-in into the archive of the New World at the archaic origin. The internecine flesh and blood entity available for "pre-view" on board the slave ship dispels an understanding of rape as an "interiorized violation" (387) (hers) while also becoming the "topic" (387) (surface and object) of obscene torture normally thought a singularly male fate.[4]

Serving a tautological function as the metonymic site/sight of social facts (turned inside out), the regressed body is also a "metaphor for value" (389): the captivated (and captivating) body fleshed (out) at the intersection of culture and biology is precisely what this *kind* of person is worth. As these dynamic mechanisms of what to name and how to value take on a life of their own in the national imaginary, this singled-out-and-displayed ("atomized") entity perennially *under*states the business of "captivity and mutilation" (388). Acculturation continues apace even after liberation (so-called) because the profitable symbolic weight of these historic conditions harms, burdens, and murders "over and over again" (388). Spillers terms this failure to tally these historic conditions the "Great Long National Shame" (388), as "sticks and bricks might break our bones, but words will most certainly kill us" (388).

For the captive community dreaming of "rigor" (388) in historical method, this lexicon marks a severe rupture that creates a form of (temporal and spatial) continuity scandalously different in nature than the dominant community's. Saddled with this rupture's extant force, active subjects may fail to materialize, but signifying difference, writing over the nominative case for "double and contrastive agencies"—Sapphire and Old Man—bequeaths "a text for living and dying, and a method for reading both through their diverse mediations" (387).

III. Dog Whistles

These (re)inscriptions empower the dominant community to distort historical experience by turning a meeting in the New World into a form of descent. An American Grammar—assiduously maintained by latter day *archons* of the flesh—takes "a wild and unclaimed richness" (393) into its "semantic and iconic folds" (389) to merely suggest (to us) the person encrypted within. In the "mighty debris of the itemized account, between the lines of the massive logs of commercial enterprise" (390), therefore, black women are not encountered. What we *are* able to garner (with our growing ability to clarify) are the bounded mannerisms and determinative bodily metrics mandated by *this* project of culture. Oceanic protocols oblige captains, explorers, and great men of learning to inculcate an obscene, inhuman, and seemingly impossible *lack* of curiosity about the " 'cargo' that bled" (390). To maintain a magisterial solipsistic self that grips the pages of the archive, a descriptive grammar writes the scene as inherently male (391); reference is made to females on the basis of an imputed social and cultural function, but their *specific* gendering per local mores is deflected as a particular case of more generalized forms of "estrangement" (391)—(from what?).

Spectral realities of the "Great Long National Shame" prop up the magical being/time of skin color by transforming difference into "an *altered* human factor" (391), a way of writing the archive that traps (or tropes) in exact denotative value what can only be an "alterity of European ego" (391). Upon bitterly opining that one would never guess the specularity and arbitrariness of the categories of exchange (391), given the actual bloody course of history, Spillers offhandedly mentions the similarity-in-difference to European mores of African climate-based living arrangements and the precision of their attendant socially measured mappings.[5] Apparently, this similarity-in-difference indicates a parallel *inclination* in the meant-to-be-enslaved of a reliance on human calculability. Notwithstanding that all who bump into each other have the aspect of perceiving difference as absolute "degradation *or* transcendence"—and not a *lateral* move—only *one* side invested in skin color as an alibi for mercantile and commercial interests.

The Middle Passage, as the facilitating movement *from* degradation *to* transcendence, cuts (out) and sews (on) live persons from one place into another—whole cloth.[6] Inequities are sealed into place by means of the following metonymic chain: Flesh & Blood Entity→ Slave→ Culture: Sapphire, Mammy, Black Woman at the Podium, Jezebel, etc. *Her* having a signifying property *plus* permits the dominant community to dissemble what it means, for the semiotic iconography put into play fronts the actual *absurdity* of this New World logic. (African persons must move backwards "nowhere" to move forward "somewhere.") As such, the "dehumanizing, ungendering, and defacing" (393) of Africans emplaces the New World's historical ground.

IV. But We Are Not Finished Yet

At this juncture in Spillers's text, there is an interruption. She tenders an example of another cultural vestibule wherein the historical weight borne by black women's intellectual production is available for pre-view. What seems to be a reviewer of her essay prior to publication insists ("It has been pointed out to me") on writing Spillers as irremediably African-American. (American to all appearances means only Anglo-clone.) Spillers interjects a response ("I would suggest") to this interjecting reviewer (recall the "ASAP" reviewer of JanMohamed and Lloyd) who applies a social metric to the ship's cargo: to grant females less space below deck is to apply gender rules to material conditions. That these are the material conditions of the Middle Passage seems irrelevant to this cold calculation (based on Vulgar Fractions?) of gendered logic by an anonymous agent of feminism: having been allotted less space, "it" was (recognized as) female.

Spillers indices exasperation and irritation at this stoppage of *her* "*intervening, intruding* tale" (403) when she explains: while females may have less space below deck, the gender rule (whose gender rule? for whom?) does not apply here, for gendering occurs in the cloistral world of the domestic ("somewhere"), and not in The Middle Passage ("nowhere"). On board these feminized vessels, the cultural project squanders written-in bodies to disgorge *un*written flesh in service of a finished "essential metaphor" (393) (New World) that puts male/female in *proper* place—unhyphenated. Lacking this form of "specificity" (393) bestowed by the naming power of the patronymic, the "*altered* human factor" (391) dragged in the slave ship's underworld (first back, then forth) purveys a "*counter*-narrative" (393) of our envisaging of domestic space.

In the beginning, the literal theft of the body (subtraction of motive will and active desire) erases family names (Mother, Daughter, Father, Son).[7] Taking place (in the middle of) nowhere, this passage *from* an African *into* an American Grammar, obfuscates the relatedness intrinsic to *that* site/sight. The actual historical condition of being culturally *un*made frays the understated descriptor of "slave ship, its crew, and its human-as-cargo" (393). In keeping with the inviolable banality of commerce, "the massive logs of commercial enterprise" expose *how* the body is written-in at the archaic origin. *For* a historically adequate archive of antiquity, however, the radical *openness* of the flesh, as (made) manifest under erasure of the body, signals the vertiginous possibilities of culture. Under the auspices of our marvelous historical pluck, the impress of undecipherable yet uncannily familiar crevices express how heterogeneity *in medias res* is explained (away) once the ship reaches shore (393). Having gained the land, the sway of the ship is transformed into the ball-busting sway of Sapphire's hips. In the underworld, therefore, are neither males nor females because both are granted due consideration "as *quantities*" (393). A belated attribution to captive persons of a feminization that enslavement in fact withheld and kept out of reach will not fill in for missing black women (394). Indeed, any effort to "undo *and* reveal" (394) furthers the perennial "anonymity/anomie" (394) of the "unknown human factor" (394), as the record's duteous tabulations "throw [. . .] no *face* in view" (395).

What does emerge across the pages is the persistent uniformity with which captive persons are portrayed across sex/gender divisions. If the trader, "[q]uite naturally" (395), has no curiosity about his cargo, then striving for the heterogeneity dislocated by the naming becomes the project of culture. In another inversion of (major) feminism, which warrants a miring movement beyond the domestic enclosure, black women mend the kinless status attributed to what is "she" only to the extent of mere "genetic reproduction" (395) of a particular kind. Within a patronymic symbolic order, the slave-child deposits us on the very border of culture, yet again at its nexus with human biology. Here, whether this entity is human and has a family, "*by the very nature of the case*" (398, emphases added), remains undefined. Any claim to kinship by the slave is, again, "[q]uite naturally" (395) prone to dissolution, usurpation, and dislocation by property relations (396), as the inviolable agency of profit maximizes kinship as proliferation.

Motherhood for the slave does not mean "female blood-rite/right" (398) but "flesh" (398) that is a sought-after commodity meant for exchange. The (white) gendered female traverses this free market of "female bodies in the raw" (398), an Ur-text that commands *this* (American) feminist subject to move in precisely the *opposite* direction—for her *own* sake. (Recall DuCille's distinction between *dis*-course and *dat* course.) If black women's mythical will substitutes for the father's absence and denial, then actual history discloses that fatherhood is in fact a "supreme cultural courtesy" (398) for those compelled to lose the natural mother, always. A conflation of gendering and mothering, therefore, accords black women, as written-in into the "not-quite spaces" (400) of (an) American domesticity, a significant presence in the cultural landscape *by virtue of category alone*, for the "actual situation" (401) the birth of a child entails for black women fundamentally destabilizes the problem of culture. *Her* dispossession (or mythical prepossession) "between the lines" (390) of antiquity's archive consolidates the selectivity of our family memory. Female gendering in this writing glosses over the determinative exception: we lose at least (our theoretical preoccupation with) the reproduction of mothering "*in the outcome*" since mothering and *un*gendering mean the same thing.

V. Lacerations, Woundings, Fissures, Tears, Scars, Openings, Ruptures, Lesions, Rendings, Punctures→ Openness of Flesh→ Heterogeneity→ Animal (An Updated Grammar)

Spillers's framing writes us into the archive on the verge of the New World where we witness the literal theft of the body; upon subtracting motive will and active desire, the implements of culture regress the body into the flesh. Once the body is turned inside out, the remnant flesh and blood entity (female flesh *ungendered*) can be made a slave who is the "essence of stillness" (401). As there is no dynamism to be found, Spillers reads in the discourse of the law a reification of personality, which authorizes us to thoughtlessly slide over what is the historical space of a "transaction" (401) (relationship?). Overburdened metaphors and overdetermined understatements eclipse a "historical dimension" that we know "*in practice*" (401) can only be a minefield of ambiguities, illogic, accidents, and surprises because it solemnizes actual human contact. Abandoning historical adequacy, the Master is condemned by the *archon* to follow that rule of law that renders the Slave unsanctioned *life*. The mythologized antithesis commanded into being is a "reverse degree zero" (401): *one* side possesses all the will in the world, while the other side is *nothing*.

By prohibiting the slave any real negativity, the ontological *and* cultural fixation that adequates property and personality betrays its anxiety-ridden lineaments. Within this sadistic spectacle, the truth content of the New World is (to be) found at the *end* of the tools of the trade, but does not manifest an "intransitive 'is.' " The mood divulged by this dream text (the Law) is explicitly subjunctive, as this rigidity of circumstance is (only) "devoutly to be wished" (402). *This* dream text respectfully picks up where Spillers leaves off in her (re)inscription of the inaugural scene of the New World. Spillers begins her palimpsestic reading of an American Grammar with names (Sapphire, Earth Mother, Jezebel, Black Woman at the Podium, etc.), which do significant cultural work in dislocating even those who use them. For the *potential for* rather than *actuality of* historical rigor and method, perhaps we can understand the cultural work done by the animal. If the law commands an artifice into being, and these names repeat the initial inaugural moments, then the actual course of history lets slip that on the other side of the culturally saturated body is the *only* kind of flesh and blood entity there is: the animal.

For the "*intervening, intruding* tale" of human exceptionalism, what lie of the "marking and branding" of humans is told? If the cultural vestibule that is the slave vessel displays how the human sequence (Father, Daughter, Mother, Son) is written in blood, then where is the flesh and blood entity that is the animal? Having (hitherto) been deposited at the threshold of nature and culture, we may encounter *another* body "*whose* flesh carries the female and the male" indistinguishably to the brink of survival. As we continue in reversed course to where the animals will (always) have been, we may notice (as if for the first time) *how* the tools of the trade install (a) Grammar that ventures to write over the planet. The historical inadequacy of *this* kind of generational passing, where bit parts, teeth, eyes, ankles, arms, and jaws *are* the "body," and bits parts, ships, and their crew *are* the "land," evinces a cured wound[8] that is also a repeatable freeze frame.

The slave vessel is that scene of the flesh where culture comes up against its own borders. Those whom it covers in a wide agglomeration of motives may endeavor to *mean* something else beyond the body as a metaphor that founds a discipline (Shetty and Bellamy 47), as the locus, repository, and receptacle for the patronymic (Butler, *Bodies* 38), or as the groundbreaking turf upon which to invent a country (Spillers, "Mama's Baby" 384). In Spillers's revision, American feminist inquiry achieves the *potential for* rather than *actuality of* gender differentiation. Our palimpsestic contribution to this (heretofore) shifted ground moves further along the array of pressure points or points of crises to account for the possible impossibility of self-preservation that is global warming. What this means is that the utter contingency of the internecine flesh and blood entity available for "pre-view" on board the slave ship affords a glimpse of *somebody else*.

VI. An (Ironic and Melancholy) "ASAP" Review

Having arrived indistinguishably at the brink of survival, we are able to spot that the human is a signifier that also seems to have no movement in the field of signification. We are for all intents and purposes plunked *into* the pure present by the "double and contrastive agencies" of Human and Animal. If the Moynihan Report uses ethnicity as a stand-in for the living—that is, ethnicity is *used* synonymously with (appreciative) culture—then the perspective recently gained by anthropogenic climate change broadens the domestic outline by reawakening our family (species) memory. Since gendering is a cultural project that occurs within the domestic enclosure, upon achieving the *potential for* rather than *actuality of* gender differentiation, we may avoid deflection by the *name* for sexual difference *in defiance of all the living*: culture. Positing the body as a signifier of agency, Spillers, on one hand, equates culture with having motive will and active desire, and, on the other, with having gender and history. As *all* are subtracted from the body to garner the flesh and blood entity, we end up with an inverted patriarchal logic whereby gendering is to *have* motive will and active desire.

In addition to being at odds with history in its real course, gendering—inverted or straightforward—depends on a prior dualism between nature and culture. An antagonistic understanding of difference put into place at the archaic origin functions as a historical alibi for human exceptionalism. Tossing aside the inherent fiction of the culturally saturated body, we may resurrect the flesh and blood entity to bear the mother's mark on our person—that is, on second thought, our personal pronouns *ought* to be used for that "*collective* function" (384) that does not *stand-in* for (all) the living, but allows for a coming-into-being that *is* for (all) the living. To gather together text and pre-text for a different set of domestic arrangements—we are here (all of us) *already* together—is to forego the symbolic integrity made tenable by a spiritualized sexual difference, which (dis)enfranchises signifying capacities at the cost of a qualitative variety of experience. What difference then does "it"—the flesh and blood entity—actually make?

If lacerations, woundings, fissures, tears, scars, openings, ruptures, lesions, rendings, punctures are cured/specified beforehand as "altered human tissue," then the project of culture that conflates Sapphire and Old Man, Slave Vessel and Laboratory, and Itemized and Objective Prose, *also* conflates Body and Culture. It is the symbolic integrity of culture that *matters* not "flesh and blood," or the "entity" that is "it." But what happens to those *other* flesh and blood entities that are also, *by the very nature of the case*, in the slave vessel and laboratory, and docketed by itemized and objective prose? *Who* are they? Spillers unleashes an inventive descriptive force by alloying being a flesh and blood entity and being "seared, divided" (387); the implications of this startling exposé, however, are preempted because the only flesh and blood entity on board the slave ship is the "human-as-cargo." At the aporetic juncture where flesh is both cargo and bloody, we catch a glimpse of how the "calculated work" of sexual difference implants the mechanism for (our) ersatz vertical secession from nature (that is, from life).

Implements of violence—"iron, whips, chains, knives, the canine patrol, the bullet"—are written-in into the archive as metonyms for the crew, who as incurious men of the trade command symbolic integrity by appending to one "body" what is *taken* from another. In this discourse of appropriation and displacement, the *only* tissue that *can* be altered is human in outline, antecedently. *Having* "eyes beaten out, arms, backs, skulls branded, a left jaw, a right ankle, punctured; teeth missing" does not apply to the "beasts of burden" (402) on board that vessel of culture whose diligent annals are missing even the (human-given) name of their species. Inasmuch as "livestock" stands in for "*all* and *any* animal(s)" (402)—the emphasis is original—animals themselves (an absurdity) are somehow the *only* ones (*all* and *any*) with symbolic integrity: an erstwhile corpse (not a flesh and blood entity), "it" is carried across, *un*remarkably intact, wherever "it" goes.

The "wild and unclaimed richness" of these oxymoronic names (Spillers does use "various" when referring to livestock) is an abundance that is only virtually domesticated. It would be imprudent to ignore the fatal effects (for us) of this virtual domestication, which calls forth "*all* and *any* animal(s)" into the academic archive of the "descriptive document" (402). Spillers marvels at how commercial logs put the slave alongside the kitchen item, the book, and various livestock in the same order of meaning (402). In this addendum to Spillers's addendum, we may detect that the "double and contrastive agencies" of Slave Vessel and Laboratory, Crew and Cargo, Objective Description and Calculated Work, and Tools of the Trade and Flesh and Blood, are mythologized by a phenomenon of "marking and branding" that is nonpareil: cruelty.

As our determinative difference from the rest of the planet, cruelty qua human exceptionalism impedes the remembrance that "livestock" and "beasts of burden"—"all and any animal(s)"—do not enact being animal(s) in accordance with our Grammar (as is devoutly wished), as if they belonged there. Our cultural project is that "prescribed internecine degradation" that ferments the (temporal and spatial) cultural continuity of the slave vessel, the laboratory, and the factory farm, by cutting (out) and sewing (on) the animal, a word that will most certainly kill us (all). If the abundance of virtual domestication contains an alarmingly and noticeably dislocated item (402), then it becomes important to ask who are these "various" yet "all and any animal(s)," for any projection of kinship (Mama's Baby) that structures itself against a damaged and maligned nature remains fundamentally bound to what it claims to have transcended (Butler, Undoing 126).

VII. Mama's Baby: The Resurrection of the Flesh

The African-American example in this codicil may hold a key to that essential particle of mother wit that is perennially understood "as a metaphor of social and cultural management" (Spillers, "Mama's Baby" 403): self-preservation. Undermining the axiomatic debasement that attaches to female cultural inheritance requires undoing the project of culture that conflates this genealogy with "brute animality" (403). As latter day archons of the flesh, we interject a renewed semantic fold or cultural iconography into the palimpsestic narrative of human life. Our dream of rigor leads us to that abiding Mother whose processes of reproduction are not considered a valid cultural heritage because "Mother Right, by definition, [is] a negating feature of human community" (402–3). To be Mama's Baby, therefore, is to reclaim our historic being for an unusual cultural text wherein we are (all) well met "in the flesh" (404).

This female blood rite/right moves beyond the traditional repertoire of symbols for a different cultural subject who experiences the ground beneath her feet as the vital and historical claim of that Mother whose disavowal condemns us all to silence. Under the auspices of this space clearing gesture, which continues to backtrack our cultural direction, the mise-en-abyme on board the slave vessel mythologizes (*all* and *any*) animal(s)—a "degradation *or* transcendence"—for our exclusive cultural project. Here, we pick up Spillers's relay for the heterogeneity that lives and breeds as *life* because the human is the odd one out. Our "highly motivated" interest in non-Eurocentric ecological justice[9] may be the middle passage to that utopian understanding of the project of culture where *all* mothers are important.[10]

Conclusion

Three Women's Texts and a Critique of Imperialism 2.0[1]

An Aesthetic Education and the Planetary Imperative

They were not bound to regard with affection a thing that could not sympathize with one amongst them[,] a heterogeneous thing.

—Charlotte Brontë, *Jane Eyre*

There are always two deaths, the real one and the one people know about.

—Jean Rhys, *Wide Sargasso Sea*

I was required to exchange chimeras of boundless grandeur for realities of little worth.

—Mary Shelley, *Frankenstein*

Nature is all on planet Earth that has no need of us and can stand alone.

—E.O. Wilson, *The Creation*

A functional change in a sign-system is a violent event.

—Gayatri Spivak, *In Other Worlds*

Until nothing is enough, nothing suffices. We (no longer we are in) the planet.

—Gayatri Spivak, *An Aesthetic Education*

I. Who Wins Loses/Who Loses Wins[2]

On the penultimate day of the COP 21 climate talks in Paris, attending scientists expressed genuine surprise that 1.5° Celsius had been built into the agreement. The talks' stated goal had always been to forge a path whereby we might hold this century's global warming to 2° Celsius. Ratcheting mechanisms for strengthening the accord over time, for that purpose, had been central to the hotly contested deliberations. It was known that the INDCs (Intended Nationally Determined Contributions to greenhouse gas reductions) amounted to 3.5° Celsius of warming this century. Future agreements on extremely robust emissions and land use controls are needed to reduce future warming to 2° Celsius—a number that while generally embraced by governments and international bodies, is more an arbitrary target than a scientifically determined guardrail for keeping the planet, its biosphere, and human civilization meaningfully safe. For instance, global warming of 2° Celsius above preindustrial levels significantly threatens numerous ecosystems including coral reef systems whose very viability comes into question—as the global coral bleaching event of 2016 demonstrates.[3] Considerable uncertainty in fact remains in terms of the effects of a corresponding level of ocean acidification on phytoplankton, the basis of the oceanic food chain and a prime producer of oxygen and absorber of CO_2 on planet Earth.

What we do know is that the global transformations in a 2° world are in any traditionally conservative sense catastrophic. While the current business as usual projections of 4.5° Celsius (8.1° Fahrenheit)—or the 3.5° Celsius result of full implementation of the ratified 2015 Paris Agreement—would likely be civilization-breaking, 2° Celsius entails massive alterations and concomitant suffering.[4] Stefan Rahmstorf of the Potsdam Institute for Climate Impact Research stated in 2014:

> One of the rationales behind 2° C was the AR4 [the IPCC's 2007 Fourth Report] assessment that above 1.9° C global warming we start running the risk of triggering the irreversible loss of the Greenland Ice Sheet, eventually leading to a global sea-level rise of 7 meters. In the 2014 AR5 [the IPCC's Fifth Report], this risk is reassessed to start already at 1° C global warming.[5]

Eric Rignot's 2014 study of the Amundson sea sector of the West Antarctic ice sheet describes this area's collapse as "unstoppable." This part of the West Antarctic ice sheet alone will raise sea levels one meter, but over a maximum two-hundred-year time frame, "its disappearance will likely trigger the collapse of the rest of the West Antarctic ice sheet, which comes with a sea level rise of between three and five meters. Such an event will displace millions of people worldwide." More recent studies have verified Rignot's untypical statement (for a scientist) that "the fuse is blown" in West Antarctica. The question is no longer *if* we will witness this scale of sea level rise barring a truly global and multifarious drawing down of actual atmospheric CO_2 on a decadal timeframe.[6]

Add to this the ongoing destabilization of the Greenland ice sheet—and the recently discovered vulnerability of the massive Totten Glacier in East Antarctica (once thought to be stable)[7]—and national boundaries in the foreseeable future will almost assuredly be changed with the likely inundation of most of humanity's great coastal cities. With current warming of .85° Celsius and other human abuses of the biosphere, species extinction rates are today likely well more than one thousand times higher than the background rate of extinction.[8] Substantially higher global temperatures, coupled with ongoing loss of habitat, pollution, population growth, and overconsumption of wildlife, may lead to a loss of 50 percent or more of Earth's flora and fauna this century.[9] Considering that the Earth required approximately ten million years to recover from five previous mass extinction events in the history of life on Earth, "the peak of destruction that humanity has initiated is often called the Sixth Extinction."[10]

In spite of the unknowns—or perhaps because of them—the insertion of a number (1.5) within a bracket into the Paris Agreement figures the unimaginable scale of the end of life as we know it.[11] The prospect of that— massive loss of biodiversity, astounding degradation of life itself—is placed in a parenthetical.[12] Even as any parenthetical text of the draft agreement signified points of major contestation, survival writ-large was contained in a bracket: 1.5° Celsius is the presently impossible ideal (survival with significant social and biological turmoil) for future temperature rises. This bracketed number was written-in into the Paris Agreement text at the last moment as a nod to the future and our present (limited) capacity for hope. The fact that 1.5° Celsius was even included at all was seen at the time as a radical move, if it is remembered that this agreement's language was approved by nearly two hundred countries. On one hand, this *is* a figure of hope because the solutions to our predicament are *known* and accessible (if not politically achievable). And yet, the fact that a figure for a stable and familiar world must be *slyly* inserted into a still contentious global agreement does not bode well for our civilization's long-term survival, whilst the scale of losses of all kinds on the slippery slope *up* the thermometer is simply unfathomable.

Allowing that scientific language describes the planet and the physical universe, survival figured as a parenthetical containing a number has an ironic way of making the planet disappear. This conclusion begins *here* with/in that parenthetical, docketed until the very end of the COP 21 climate talks, as it telescopes the inverted telos of an irreducibly humanized planet. We are planet Earth; but the planet itself, as (our) absolute alterity, is dislocated within brackets, an epistemograph that takes us to the edge of the inconceivable and (virtually) domesticates it (via calculus not "sign" of civil society qua sexual difference). Under the best of circumstances, this (doubly) inversionary teleology of the Anthropocene—domestic$\rightarrow$ calculus$\rightarrow$ planet$\rightarrow$ human—has led us to an aporetic curtain call for human civilization:[13] even though destroying our only means of self-preservation ought to be illogical *and* unnatural, we are forced to imagine an unimaginable world.

Although the planet's radical alterity cannot be grasped by any human paradigm of comprehension, we can turn to what Spivak terms "an aesthetic education." Conceiving (of) ourselves as a planetary accident stretches our availability to undergo *in some way* the experience of the impossible by enabling a cosmogonic peek at our not-quite-not-a-relation with radical alterity: "Planetary imaginings locate the imperative in a galactic and para-galactic alterity . . . that cannot be reasoned . . . as the self's mere negation" (*Aesthetic* 140–41). As this not-quite-not-a-relation with radical alterity is underived from identitarian systems, an effort to not just imagine but to grasp the unimaginable is asymptotic, for we are not isomorphic with the planet we live on.

Spivak's understanding of an "aesthetic education" is valuable because it trains us to imagine ourselves as a planetary accident. In her canonical essay, "Three Women's Texts and a Critique of Imperialism" (1985), she reads *Jane Eyre* (1847), *Wide Sargasso Sea* (1966), and *Frankenstein* (1818) to criticize nineteenth-century feminist individualism and the domestication of the imperial social mission. In this conclusion, we will also turn to three exemplary women's texts that stage an encounter with the inassimilable. By way of an exegetically created cosmogonic peek at our not-quite-not-a-relation with radical alterity, these women's texts show us *how* a world is (un)made by the ubiquitous business of making (a) human being(s). *Their* effortful figuration of the impossible may be paradigmatic for the imaginative labor required to understand planetarity as our ascension to nature and not our debasement.[14]

II. The Planetary Imperative:
Postcoloniality$\rightarrow$ Heterogeneity$\rightarrow$ Planet$\rightarrow$ Alterity

In the beginning, what we appreciate ("first of all" à la Shetty, Bellamy, and Spillers) is a founding gap, "*in* being human . . . *from* planetary discontinuity" (Spivak, *Aesthetic* 342). The galactic and para-galactic scale of the planetary scene grounds a planetary accident (vis-à-vis an exceptional human being) *in* being human, which hinders the arithmetic that underwrites effortless generalizability: colonial/postcolonial; colonizer/native; modernity/tradition; logic/rhetoric; and, individual/collective (*Death* 42, 81). An effortful figuration of an inviolate *limit*—that is, a going native that *un*plugs (our) cultural saturation—conveys and upholds a *substantive* being human, for if "we imagine ourselves . . . as planetary creatures . . . alterity remains underived from us . . . it contains us as much as it flings us away" (73).[15] Since radical alterity is neither continuous nor discontinuous from us, the perspective that comes *in* being human may validate a discursive shift that further expands Mother Right.[16]

Instead of cathecting globalization's system of exchange, a planetary accident follows its rhetorical logic (72, 61) to dislocate cultural origin: what emerges is a perpetual (re)opening of the future anterior, which empowers us to apprehend (our) utter contingency (88). Planetarity as the project of thinking ground is perforce a catachresis that invaginates the geo-graphy of finance capital because the planet's alterity is absolute—that is, wholly other. If Reason abjures the unbreachable to feign totality as being-together *au fond*, collectivity for a planetary accident is secured (or is perhaps a "gift") via a not-quite-not-a-relationship to radical alterity (*Aesthetic* 104, 109–11). The source of the planetary imperative is a vestibular timing and spacing that pre-views (our) cultural continuity: *in* being human, before "[then] 'humanistic' training in [now green] consumerism" ("Subaltern" 272), a metonymic instantiation of the same (we the planet), there is heterogeneity.

At the brink of the abyss, working "to re-imagine the subject as planetary accident" (*Aesthetic* 338), an aesthetic education non-coercively rearranges desires via opening up the future anterior—"again and again" (348). *That* scale of being human limns alterity ("the outer") as beyond creaturely dialectics (339), for we cross an aporia by entering another's (trace of) idiom at "ground level" (111). In other words, *experiencing* the unthinkable *scale* of loss in a humanized world is "coming as close as possible to accessing the other as the self" (113) to bring Reason to crisis for responsibility and reparation (104). An aesthetic education trains the imagination to supplement institutionally validated agency (postcoloniality, nation-state, liberal humanism, etc.) to espy *in some way* "life as pure immanence" (432). Exerting an almost gravitational force, coming upon *this* unrepeatable difference makes vividly tangible the inaccessible scale of suffering and loss refracted into a calculus by the COP 21 Paris Agreement. Part of singularity's power in the world involves its contravention of any sense of scale; even so, legitimizing a cosmogonic peek at our not-quite-not-a-relation with radical alterity is part of "an effortful project of developing something de-formed and de-constituted, fragmented into disjointed joinings, through a species of prayer to be haunted . . . the strengthening of the imagination to learn broadly" (201).

III. The Square Root of Minus One[17]

I am indebted of course to Spivak's analysis of that history of slavery and colonialism that also calls itself feminism. She reads feminist individualism, which operates on the registers of childbearing and soul-making, as an allegory *and* motor for the epistemic violence of imperialism ("Three Women's" 244–45). The mechanics of the production of Europe and its not-yet-human Other, and attendant metaphysics of presence ("the selfed Other . . . the Othered self"), contract the native's heterogeneity into Europe's self-consolidating Other (247, 250, 253). When Spivak's essay was published, we were still witnessing early days in postcolonial theory's institutionalization. That postcolonial migrants became native informants for globalization is part of this institutional history: "[T]he undoing of the colonizer/colonized binary by economic fact gives us the genealogy of globalization in its current manifestation, before postcolonialism or liberal multiculturalism began" (*Death* 53).

Following Spivak's critique of postcolonial reason—that is, of institutionally validated agency that appropriates and displaces decolonizing terrain and usurps postcoloniality *tout court*—I turn to three women's texts that cannot be accommodated in globalization's cultural alibis of multiculturalism and sustainable development. We *experience* what remains (un)mediated, (un)reconciled, and terribly alone, and that aesthetic education discloses collectivity via "the singular and the unverifiable" (*Aesthetic* 2). I suggest that these women's texts elucidate how we may understand ourselves as a planetary accident and not as the culmination of (*all* and *any*) life on Earth.

Bessie K.

Yale University's Fortunoff Video Archive of Holocaust Testimonies maintains a video of a woman named Bessie K. She speaks to the unseen, highly trained interviewer while her husband is a silent presence beside her. We as audience face her and her story directly. She describes the cattle trains and then the selections at Auschwitz:

> I didn't know what was happening actually. I saw them taking away the men separate, the children separate, and the women separate. So I had a baby. I took the coats . . . and I wrapped them around the baby. And I put it . . . on the left side. Because I saw

that the Germans were saying left to right. And I went through with the baby, but the baby was short of breath, so it started to choke and it started to cry. So the German called me back and he says, "What do you have there?" in German. // Now, I didn't know what to do, everything was so fast, happened so suddenly. I wasn't prepared for it. To look back, the experience[,] . . . I think I was numb or something happened to me. I don't know. I wasn't there even. And, um, he stretched out his arms, I should hand him over the bundle. I hand him over the bundle and this was the last time I had the bundle. // When I look back, I don't think I had anybody with me. I was alone. I was within my self. Since that time, I think all my life I've been, alone even when I met Jack. . . . I think to me, I was dead. . . . I didn't want to hear nothing, I didn't want to know nothing. . . . // In Stuttgart I found the doctor who operated on me, in the Ghetto. And they brought us in there and when she saw me there[,] . . . she was so happy to see me. Right away she said to me, "Where's the baby? What happened to the baby?" And right there, I said, "What baby?" I said to the doctor, "What baby?" I didn't have a baby. I don't know of any baby. That's what it did to me. (Laub 193)

In the video, there is a shift when her baby becomes "the bundle"; Bessie K.'s gaze unfixes itself from the interviewer and looks through him, the camera, us across time, and into the unlivable horror of her baby becoming a bundle that she no longer has.

The word "bundle" coalesces into a node, a singularity, wherein the scale of genocide concenters upon a baby in its mother's arms become a bundle in the hands of a Nazi. The baby is gone—*as if*, for Bessie K., she had forgotten it—or worse, forgotten it *as a baby*: "That is what *it* [all of it] did [to her]" (193). But the baby was there *as a baby* just beneath the surface of her memory. Something unwelcome lodges in us—a word: "bundle," at which point we experience what is utterly accessible and utterly beyond us. Bessie K. shapes genocide into a "bundle" containing a baby whose atrocious namelessness breaches particularity leaving a persistent and haunting presence.

Beloved

Beloved is a ghost story centered on the act of a mother slitting the throat of her nameless "crawling-already? girl" (Morrison 110) to protect her from slavery; it affirms the permeability of worlds: life/death, fiction/reality, human/animal, love/hate. But Sethe's memory, its non-narrative, non-linguistic disruptiveness, also becomes an actual force in the world. To her daughter Denver's delight, Sethe retells the story of Denver's incredible birth while on the run from Sweet Home. Sethe utters what Denver registers as "a truth for all time"—that "[a]nything dead coming back to life hurts" (42):

> "I was talking about time . . . Some things go. Pass on. Some things just stay. I used to think it was my rememory. . . . Some things you forget. Other things you never do. . . . Places, places are still there. If a house burns down, it's gone, but the place—the picture of it—stays . . . out there, in the world. What I remember is a picture floating around out there outside my head. I mean, even if I don't think it, even if I die, the picture . . . is still out there. Right in the place where it happened."
>
> "Can other people see it?" asked Denver.
>
> "Oh, yes. Oh yes, yes, yes. Someday you be walking down the road and you hear something or see something going on. So clear. And you think it's you thinking it up. A thought picture. But no. It's when you bump into a rememory that belongs to somebody else. Where I was before I came here, that place is real. It's never going away . . . and what's more, if you go there—you who never was there—if you go there and stand in the place where it was, it will happen again; it will be there for you, waiting for you. So, Denver, you can't never go there. Never. Because even though it's all over—over and done with—it's going to always be there waiting for you. That's how come I had to get all my children out. No matter what." (43–44)

Morrison figures the inconceivable, the cascade of horrors, and the domestic love story in this context, as a "place." But where is this "place"? Anywhere. If anywhere, where might this spot be? Here, of course.

What we picture is an incessant human stream flowing around, over, through, and past the perpetual, almost geologic presence of the terrible— that is, a rememory is powerful enough to exist outside of the mind at once inhabiting and being place. But it is the word "place" that turns Sweet Home from haunting specter to harrowing experience. Sweet Home breaches particularity; a change occurs, an incarnation of sorts, where a psychological interior ("what I did, or knew, or saw") enters the "real" world. There (anywhere and everywhere) it waits (for us). It does not fade with time. The ordinary quality of "place" stakes a claim about the scale of loss and suffering in a thoroughly human-determined world: slavery, another (yet the same) Anthropocene.[18] If you go there—to any "place"—it will be there, waiting for you.

Douloti

As Spivak points out, Douloti was bountiful. Bought for three hundred rupees (approximately five dollars), in thirteen years of being prostituted as a child by her pimp/husband/lord, she brought in a hundred thousand rupees and counting (*Outside* 88). In fact, in Mahasweta Devi's story, Paramananda Misra is known as the "son-in-law of the village" (*Imaginary* 47) because he saves fathers from bond-slavery by marrying their daughters. The name India qua nation-state dislocates the immense heterogeneity of decolonizing terrain, as does museumized culture in US multiculturalism (*Outside* 78–79). Devi's story, then, is about the inconceivable inhabitants of this dislocated place, which the transcoding/embedding of usurer-capital crosses (out).

Spivak reads Douloti as a figuration of "the impersonal indifference of the space of the woman-in-difference elsewhere" (83). When we go there, to these places (Bhilai, Bokoro, Jamshedpur, Palamu, Matangi, Jaggali, Mala-jangam, Mahar, Chamar, Nagesia, etc.), where the lines of mobility stop, we find that the woman's body bears the brunt of absolute desecration (82, 84). "Because of nothing, nothing, nothing," usurer-capital fabricates the *kamiyas* (or *seokia, haroaha, Gothi, halpati, jeetho, sagri, bhumidases, Nadapu*, etc., a not-quite-not-a-collectivity), who can miraculously turn one rupee into thousands (*Imaginary* 50, 47). This encroachment of capital—that is, the usurer's loan—is described as "the troops of blood-seeding" (48). Devi's story, therefore, stages a relay of disfiguring dislocations: body is land; land is map; map is dead, rotting flesh; Mother India *is* a dirty, *kamiya* whore, all used up, "by the thousands" (48).

But it is the word "bountiful" that allows us to imagine the unfathomable scale of caste-based exploitation; its utter perversity roils (now Global) India's Unity in Diversity. When Paramananda Misra visits Douloti's father, Crook Nagesia, he refers to himself as doing the work of Narayana. My almost-forgotten schoolgirl Sanskrit and pedestrian Hinduism translates Narayana as all-pervading God (also known as Vishnu). Paramananda says that he searches for a Goddess Laxmi to work by his side (46). Again, my pedestrian Hinduism registers Laxmi as Vishnu's consort and the goddess of wealth and prosperity. She is the goddess that we wait for on Diwali (keeping all household lights on), as we recreate the God Rama's (an avatar of Vishnu) and his wife Sita's (an avatar of Laxmi) return from exile. The Vishnu/Laxmi pairing turns into Rama/Sita; the Rama/Sita pairing turns into Paramananda/

Douloti; the Paramananda/Douloti pairing turns into Agri-capitalist-Proprietor-Collector-Railway Inspector-Regulator-Police Officer (that is, "someone called India" or "Gormen" [Government] [65, 72]) /*kamiya*-whore.

Douloti is the "last instance" (*Outside* 82) in *this* relay of bounty's blood-seeding (or genealogy of reincarnations), which is homologous to capital and its downward transcoding trajectory, and she *is* "elsewhere." She is dislocated into the shadows, an inverted transcendental goddess who is strictly speaking the origin of capital *in* India: consort to (her) Vishnu/whore to (her) pimp. No postcolonial feminist individualism is (to be) found here. As mentioned, her skeletal body is bountiful, but she is no goddess, only her (the goddess's) nadir. Laxmi bestows her prosperity from above in magnificent rays of light; Douloti bestows her prosperity (her initially extremely marketable/desirable virgin body) down below in Rampiyari's whorehouse.

A brutal rape is her entry into the circuitry of capital and nationhood. When she dies spread-eagled over a chalk-drawn map of India (a map I had to learn to draw in tenth grade for matriculation), her "body hollow with tuberculosis, the sores of venereal disease all over her frame, oozing evil-smelling pus" (*Imaginary* 92), she breaches particularity by bringing dualisms to crisis; she turns "India" inside out: light/shadow; health/disease; colonial/postcolonial; goddess/whore, etc. That bountiful body, a "tormented corpse, putrefied with venereal disease, having vomited up all the blood in its desiccated lungs" (94), a gift to the last, ought to be worshipped. To sum up, she made thousands and thousands and thousands from "nothing, nothing, nothing" (50). *She* is the capitalist's dream goddess.

IV. Staging the Failure of a Response

How do we archive extinction? Johan Rockstrom underscores that the Anthropocene "alters our worldview" as profoundly as the Copernican revolution (observation of the heliocentric solar system) or Darwinian evolution (4). But the "planetary stability our species has enjoyed for 11,700 years, that has allowed civilization to flourish, can no longer be relied upon" (5). According to Marco Lambertini, "Wildlife populations have already shown a concerning decline, on average by 58% since 1970 and are likely to reach 67% by the end of the decade" (6). Regarding the Holocene epoch, E.O. Wilson says: "Begun 11,700 years ago, when the latest of the continental glaciers began to retreat, it brought a milder climate and what may have been briefly the highest peak in numbers of species in the history of life" (*Half-Earth* 8). Wilson's book *Half-Earth* (2016), about the end of biodiversity and a last-ditch goal to alter the future, is itself a novel act of mourning, though one that eschews image for contact and conventions for facts.

Wilson's mourning—a kind of lamentation buttressed by clear-eyed knowledge and unsentimental reason—operates on two timeframes, an immediate now and a not-so-distant future. In a chapter called "Elegy for the Rhinos," Wilson lays out the grim reality of the five species of rhinos, whose overall numbers have plummeted from over a million to twenty-seven thousand in a hundred years, nearly all of whom are southern white rhinos (29). With six remaining northern white rhinos in zoos, this species is "functionally extinct" (29). The western black rhino is actually extinct, with no individuals even in captivity; the last four individuals in Cameroon died at the start of the new millennium, closing out "millions of years of evolutionary glory" (31). The Javan rhino is "the rarest large land mammal in the world" (31), with perhaps thirty-five individuals in a small park in Java. The Sumatran rhino is similarly imperiled. Yet, the statistics and exponential curve of the rhinos' disappearance due to poaching fail as an expression of mourning for Wilson. He recounts his personal contact with two of the last Sumatran rhinos at the Cincinnati Zoo: "Drawing close, I asked [the zoo director] if I could touch them. He nodded, and I did so, once each, quickly and softly, with the tips of my fingers. My feeling at that moment was spiritual and lasting, one I can't explain in words to you or to myself" (33). The evanescence of a touch remembered and described acknowledges that life is here now, but in an instant gone. The human is left alone at the edge of absence and silence.

In Louie Psihoyos's film *Racing Extinction* (2015), Dr. Christopher W. Clark of the Cornell Bioacoustics Research Program and the Macaulay Library at the Cornell Lab of Ornithology says: "As we listen more and more around different parts of the planet, whether it's [the] frozen Arctic Ocean or the deepest jungles of Central Africa, the whole world is singing, but we've stopped listening." The Cornell Bioacoustics lab is an archive of animal sounds recorded in various media since the 1930s. It preserves not just the traces of many now-gone creatures, but it enacts the moment of their disappearance into nothingness. Dr. Clark plays a recording of the last observed Kauai O'o, a songbird native to Hawaii. He emphasizes that these birds mated for life. This male should be singing a duet with his mate. Except that in the recording, whose sounds are also graphically transcribed on a computer screen, we hear and see the male's song and then silence. Dr. Clark says:

> That's the last male of a species singing for a female who will never come. He is totally alone and now his voice is gone. In the brief lifetime of this collection, seventy years or so, many of the

species that were recorded are now extinct, so the repository is a
living example of the massive rate of extinction that's happening.

At another point, he adds a common metaphor: "I compare the world's sounds
to a symphony. Little by little, one by one, the musical instruments—in this
case species—are being removed, driven to extinction. And then you end up
with . . . empty silence."

Stating the obvious, the call of the last Kauai O'o registers his unmitigated
solitude accompanied only by the immediacy of his species' extinction. On
hearing this perfectly normal, expectant, yet incomplete sound, we potentially
extend ourselves into the moment's poignancy; we just might experience
a foreshadowing of the Eremocene (or what E.O. Wilson calls the "Age of
Loneliness") on hearing the recorded presence of a solitary creature that is
gone. But, again, what does it take to make a connection? Sometimes it seems
that we register Nature only in its passing. To imaginatively extend ourselves
toward the last of its kind—now representative of the entire species—we need
to appreciate at once both the call out and the silence that answers unrelent-
ingly back. A further, final, example of this remarkable need for a physical
(tactile, acoustic, or sighted) engagement with presence—or the story of the
close call—to begin to register absence, though never the absolute absence
that is extinction, may be found in the work of Joel Sartore.

His Photo Ark project has photographed over six thousand animal
species and counting in sumptuous, black- or white-backed, high-resolution
studio photographs. The aim, he says, is to "document biodiversity, show
what's at stake, and to get people to care while there's still time."[19] This project,
in conjunction with National Geographic, starts with the recognition of loss
on a massive scale, immediate and threatened, but seeks principally to create an archive of "intimate portraits of an estimated 12,000 species of birds,
fish, mammals, reptiles, amphibians and invertebrates."[20] Upon completion,
Photo Ark "will serve as an important record of each animal's existence, and
a powerful testament to the importance of saving them." Such a mission is
not unlike the Encyclopedia of Life (eol.org) whose goal, as articulated by
E.O. Wilson, is to maintain an ever-expandable webpage for every species now
or recently existing on planet Earth, where, ultimately, everything we know
about the species might be stored or linked to in perpetuity. EOL is infor-
mational—but, of course, by representing biodiversity and its state of crisis, it
may also forward the project of preserving Nature against its disappearance.

Sartore's undertaking is as intimate as EOL is vast. It is in the intimacy
and immediacy of these living animals' portraits that we might come to know
our connection with them and life writ-large. As "a record of each animal's
existence," Photo Ark is not meant as an archive of memorials—Sartore's

subjects are very much alive, even if many or even most go extinct over the course of this century. The vitality and exultant beauty of these creatures is hardly mournful; each is presented at the same equal scale so a rhino fills the portrait as much a butterfly. Yet, Photo Ark may wind up serving as one of the most affecting testimonials to human destructiveness. When we look at these portraits of living animals, we see them in the familiar frame of portraiture and for a moment we are equals. Only then do we register the uncanny sense that we are seeing individuals *as individuals*—who are also representative of their kind. And, at that point, the aesthetic nature of these creatures, the beauty of their evolutionary wonder, begins to sift into our appreciation of these photographs. However, the fact of these animals' containment—for the moment of the photo—acts as a reminder that we dominate them completely. We control their existence. We can record this existence—and do something to ensure its continuity—or we can record existence against the white or black backdrop of the annihilation facing many or most of these beings. These photos have the ability to cut through sentiment, to move past understanding, to reach a level of connection (albeit momentarily) such that in the image we see at once Nature and ourselves.

As we are a planetary accident, we are at once an accident unto the planet. We are the meteor strike in every sense, except that we are fully aware of what we are doing. Despite our knowing of our actions, Nature's scale—and, hence, the scale of our triumph—entirely eludes us even now. While the Holocene's 11,700 years of remarkable climactic stability may very well have played a significant role in human communities around the world developing agriculture and civilization as we know it, the sixth extinction may be our supreme legacy, with the Anthropocene encircled as the moment when a single species for the first time in Earth's 4.5 billion-year history (and life's 3.8 billion-year history) has left a geologic trace in the planet's very crust.

While consideration is due to whether our legacy is in the radioactive global fallout of above-ground nuclear tests, the overloading of our atmosphere with CO_2, the acidification of the global ocean, the clotting of planetary waters and soils with plastic and other poisons—all being intrinsic to our nature—our final calling card may yet be in the ever vaster silence that contains and suffuses our racket and which will be apparent in the geologic record millions of years from now as the thoroughgoing end of the line for much of life.

While we are leaving our chemical traces in planetary geology, we are creating vast clearances in the future fossil record, testimony to the silence of absence. How are we to wrap our heads around extinction in all its senses? Clearly, its ultimate and infinite aspect defies our Paleolithic conceptual capacities. The scale of not just the extinction of potentially millions of species determined by the deaths of countless individual living entities, but the boundless loss of singularity itself, defined as the last creature before the abyss of its extermination as individual and kind, defies our sensate registration and analyses. Wilson cautions,

> We need a much deeper understanding . . . than the humanities and science have yet offered. We would be wise to find our way . . . out of the fever swamp of dogmatic religious belief and inept philosophical thought through which we still wander. Unless humanity learns a great deal more about global biodiversity and moves quickly to protect it, we will soon lose most of the species composing life on Earth. (*Half-Earth* 3)

Disentangling human beings from extinction and silence may be *that* separation from nature that is truly worthy of its proper name. After all, we are just a species.

Coda

As he said this, Socrates put his feet on the ground and remained in this position during the rest of the conversation.

—Plato, *Phaedo*

But hush, for I have lost the theme. . . .
A stricken rabbit is crying out
And its cry distracts my thought.

—William Butler Yeats, "Man and the Echo"

Death begins with the shoes . . .

—Primo Levi, *Survival in Auschwitz*

This book's naïve perspective attempts to tell the unfortunately neglected story of our subject matter. Inculcating our historical responsibility towards heterogeneity is precisely what is meant by postcoloniality. A proportional footstep becomes the placeholder for thinking on a human scale because our genealogical endeavors never begin anew; our attempts to understand are always part of a much older legacy. The boundaries over which we become "suicidally passionate" necessarily tread upon "craggy, boggy, overgrown, and overbuilt terrain" (Robinson 7, 12). With every step, we traverse "geologies, biologies, myths, histories, politics" (12). As Robinson states,

> Let the problem be symbolized by that of taking a single step as adequate to the ground it clears. . . . To forget these dimensions . . . is to forgo our honour as human beings, but an awareness of them equal to the involuted complexities under foot . . . [is] a crushing backload . . . to carry. Can such contradictions be

forged into a state of consciousness even fleetingly worthy of its
ground? (12)

The world insists (without insisting) that we tread lightly. As bearers of this
"ecological imperative" (12), we may reconcile what is silently underfoot with
the shock and awe of what is transiently up above from this impossible place
of un-dividedness.[1] To be this measure against the wastefulness that is a
forgetting of dimensions is to be a subject that matters.

Notes

Introduction

1. See for example the racism in Geoffrey Bennington's review, "Embarrassing Ourselves," *Los Angeles Review of Books*, March 20, 2016 (https://lareviewofbooks.org/article/embarrassing-ourselves/#).

2. See Dipesh Chakrabarty, "Postcolonial Studies and the Challenge of Climate Change," *New Literary History* 43, no. 1 (Winter 2012): 1–18; "The Climate of History: Four Theses," *Critical Inquiry* 35, no. 2 (Winter 2009): 197–222.

3. An intellectual experience begins "without the delusion that [one] already has possession of the matter to which the concept refers" (188). One recognizes the depth of the subject matter by breaking through existing circumstances. Speculation's freedom "goes beyond what it can legitimately cover" (189), its "open and unprotected nature . . . interpret[s] phenomena . . . unarmed" (193). Eliminating all qualitative features of the subject matter ensures the system's pyrrhic but "murderous success" (195). The subject's qualitative variety of experience of the object, of its particularity, beyond this object's definition as particular by the system's disavowed ideology, may lead to living in the world. To learn something, subjects recognize that "truth is shifting and fragile, thanks to its temporal substance" (199). To give witness to a "process of becoming [that] dwells in the object" (206) is to clear an apocryphal pathway for philosophers of the future. See "Appendix: Towards a Theory of Intellectual Experience" in *Lectures on Negative Dialectics* (183–210).

4. I would like to thank Reader A for the term "family resemblances."

5. As Jacqui Alexander and Chandra Mohanty recount,

> We both moved to the United States of North America over fifteen years ago. None of the racial, religious, or class/caste fractures we had previously experienced could have prepared us for th[is] painful terrain. . . . We were not born women of color, but became women of color here. From African-American and U.S. women of color, we learned the peculiar brand of U.S. North American racism. . . . [S]olidarity is necessary, even if that means grappling with the differences between oppositional and relational consciousness. (*Feminist Genealogies* xiv)

6. I became a US citizen in June 2017.

7. Spillers iterates, the "rabid fear and revulsion . . . this vicious epiphenomenon, which we have not yet understood . . . [is] a peculiar combination of passions that I would call 'racist' and 'sexist' only if I were caught in a fit of impatience" (*Black, White* xii).

8. See Spivak's, "The Setting to Work of Deconstruction" in *A Critique of Postcolonial Reason: A History of the Vanishing Present*, Cambridge, MA: Harvard University Press, 1999, 423–31.

9. See Rodolphe Gasché, *Europe, or the Infinite Task: A Study of a Philosophical Concept*, Stanford, CA: Stanford University Press, 2008.

10. Obviously, empirical analysis is one of the things feminism does best.

11. When discussing my dissertation, Sally Kitch and Mary Fonow state, "Our final exemplar . . . achieved what we consider epistemological and methodological success in perhaps the most difficult way possible. That is, the writer managed to use a single case study as significant evidence for addressing large questions essential to . . . knowledge production" (122). (See "Analyzing Women's Studies Dissertations: Methodologies, Epistemologies, and Field Formation," *SIGNS: Journal of Women in Culture and Society* 38, no. 1 [2012]: 99–126).

12. See, for example, Ania Loomba, "Dead Women Tell No Tales: Issues of Female Subjectivity, Subaltern Agency and Tradition in Colonial and Post-Colonial Writings on Widow Immolation in India," *History Workshop Journal: HWJ* 36 (Autumn 1993): 209–27; Benita Parry, "Problems in Current Theories of Colonial Discourse," *Oxford Literary Review* 9, issue 1, 27–58.

13. An excellent reading of this essay is Ritu Birla's "Postcolonial Studies: Now That's History" in *Can the Subaltern Speak?: Reflections on the History of an Idea*, edited by Rosalind C. Morris, 87–99, New York, NY: Columbia University Press, 2010.

14. This essay and its revised version in *A Critique of Postcolonial Reason* (1999) will be taken up again in chapters 3, 8, and 9.

15. Kumkum Sangari retorts:

> The disavowal of the objective and instrumental modalities of the social sciences occurs in the academies at a time when usable knowledge is gathered with growing certainty and control by Euro-America through advanced technologies of information retrieval from the rest of the world. . . . [T]he operations of neo-colonialism . . . continue to be confidently carried out abroad and . . . "return" as the crisis of meaning, representation, legitimation at home. ("Politics" 244)

16. See Spivak's discussion of Deleuze and Guattari's *Anti-Oedipus* (1972) in the "Philosophy" section of *A Critique of Postcolonial Reason* (1999), 1–111.

17. See also Sangeeta Ray's discussion of Spivak's interview in the chapter "Reading Singularity, Reading Difference: An Ethics of the Impossible" in *Gayatri Chakravorty Spivak: In Other Words*, Malden, MA: Wiley Blackwell, 2009, 67–106.

18. See also Spivak's "Translator's Preface," *Imaginary Maps*, Kolkata, India: Thema, 2001, xvii–xxvii.

19. I realize that using this poem may be clichéd but I would argue is culturally *a propos*. For example, the highly lauded series *Breaking Bad* has an episode titled "Ozymandias." Here is Bryan Cranston, who plays the lead character, reciting the poem: https://www.youtube.com/watch?v=T3dpghfRBHE.

20. For a superb analysis of immanence and transcendence see Susan Abraham's "The Pterodactyl in the Margins: Detranscendentalizing Postcolonial Theology" in *Planetary Loves: Spivak, Postcoloniality, and Theology*, edited by Stephen D. Moore and Maya Rivera, 79–101, New York, NY: Fordham University Press, 2011.

Chapter One

1. See Deepika Bahri, "Once More with Feeling: What Is Postcolonialism?," *Ariel* 26, no. 1 (1991): 51–82; Ann McClintock, "The Angel Of Progress: Pitfalls of the Term Post-Colonialism," *Social Text* 31 and 32 (Spring 1992): 84–98; Ella Shohat, "Notes on the 'Postcolonial,'" *Social Text* 31 and 32 (Spring 1992): 99–113; Arif Dirlik, *The Postcolonial Aura: Third World Criticism in the Age of Global Capitalism*, Boulder, CO: Westview Press, 1997.

2. Varadharajan reduces this historically specific object to the "radically other" (*Exotic* 81). In contrast, Adorno demonstrates how subjects posit radical sameness *as* radical otherness in their categorial performance because conceptual systems privilege their own perpetuation. Within totalizing and abstract systems, subjectivity is construed as totalizing and abstract.

3. Here, Varadharajan uses Adorno's criticism of Heidegger. As Heidegger's anti-Semitism and Nazism are indubitable, Varadharajan's use of this phrase while referring to Spivak seems gratuitous.

4. See Sara Suleri, "Woman Skin Deep: Feminism and the Postcolonial Condition," *Critical Inquiry* 18 (1992): 757–69.

5. Varadharajan appropriates and displaces other scholarly traditions, such as Latin-, Native-, and African-American, which are subsumed under the rubric of postcolonial criticism.

6. For examples of materialist criticisms of postcolonial theory, see Aijaz Ahmad, *In Theory: Classes, Nations, Literatures*, New York, NY: Verso, 1992; Benita Parry, "The Institutionalization of Postcolonial Studies" in *The Cambridge Companion to Postcolonial Literary Studies*, edited by Neil Lazarus, 66–80, New York, NY: Cambridge University Press, 2004.

7. Ganguly conducts no substantive engagement with other minority traditions.

8. Lazarus makes no mention of postcolonial theory's problematic relationship with Latin-, Native-, and African-American scholarly traditions.

9. See, for example, Edward Said, "Adorno as Lateness Itself" in *Adorno: A Critical Reader*, edited by Nigel Gibson and Andrew Rubin, 193–208, Hoboken, NJ: Blackwell, 2002.

10. Dallmayr excludes any indebtedness postcolonial theory might have to Latin-, Native-, and African-American scholarly traditions.

11. Whites were the beneficiaries of apartheid and its perpetrators, but the majority of those who participated in the Truth and Reconciliation Commission were black. See the documentary *Long Night's Journey into Day* (Iris Films, 2000).

12. Bahri asserts, the postcolonial text is "regarded as an efficient substitute for otherwise time-consuming investigations into history, politics, economics, et al" (*Native* 11).

13. According to Bahri, "Against the dominant notion of 'native intelligence' as minority and Third Word informancy stands the . . . aesthetic cognition of literature in its conflicted relation to the logic of what Marcuse conceives of as the world of work and power" (*Native* 7).

14. Bahri maintains, "The charge of . . . representation has come to rest increasingly on . . . postcolonial experience that is available through canonical literary postcoloniality" (*Native* 11). Hence, "it is the postmodern and the First World centric senses of migrancy and hybridity that tend to predominate in an understanding of the postcolonial" (175).

15. The postcolonial text is "castigated for failing to provide a revolutionary vision and a program for change while numerous examples of political and ecological activism in the postcolony scarcely register a meaningful presence in metropolitan discourse." At the same time, "certain sorts of postcolonial production remain unintelligible or discursively and otherwise incapable of being *dans le vrai*" (Bahri, *Native* 37).

16. Bahri suggests that "the aesthetic and semiotic field can and does overlap with political signification, but . . . [not] by transparence or equivalence" (*Native* 12).

17. These played out roles seem to be why I believe Adorno has never quite been forgiven for his treatment of jazz, as this moment continues to be seized upon. Regardless, the uncanny familiarity of his critiques of modernity and the role of art is recognized. See, for example: Robert W. Witkin, "Why did Adorno 'Hate' Jazz?," *Sociological Theory* 18, no. 1 (March 2000): 145–70; William P. Nye, "Theodor Adorno on Jazz: A Critique of Critical Theory," *Popular Music and Society* 12, issue 4 (Winter 1988): 69–73; J. Bradford Robinson, "The Jazz Essays of Theodor Adorno: Some Thoughts on Jazz Reception in Weimar Germany," *Popular Music* 13, no. 1 (January 1994): 1–25; Carol Hamilton, "All That Jazz Again: Adorno's Sociology of Music," *Popular Music and Society* 15, no. 3 (Fall 1991): 31–40; Evelyn Wilcock, "Adorno, Jazz, and Racism: 'Über Jazz' and the 1934–7 British Jazz Debate," *Telos* 107 (Spring 1996): 63–80.

Chapter Two

1. I take to heart Kwame Anthony Appiah's call for space clearing gestures in "Is the Post- in Postmodernism the Post- in Postcolonial?," *Critical Inquiry* 17, no. 2 (Winter 1991): 336–57. See also Amy Allen, *The End of Progress: Decolonizing the Normative Foundations of Critical Theory*, New York, NY: Columbia University Press, 2016.

2. Varadharajan aptly depicts this substitution of rhetoric for meaningful understanding of reality:

The very process that exposes the illusory mastery of the subject fore-closes upon the resistance of the object. If the subject is always already discontinuous with itself and its identity only a necessary illusion, is the power exerted in the name of that fiction of identity and mastery equally illusory? If the subject was never whole and undivided, was the object never powerless, traduced, and excluded? Whom shall the object hold accountable for its suffering? The displacement of the subject can all too easily become a convenient ploy to withhold subjectivity from those for whom it has never been anything but an illusion. (*Exotic* 20)

3. Adorno establishes,

[T]he depravation of theory could not have happened, had there been no apocryphal dregs in it. In their summary treatment of culture, from the outside, the functionaries who monopolize [theory] would clumsily feign superiority to culture, thereby rendering aid to universal regres-sion. Those whose expectations of imminent revolution made them wish to liquidate philosophy were impatient enough with its demands to lag behind philosophy even then. The apocryphal part of materialism reveals the one of high philosophy, the untruth of sovereignty of the spirit which the reigning materialism disdains as cynically bourgeois society used to do in secret. Idealistic majesty is the apocryphal imprint. (*Negative* 204)

4. Adorno states,

By itself, the logically abstract form of "something," something that is meant or judged, does not claim to posit a being; and yet, surviving in it—indelible for a thinking that would delete it—is that which is not identical with thinking, which is not thinking at all. The *ratio* becomes irrational where it forgets this, where it runs counter to the meaning of thought by hypostasizing its products, the abstractions. The commandment of its autarky condemns thinking to emptiness, and finally to stupidity and primitivity. (*Negative* 34)

5. Ron Suskind reports, in "Without a Doubt," *New York Times Magazine*, Sun-day, October 17, 2004, that a Republican aide, when questioned about what he meant by his opposition to "the reality-based community" comprised of people who "believe that solutions emerge from . . . judicious study of discernible reality," responded by saying, "That's not the way the world really works anymore. . . . We're an empire now, and when we act, we create our own reality." As the library and museum in Baghdad burned, Donald Rumsfeld declared: "Stuff happens" (Sean Loughlin, April 13, 2003, www.cnn.com). See also Edward Said's analysis of the invasion of Iraq (*Culture* 282–336).

6. Adorno observes,

In a world which, permeated through and through with the structures of social order, is so heavily weighted against all individualistic tendencies that the individual has little other choice but to accept them for what they are, naïvety continually grows apace and takes on sinister connotations. What is forced upon the individual by an all-pervasive apparatus of his own construction, and in the toils of which he is held enmeshed, to the virtual exclusion of all spontaneous impulse, becomes natural to him. The reified consciousness is entirely naïve, and yet it has also lost its naïvety completely. The task before philosophy is to break up the seemingly obvious and the apparently incomprehensible. ("Why Philosophy?" 48)

7. According to Adorno, the

invariants, whose own invariance has been produced, cannot be peeled out of the variables as if all the truth were at hand, then. Truth has coalesced with substance, which will change; immutability of truth is the delusion of *prima philosophia*. The invariants are not identically resolved in the dynamics of history and of consciousness, but they are moments in that dynamics; stabilized as transcendence, they become ideology. . . . Ideology lies in the substruction of something primary, the content of which hardly matters; it lies in the implicit identity of concept and thing, an identity justified by the world even when a doctrine summarily teaches that consciousness depends on being. (*Negative* 40)

8. I refer to Czeslaw Milosz's poem, "It looks as if *that*, ready, formed in every detail, waited nearby, at a hand's stretching, and had I caught it, I would not have drawn the thing out of nothingness all around, but taken, as if from a shelf, an object already existing" ("That" 51).

9. In his opening salvo, Adorno contends,

Having broken its pledge to be as one with reality or at the point of realization, philosophy is obliged ruthlessly to criticize itself. . . . The introverted thought architect dwells behind the moon that is taken over by extroverted technicians. . . . The discrepancy (decayed into commonplace) between power and any sort of spirit has grown so vast as to foil whatever attempts to understand the preponderance might be inspired by the spirit's own concept. The will to this understanding bespeaks a power claim denied by that which is to be understood. (*Negative* 3–4)

10. One could be tempted to think of negative dialectics as a genealogy (see, for example, Nietzsche's *Ecce Homo*), or as what Foucault later terms "marginalized and subjugated knowledges." Neither Nietzsche nor Foucault centralize the imagination as the most critical activity of genealogy, and, as this book argues, for bearing witness to the contemporaneous sense of nonidentity and difference, "stalled in the pre-articulate"

(to use Seamus Heaney's phrase). Negative dialectics entails an incapacitation. As an imaginative exercise, it turns the familiar into the obscure. Difference rushes forth whilst also leading back to what will (always) have been.

11. Adorno affirms, "In truth, all concepts, even the philosophical ones, refer to nonconceptualities, because concepts on their part are moments of the reality that requires their formation, primarily for the control of nature" (*Negative* 11). Furthermore,

> In Marx the principle of *domination of nature* is actually accepted quite naïvely. According to the Marxian way of seeing, there is something of a change in the relations of domination between people—they are supposed to come to an end, that is, domination should disappear—but the unconditional domination of nature by human beings is not affected by this, so that we might say that the image of a classless society in Marx has something of the quality of a gigantic joint-stock company for the exploitation of nature. . . . The fact that, to Marx, the labour performed by animals does not lead to the production of surplus value—even though the costs of reproduction are lower in animals than the time or energy expended—the fact that . . . their labour produces no surplus value is merely the crassest symbol of this. . . . If there is only *one* truth, it is not possible to criticize radically the principle of domination on the one hand, while unreservedly acquiescing in it in an undialectical manner on the other. . . . [F]or a seriously liberated vision of society . . . the relationship to the domination of nature has to be changed if it is not constantly to reproduce itself in the internal forms of society. (*Lectures* 58–59)

12. As per Adorno,

> The system . . . has its primal history in the pre-mental, the animal life of the species. Predators get hungry, but pouncing on their prey is difficult and often dangerous; additional impulses may be needed for the beast to dare it. These impulses and the unpleasantness of hunger fuse into rage at the victim, a rage whose expression in turn serves the end of frightening and paralyzing the victim. In the advance of humanity this is rationalized by projection. . . . The more completely his actions follow the law of self-preservation, the less can he admit the primacy of that law to himself and to others; if he did, his laboriously attained status of a *zoon politikon* would lose all credibility. (*Negative* 22–23)

13. Adorno uses the term "inescapably and fatefully" to describe how "contradictoriness" moves through the system as though a force of nature or a Greek tragedy (*Negative* 6).

14. Adorno emphasizes how the principle of identity is not (merely) a cogitative law but real. He remarks,

The alleged social relativity of views obeys the objective law of social production under private ownership of the means of production. Bourgeois
skepticism, of which relativism is the doctrinal embodiment, is obtuse.
But the perennial anti-intellectualism is more than an anthropological
trait of bourgeois subjectivity. It is due to the fact that under the existing
conditions of production the concept of reason, once emancipated, must
fear that its consistent pursuit will explode those conditions. That is why
reason limits itself; throughout the bourgeois era, this spirit's accompanying reaction to the idea of its autonomy has been to despise itself. The
spirit cannot forgive itself for being barred, by the constitution of the
existence it guides, from unfolding the freedom inherent in its concept.
The philosophical term for this prohibition is relativism. (*Negative* 37)

15. Adorno states,

Without concepts, that experience would lack continuity. By definition, the part it takes in the discursive medium makes it always more
than purely individual. The individual becomes a subject insofar as its
individual consciousness objectifies it, in the unity of the self as well as
in the unity of its experiences; to animals, presumably, both unities are
denied. Because it is general in itself, and to the extent to which it is
general, individual experience goes as far as the universal. (*Negative* 46)

16. Adorno advises,

Dialectics alone might settle the Greek argument whether like is known
by like or by unlike. If the thesis that likeness alone has that capacity
makes us aware of the indelible mimetic element in all cognition and all
human practice, this awareness grows untrue when the affinity—indelible,
yet infinitely far removed at the same time—is posited as positive. In
epistemology the inevitable result is the false conclusion that the object
is the subject. Traditional philosophy believes that it knows the unlike
by likening it to itself, while in so doing it really knows itself only. The
idea of a changed philosophy would be to become aware of likeness by
defining it as that which is unlike itself. (*Negative* 150)

17. As Michel Foucault has also privileged the "historical dimension" in his
analyses (see, for example, *Society Must Be Defended*, 43–64, 55, 170), his criticism
of the Frankfurt School is important to invoke. Foucault acknowledges that Frankfurt
School theorists made similar statements earlier than his own work and ought to be
studied for the domination that results from reason itself and the effects of power as
they relate to a particular rationality. In fact, he underlines that had he encountered
them earlier perhaps he would have devoted himself to commenting on their work
entirely. Yet, their conception of the subject seems traditionally philosophical to Foucault

as it emerged from Marxist humanism (*Power* 273–74). Foucault goes on to characterize their work as the recuperation of a lost identity, to detect an essential truth, or to release our captive nature. But, the task is to do something completely different: "we need to produce something that doesn't exist yet, without being able to know what it will be" (275). His quest for "total innovation" (275) differs from what he considers the Frankfurt School's metaphysical impulse that sought to undo alienation from our "fundamental essence" (275). Unlike Foucault's own historical-genealogical emphasis, Frankfurt School theorists "weren't doing much history in the full sense." In fact, "they are eaters of history as others have prepared it . . . [because] they consider that the work of the professional historian supplies them with a sort of material foundation that can explain phenomena of a different type which they have called 'sociological' or 'psychological' phenomena" (276). While Foucault's criticism is fair enough, one could counter that Adorno seems to understand metaphysics as historicity, which is itself quite unlike a prepackaged view of history.

18. Adorno reveals,

> The constellation illuminates the specific side of the object, the side which to a classifying procedure is either a matter of indifference or a burden. The model for this is the conduct of language. Language offers no mere system of signs for cognitive functions. Where it appears essentially as a language, where it becomes a form of representation, it will not define its concepts. It lends objectivity to them by the relation into which it puts the concepts, centered about a thing. Language serves the intention of the concept to express completely what it means. . . . By gathering around the object of cognition, the concepts potentially determine the object's interior. (*Negative* 162)

19. See also *Negative*, 42, 47, 158, 180, 207.

20. By negativity, Adorno refers to the critical force unleashed through self-reflection, which moves beyond derivativeness:

> In itself, and prior to every particular content, thought is negation, resistance to whatever imposes itself. . . . If nowadays ideology more than ever encourages thought towards the positive, it nevertheless astutely registers the fact that thought runs counter to positivity. . . . The effort implicit in the concept of thought . . . is itself this very negativity, a revolt against any demand that it should defer passively to every immediate. . . . The forms of thought aspire to more than what merely exists. (*Lectures* 191)

21. This kind of approach does not preclude yoking heterogeneity to worldliness. Edward Said's concept of worldliness refers to the specific material context of the text or critic, which determine the textuality of the text. The text is not an autarkic object insulated from the world as a world in itself: "[T]exts have ways of existing that even

in their most rarefied form are always enmeshed in circumstance, time, place, and society—in short, they are in the world, and hence worldly" (*World, Text* 35). Worldliness as the material anchoring of the text delves deeper *into* the text. Exegetical labor as generating an apocryphal genealogy delves deeper *out* of a text. Worldliness moves towards the text; exegesis moves towards reality.

22. Adorno explains,

> The subjective preconception of the material production process in society—basically different from its theoretical constitution—is the unresolved part, the part unreconciled with the subjects. Their own reason, unconscious like the transcendental subject and establishing identity by barter, remains incommensurable with the subjects it reduces to the same denominator: the subject as the subject's foe. The preceding generality is both true and untrue: true, because it forms that "ether" which Hegel calls spirit; untrue, because its reason is no reason yet, because its universality is the product of particular interests. This is why a philosophical critique of identity transcends philosophy. But the ineffable part of the utopia is that what defies subsumption under identity—the "use value," in Marxist terminology—is necessary anyway if life is to go on at all, even under the prevailing circumstances of production. The utopia extends to the sworn enemies of its realization. Regarding the concrete utopian possibility, *dialectics is the ontology of the wrong state of things.* The right state of things would be free of it: *neither a system nor a contradiction.* (*Negative* 10–11, emphases added)

Chapter Three

1. Spivak's previous discussion of the Rani of Sirmur was published in the "Rani of Sirmur: An Essay in Reading the Archives," *History and Theory* 24, no. 3 (October 1985): 247–72.

2. In traditional anthropology, the native informant is "a figure who, in ethnography, can only provide data . . . [or] can only be read, by definition, for the production of definitive descriptions" (Spivak, *Critique* 49). Spivak transforms this "impossible (because historically and discursively discontinuous) perspective" into an interruptive *reader's* perspective (33, 67), which requires tracking a perspective "lost" to the archive. This impossible counter-narrative provides the conditions of possibility for the difference of the present from itself.

3. When discussing Kant, Spivak states,

> The possibility of the production of the native informant by way of the colonial/postcolonial route . . . is lodged in the fact that, for the real needs of imperialism, the in-choate in-fans ab-original para-subject cannot be theorized as functionally *completely* frozen in a world where teleology is schematized into geo-graphy (writing the world). This limited

access to being-human is the itinerary of the native informant into the post-colonial, which remains unrecognized through the various transformations of the discussions of both ethics and ethnicity. Thanks to this sanctioned inattention, the philosopher's duty, articulated in its place, seems to apply to all men, in the interest of being able to presuppose equality: it is the philosopher's duty to help men turn the fearful abyss of Nature the mother into the sublime, through reason, with the use of the assumption of God the father (though with no cognizable ground of his presence)—to resolve practically the contradiction between what *can* be known and what *must* be thought. (*Critique* 30)

I will return to Spivak's concern with the itinerary of "being-human" and the "philosopher's duty" in the conclusion.

4. Spivak stresses,

In financialization, however, women's micro-enterprise—credit-baiting without infra-structural involvement—opens the poorest women into direct commercial exploitation by the international commercial sector through the alliances between Women's World Banking and unexamined universalist feminism. We cannot . . . notice only the exacerbation of wage labor as the result of globalization. The credit-baiting can be offered as a "solution." The exacerbation of wage labor for women—the feminization of labor—happened as capital was on the way to globalization through the computerization of stock exchanges and postfordist homeworking, and so-called free trade initiatives. World trade is now the second in command of the full financialization of the globe. (*Critique* 220)

5. All of the archival sources Spivak cites are at the India Office Library in London (see *Critique* 211, note 26).

6. As I read Spivak's text, I add more details in my mind's eye. "Dark" and "Golden" are my romantic figurations.

7. Spivak is quoting Birch (*Critique* 213; Spivak also cites an extract from Bengal Secret Consultations [n.d.], Board's Collections, 1819–1820 [see Spivak's note 29]).

8. Spivak refers to Bengal Secret Correspondence, September 27, 1815 (see Spivak's note 30).

9. Spivak provides the deleted passage authored by the court of directors but removed by the board of control of the Company (*Critique* 215–16, second parenthetical insertion mine; note 32: Draft Military Bengal, December 18, 1819, Dispatches to Bengal 82, collections 13, 990–14,004).

10. Spivak accentuates this moment,

Continuing our Freudian or wild-psychoanalytical fantasy, we see here something approaching the plan to produce the image of the European Master as a (paranoid schizophrenic) super-ego—a fearful figure where desire and the law must coincide: our desire is your law if you govern in our name, even before that desire has been articulated as a law to be obeyed. (*Critique* 216–17)

11. Spivak is citing from Bengal Secret Correspondence, August 2, 1815 (*Critique* 225, note 48).

12. Spivak refers to Edward Thompson's influential colonial account, *Suttee: A Historical and Philosophical Enquiry into the Hindu Rite of Widow-Burning*, 132.

13. Letter from Birch to Metcalfe, which was included in Metcalfe to Adam, March 5, 1816 in Board's Collections, 1819–1820, extract from Bengal Secret Consultations (*Critique* 204, note 64).

14. This staid impermeability is what Marlowe calls "The Idea" (Conrad 7).

15. Letter from Birch to Metcalfe, which was included in Metcalfe to Adam, March 5, 1816, in Board's Collections, 1819–1820, extract from Bengal Secret Consultations (*Critique* 234).

16. Although this takes me beyond my expertise, I will note that Spivak models this sentence on Freud's "a child is being beaten" and provides a clue to her auto-critique because the analysand who produces this sentence is a narcissist.

17. Colonial subjects who colluded with British manipulation of India's Vedic past to concoct a singular Hindu tradition, as found in the *Rg-Veda* and the *Dharmasastra*, were granted "honorary whiteness." As a result of this not-quite-not-a-collaboration with colonial subjects regarding the widow's plight, the British abolished *sati* in 1829 (*Critique* 284–86).

18. Spivak notes,

The word in the various Indian languages is "the burning of the *sati*" or the good wife, who escapes the regressive stasis of the widow in *brahmacarya*. This exemplifies the race-class-gender overdeterminations of the situation. It can perhaps be caught even when it is flattened out: white men, seeking to save brown women from brown men, imposed upon those women a greater ideological construction by absolutely identifying, within discursive practice, good-wifehood and self-immolation on the husband's pyre by an ignorant (but sanctioned) synecdoche. (*Critique* 303)

19. Spivak avers,

Between patriarchy and imperialism, subject-constitution and object-formation, the figure of the woman disappears, not into a pristine nothingness, but into a violent shuttling that is the displaced figuration of the "third world woman" caught between tradition and modernization, culturalism and development. . . . The case of *suttee* as exemplum of the woman-in-imperialism would challenge and deconstruct this opposition between subject (law) and object of knowledge (repression) and mark the place of "disappearance" with something other than silence and nonexistence, a violent aporia between subject and object status. (*Critique* 304)

20. The subaltern as the proper name for woman (and, hence, feminism) and subaltern space as the proper name for decolonization (and, hence, history) has two specific outcomes: the postcolonial can no longer be conflated with the native migrant seeking class advancement in the metropolis, and the problem of subject-constitution cannot be separated from the international division of labor. In this way, "what had seemed the historical predicament of the colonial subaltern can be made to become the allegory of the predicament of *all* thought, *all* deliberative consciousness, though the élite profess otherwise" (*Other* 204).

21. Spivak discusses persuasion in her section on Hegel and the *Shrimadbhaga-vadgita*. The Lord Krishna in the guise of Arjuna's friend and charioteer persuades Arjuna to kill his kin by revealing himself as Law since seeing is believing (Arjuna makes the errant request of self-revelation to Krishna). Krishna indulges Arjuna and, by revealing Himself "as containing the universe" (*Critique* 55), encourages him to perform his duty as a *Kshatriya*. As Law, Krishna is killing his kin not Arjuna. Friendship as obligation/indulgence constructs through persuasion a Hindu-Aryan myth whereby killing becomes the metonym of action as such: there is no killing; I (Krishna) am killing, you (Arjuna) are not. It is written (38, 50–56).

22. Spivak provides the text of the complete letter dated May 22, 1815 from Adam to Metcalfe. An excerpt reads:

> While, therefore, the Governor General in Council cannot direct any authoritative or compulsory interference in this case, His Lordship in Council is ardently desirous, that every means of influence and persuasion should be employed to induce the Ranee [*sic*] to foregoe [*sic*] her supposed determination. His Lordship in Council is induced to hope, that the circumstance of her being actually engaged in the administration of the Government of her Son[,] . . . together with the actual *separation of interests* which must now be deemed to subsist between her and her husband, may if explained and represented with suitable skill and address to the Pundits and Brahmins whose authority is likely to sway the Ranee's [*sic*] opinion, lead to such a declaration on their part as would satisfy her mind and lead her to adopt a different resolution. . . . The Governor General in Council authorizes Captain Birch to refuse to convey any message from Kurrem Perkash [*sic*] [her husband] to the Ranee [*sic*] [to the effect that she should accompany him to a more distant place of banishment], and to signify to him as well as to the Ranee [*sic*] herself . . . that the paramount duty of watching over the interests of the minor Rajah and his subjects must supersede any obligation of duty toward her husband which under other circumstances might render her complying with his wishes expedient and proper. (*Critique* 236–37)

Chapter Four

1. Simone de Beauvoir argues, "Enough ink has been spilt in quarreling over feminism, and for the time being the matter is closed. But still it is talked about, although it seems that the voluminous nonsense uttered during this century has done little to clarify the problem. After all, is there a problem? And if so, what is it? Are there women, really?" (*The Second Sex* vii). The contributions and achievements of black women's writing and criticism contradict its invisibility.

2. R. Radhakrishnan's "Ethnic Identity and Post-Structuralist Difference" appears in the same issue of *Cultural Critique* and discusses the larger debate on Derrida and politics (199–220).

3. It must be recorded that in fact Christian does not disarticulate social existence (alienation) from real struggle (discursive and material).

4. See Robert Edgar, *Sanctioning Apartheid*, Trenton, NJ: Africa World, 1990; Pauline Baker, *The United States and South Africa: The Reagan Years*, Ford Foundation, 1989; Stephen Ellis and Sechaba Tsepo, *Comrades against Apartheid: The ANC and the South African Communist Party in Exile*, Bloomington: Indiana University Press, 1992.

5. See Audre Lorde, "Apartheid U.S.A," *Freedom Organizing Series* 2, Latham, NY: Kitchen Table: Women of Color, 1986; George M. Fredrickson, "African Americans and African Africans," *New York Review of Books*, September 26, 1991.

6. DuCille refers to the "gap between [a] stated wish to avoid appropriating and objectifying the work and images of African American women . . . and the degree to which [the] text fosters rather than avoids such appropriations" ("Occult" 620).

7. Awkward reads both Barbara Christian and African-American feminist literary critic Barbara Smith in this essay. In particular, he reads Smith's "Toward a Black Feminist Criticism" (1978).

8. Audre Lorde cautions, "For the master's tools will never dismantle the master's house. They may allow us to temporarily beat him at his own game, but they will never enable us to bring about genuine change" (*Sister/Outsider* 112).

9. See *All the Women Are White, All the Men Are Black, But Some of Us Are Brave: Black Women's Studies*, edited by Gloria T. Hull, Patricia Bell-Scott, and Barbara Smith, New York, NY: City University of New York Press, 1982; Evelyn Hammond, "Black (W)holes and the Geometry of Black Female Sexuality," *Differences* 6, issue 2–3 (1995): 126–45.

10. At the White House Correspondent's dinner, Conan O'Brian did a wonderful segment on Paul Ryan blaming Barack Obama's second term on "urban" voters. Apparently, in Ryan's opinion, minorities voted for Obama whereas Americans voted for Mitt Romney. When Conan is asked how he likes his coffee, he responded, "no milk, no sugar, just urban" (April 27, 2013) (http://abcnews.go.com/Politics/video/conan-obrien-compares-correspondents-dinner-school-cafeteria-19059465).

11. Carby also points to segregation in the public-school system (14), which is modeled after post-apartheid South Africa.

12. As Spivak points out, "It is perhaps because there is a semi- or relative autonomy to the discursivity of cultural explanations that it can recode the abstract in

general; and the transnational dominant can write 'everything in *our* social life,' and theirs, as 'cultural.' For us, the dominant culture; for them, heterogeneity and cultural relativism" (*Critique* 315–16). A counter "political practice for the intellectual would be to put the economic 'under erasure,' to see the economic factor as irreducible as it reinscribes the social text, even as it is erased, imperfectly, when it claims to be the final determinant or the transcendental signified" (266).

13. I will attempt such a recoding and production of unity though an alternative citation of black women's writing and criticism at the end of chapter 5.

14. For Spivak, transnational literacy is not like having disciplinary expertise, but involves a larger "sense of the political, economic, and cultural position of the various national origin places in the financialization of the globe" ("Talk" 295). It "keeps the abstract, the economic, visible under erasure. Yet it cannot afford to ignore the irreducible heterogeneity of the cultural in the name of a 'cultural dominant' simply because it is dominant" (*Critique* 315). See also "Crossing Borders" in *Death of a Discipline*, 1–25.

15. Here, I deploy Spivak's objection to the "uncritical assumption . . . that the collective subject is isomorphic with social structures of cultural explanation" ("Love, Cruelty" 4).

16. Spivak is discussing Foucault and changes "discourse" to "culture" (*Critique* 356).

17. See bell hooks, "Dialectically Down with the Critical Program," in *Black Popular Culture: A Project by Michele Wallace*, edited by Gina Dent, 48–55, New York, NY: Bay Press, 1992.

18. Angela P. Harris criticizes mainstream feminism's "nuance theory": "Nuance Theory . . . assumes the commonality of all women—differences are a matter of 'context' or 'magnitude,' that is, 'nuance.'" An additive example-of-the-same-only-worse approach prevents complex analyses of socio-cultural structures and erases important strategies of resistance. Women of color are "bleached" into being "white women, only more so." Thus, "'black' is an intensifier: If things are bad for everybody (meaning white women), then they're even worse for black women. Silent and suffering, we are trotted onto the page (mostly in footnotes) as the ultimate example of how bad things are" ("Essentialism" 244–45).

19. Spivak examines how rejecting neocolonialism as the condition of possibility for Euro/US-centric migration further obscures postmodernity as facilitating the passage from modern colonialism to postmodern neocolonialism, as if postmodernity has "a kind of built-in critical moment." Postcolonial migrancy is a part of postmodern neocolonialism: if "colonialism was modernization/ism," then "postcolonialism is resistance to postmodernism; *or*, the 'true' postmodernism; now, only the postmodern postcolonialist is the triumphant self-declared hybrid" (*Critique* 361).

20. As Ann DuCille wryly comments, "The privileged white person inherits a wisdom, an agelessness, perhaps even a racelessness that entitles him or her to the raw materials of another's life and culture but, of course, not to the Other's condition" ("Occult" 615).

21. Similarly, Spivak argues against an approach that designates an already identified (new) object of inquiry for the purpose of accrediting and certifying universities

(*Outside* 55–56). Because conceptual cultures inhibit substantive criticism to control how they are represented, Spivak prioritizes heterogeneity (*Other* 114).

22. And *here* we see where both Christian and Spivak end up in their anguish: if the "exclusivist ruses of theory reflect a symptom and have a history," then one tries to locate the "absolute limit of the place where history is narrativized into logic" (*Other* 113, 207).

23. Christian identifies the constitution of a *topos*—that is, what Michel Foucault terms an "epistemological field" (*The Order* xx–xxii)—which creates historical plausible deniability via the inaugurated antagonistic difference of major and minor.

24. In conducting this examination of JanMohamed and Lloyd's Introduction, I draw a parallel between Christian's relegation to the pre-political (or political *plus*) and Spivak's analysis of the New Subaltern. I realize that the comparison is geopolitically spurious. But, I mark a possibility for undermining the antagonisms between African-American and postcolonial feminisms. Like Spivak, Christian centers the actual direction of the flow of ideas: major to minor. I suggest that black women scholars occupy an analogous position with the New Subaltern. The New Subaltern appropriates and displaces economic citizenship by rupturing narrative continuity in the logic/story of globalization (Spivak, *Critique* 69, note 86). In the active pursuit of the New Subaltern, the new intellectual capital agreements of the GATT are patenting the traditional knowledge of Southern indigenous and rural peoples. This patented knowledge is then sold back to these communities. No attempt is made to learn from below the "biorhythms that persistently deconstruct the opposition between human and natural" (383) because extracting surplus value is presented as a valuation of local cultural dynamism (*Other* 96).

Chapter Five

1. I focus exclusively on scholars of Indian origin of which I was one at that time.

2. See "Lyndon B. Johnson: Special Message to the Congress on Immigration," available at http://www.presidency.ucsb.edu/ws/index.php?pid=26830; Jennifer Ludden, "1965 Immigration Law Changed the Face of America," May 9, 2006 (http://www.npr.org/templates/story/story.php?storyId=5391395); "Poor Countries' Brain Drain," *The Economist*, November 3, 2005.

3. See Jasbir K. Puar and Amit S. Rai, "The Remaking of a Model Minority: Perverse Projectiles Under the Threat of (Counter) Terrorism," *Social Text* 80, 22, no. 3 (Fall 2004): 75–104.

4. With neocolonial migrancy as one of its constitutive conditions, the presuppositions that ground postcolonial discourse are "metropolitan." This is the constituency it represents and serves. Even though such discourse's "language skills are rudimentary," it is "full of subcultural affect" (Spivak, "New Subaltern" 331).

5. See Arif Dirlik's "The Postcolonial Aura: Third World Criticism in the Age of Global Capitalism," *Critical Inquiry* 20 (Winter 1994): 328–56.

6. Lata Mani (discussed in chapter 8) published her essay in the second special issue of *Cultural Critique*. See "Contentious Traditions: The Debate on Sati in

Colonial India," *Cultural Critique*, The Nature and Context of Minority Discourse 2, no. 7 (Autumn 1987): 119–56.

7. Patricia Hill Collins, like Christian, counters the rendition of black feminist thought as experiential knowledge "in a political context that has challenged its very right to exist" (3–4). She heeds Christian's warning that "critics of the future may have to reclaim the writers we are now ignoring, that is, if they are even aware these artists exist" ("Race" 58). Black women surface as *victims* not *producers* of knowledge because of "the invisible power lines that make and unmake the visible" (Spivak, "Globalicities" 74).

8. There are many feminist critiques of Homi Bhabha. See, for example, Ann McClintock's *Imperial Leather: Race, Gender, and Sexuality in the Colonial Contest*, London, UK: Routledge, 1995; and Rey Chow's *Writing Diaspora: Tactics of Intervention in Contemporary Cultural Studies*, Bloomington, IN: Indiana University Press, 1993.

9. Postcolonial migrants become complicit in the "spectralization of the rural," which involves "conversion of 'the rural' into a database for pharmaceutical dumping, chemical fertilizers, patenting of indigenous knowledge, [and] big dam building," etc. The rural is the "forgotten front of globalization," which uses the urban because the "material wretchedness of [rural] normality" is not regarded as the result of "remote depredations of capitalist exploitation without capitalist social productivity" (*Death* 92–93).

10. In Spivak's estimation, the appropriation of the name "third world" by first world minorities is "terrifying" (*Outside* 16). How does this national identity pit itself against other identities? What role do postcolonial theorists play as the exceptional (by definition) native informants who save the anthropologist his/her trip to the periphery? (*Critique* xii).

11. I marshal Spivak's own mobilization of catachresis:

> History, rather than being a transcendental signifier for the weight of authority (or the authoritative explanation) is a catachresis, a metaphor that has no literal referent. Here the position of the architect-subject is defined by a distancing and differentiation from (rather than an efface-ment of) a dominant narrative of history. (*Critique* 331)

12. Freud describes a game played by "a good little boy" in which he throws a reel attached to a string away from himself while saying something representing "fort" or "gone" (13–14). He subsequently draws the reel back by its string while announcing "da" or "there" (14). Freud sees this game as the child's compensatory response to his mother's departure, "the instinctual renunciation (that is, the renun-ciation of instinctual satisfaction) which he had made in allowing his mother to go away without protesting . . . by himself staging the disappearance and return of the objects within his reach" (14).

13. Spivak clarifies,

> Deconstruction considers that the subject always tends towards centering and looks at the mechanism of centering among randomness; it doesn't

say there is something called the decentered subject. . . . To think about the danger of what is useful, is not to think that the dangerous thing doesn't exist. (*Outside* 10)

She emphasizes a "strategic use of essentialism . . . the usefulness of catachresis" (162).

14. This is a play on Trinh T. Min-Ha's book, *Woman, Native, Other: Writing Postcoloniality and Feminism*, Bloomington, IN: Indiana University Press, 1989.

15. See DuCille's discussion of Jane Gallop's racist sexism towards black literary critic Deborah McDowell ("Occult" 608–12), especially when Gallop makes what Christian terms "high" and "low" the same: Frenchmen and black women are the "people [Gallop] feels inadequate in relation to and tries hardest to please" (608). Perhaps this uncanny moment—Gallop's comfort with identifying Derrida's *Of Grammatology* (1967) as Spivak's text—may be the "intentional phallacy" that is the race for theory.

16. An excellent example of this gesture of white appropriation and displacement is Tina Fey's proclamation on *Saturday Night Live* (February 23, 2008) that "bitch is the new black." This led to a rejoinder by Tracy Morgan (March 15, 2008) that "bitch may be the new black, but black is the new president, bitch!"

17. See Linda Martín-Alcoff's thorough examination of the stereotypes surrounding identity politics in *Visible Identities: Race, Gender, and the Self*, Oxford, UK: Oxford University Press, 2005.

18. See, for example, *Words of Fire: An Anthology of African-American Feminist Thought*, edited by Beverly Guy-Sheftall, New York, NY: New Press, 1995; *The Black Woman: An Anthology*, edited by Toni Cade Bambara, New York, NY: Penguin, 1970; *Third World Women and the Politics of Feminism*, edited by Chandra Mohanty, Lourdes Torres, and Ann Russo, Bloomington, IN: Indiana University Press, 1991; *Making Face, Making Soul/Haciendo Caras: Creative and Critical Perspectives by Feminists of Color*, edited by Gloria Anzaldúa, San Francisco, CA: Aunt Lute Books, 1990; *This Bridge Called My Back: Writings by Radical Women of Color*, edited by Cherríe Moraga and Gloria Anzaldúa, Waterdown, MA: Persephone Press, 1981.

19. The news item she references is "A Challenge in India Snarls Foreign Adoptions" by Raymond Bonner, *New York Times*, June 23, 2003 (http://www.nytimes.com/2003/06/23/world/a-challenge-in-india-snarls-foreign-adoptions.html).

20. DuCille objects, "Where gender and racial difference meet in the bodies of black women, the result is the invention of an Otherness, a hyperstatic alterity" ("Occult" 592).

21. Per JanMohamed and Lloyd, hegemonic subjects privilege "efficacious use of power" more than interrupting abuse; the exploited privilege the devastation of misuse. I discuss this utopian potential in the second part of the book differently from their humanist vision.

22. Understanding European modernity requires tracking, as specified by Dipesh Chakrabarty, how it played out in the colonies: "Historicism—and even the modern, European idea of history—one might say, came to non-European peoples in the nineteenth century as somebody's way of saying 'not yet' to somebody else" (8).

23. In an essay on the poet Seamus Heaney and war, Brendan Corcoran notes that Adorno's statement that "to write poetry after Auschwitz is barbaric" has become

"one of modern poetry's most clichéd and misused phrases," especially because Adorno's own reassessment of his statement is too often left out of the discussion about the role and responsibility of art—or philosophy—in the aftermath of atrocity (694). He states,

> Fortunately, in a 1965 lecture, Adorno addressed the widespread mis-apprehension that lingers still: "I once said that after Auschwitz one could no longer write poetry, and that gave rise to a discussion I did not anticipate. . . . I would readily concede that, just as I said that after Auschwitz one could not write poems—by which I meant to point to the hollowness of the resurrected culture of that time—it could equally well be said, on the other hand, that one must write poems, in keeping with Hegel's statement in his *Aesthetics* that as long as there is an awareness of human suffering among human beings there must also be art as the objective form of that awareness." (694–95) [Adorno, *Metaphysics: Concept and Problems*, translated by Edmund Jephcott, edited by Rolf Tiedemann, 110–11, Stanford, CA: Stanford University Press, 2000.]

When it comes to a reading of Heaney's poetry examining war, Corcoran finds Adorno's rejoinder that he is "on the side of art" salutary because in both Adorno and Heaney what is at stake is nothing short of, in Adorno's words, "the possibility of any affirma-tion of life" (695). Yet, such an "affirmation" for the poet, like the philosopher, is only possible if, in Heaney's words, the "overmastering power" of horror is "acknowledged and *unconceded*" (695). For Corcoran's examination of Heaney, what is most important is the poet's clear-eyed recognition of the necessity of poetry to engage the atrocities of history if poetry is to fulfill its life-affirming mandate.

24. I am reminded of Marlow's statement, "True, by this time it [Africa] was not a blank space any more. It had got filled since my boyhood with rivers and lakes and names. It had ceased to be a blank space of delightful mystery—a white patch for a boy to dream gloriously over. It had become a place of darkness" (Conrad 8).

25. See Spivak, "Transnationality and Multiculturalist Ideology," 84.

26. See LeDœuff, *Hipparchia's Choice*, xii.

Chapter Six

1. According to Wilson,

> Scientists estimate that if habitat conversion and other destructive human activities continue at their present rates, half the species of plants and animals on Earth could be either gone or at least fated for early extinction by the end of the century. A full quarter will drop to this level during the next half century of climate change alone. The ongoing extinction rate is calculated in the most conservative estimates to be about a hundred

times above that prevailing before human appeared on Earth, and it is expected to rise to at least a thousand times greater or more in the next few decades. (*The Creation* 4–5)

The International Union for the Conservation of Nature (IUCN) puts out an annual Red List of endangered species. The IUCN reports that

the rapid loss of species we are seeing today is estimated by experts to be between 1000 and 10,000 times higher than the "background" or expected natural extinction rate (a highly conservative estimate). Unlike the mass extinction events of geological history, the current extinction phenomenon is one for which a single species—ours—appears to be almost wholly responsible. http://cmsdata.iucn.org/downloads/species_extinction_05_2007. pdf

2. Adorno understands "metaphysics in a precise sense as the unity of a critical and a rescuing intention" (*Metaphysics* 51).

3. Bill Bryson describes the genesis of everything:

[F]rom nothing, our universe begins. In a single blinding pulse, a moment of glory much too swift and expansive for any form of words, the singularity assumes heavenly dimensions, space beyond conception. The first lively second . . . produces gravity and the other forces that govern physics. In less than a minute the universe is a million billion miles across and growing fast. There is a lot of heat now, 10 billion degrees of it, enough to begin the nuclear reactions that create the lighter elements—principally hydrogen and helium, with a dash (about one atom in a hundred million) of lithium. In three minutes, 98 percent of all the matter there is or will ever be has been produced. We have a universe. . . . [W]hether the moment of creation was ten billion years ago or twice that or something in between . . . for reasons unknown, there came the moment known to science as $t=0$. We were on our way. (*Everything* 28–29)

Also see Lawrence Krauss's *A Universe from Nothing: Why There Is Something Rather than Nothing*, New York, NY: Free Press, 2013.

4. Adorno emphasizes that the "contingent a-priori" recognizes that although there are "determinants which are valid . . . absolutely and necessarily," they are so "only on condition [of] some sensible matter," because even in the claim that the "a priori is always purely mental[,] . . . within this something, no matter how pale, sublimated, abstract, spiritualized it may be, there is ultimately a reference to some sensible matter" (*Metaphysics* 53–54).

5. Due to this "hellish circle," the "content of mind, that which itself is not mind, the not-I, nevertheless *is* mind" and we are left with a relationship to the world

that is "statically, hierarchically ontological, and *not* dialectical" (Adorno, *Metaphysics* 93). Adorno has an interesting moment in this lecture wherein he reveals his own ideological investment in cordoning off the genesis of metaphysical thought. As he discusses the reduction of thought to "one single, immense tautology" (94), he comments,

> And the god who actually thinks nothing but himself is not wholly unlike the navel gazer . . . who gives us the feeling that he represents being and reflects on being; and that what being says to him is only: being, being, being. I should say in fairness that this joke is not my own but goes back to an admittedly somewhat different formulation of Hegel's. In a polemic against Jacobi he remarked that the thought which immersed itself in the concept of being reminded him of the Tibetan rite of the prayer-wheel, in which the worshippers constantly say nothing but "om," "om," "om." I don't wish to be disrespectful of Aristotle [*sic*], but if for a moment one steps outside the intellectual edifice—I almost said, the cathedral—which is his thought, such ideas do enter one's mind. (94)

The disrespect only extends to Aristotle and not to the world's other great metaphysical traditions! What remains crucial, however, is Adorno's concern with the thwarting of self-reflection, which leads to "actual uniformity, indeed monotony, in which nothing differs from anything else" (97).

6. Adorno critiques the "unburdening of the empirical world" or "the sacrifice of the empirical" in metaphysical inquiry (*Metaphysics* 95).

7. Significant difference is ineffective and powerless but the difference ("base, insect-like, filthy, subhuman and all the rest") signified by our concepts is treated as "anathema." As a result, our "ideals have, to an almost inconceivable degree, become a screen for vileness," or simply a "cover for baseness, exploitation, oppression, and evil" (Adorno, *Metaphysics* 123).

8. This fateful and unlawful aspect is Adorno's opening salvo:

> No theory today escapes the marketplace. Each one is offered as a possibility among competing opinions; all are put up for choice; all are swallowed. There are no blinders for thought to don against this, and the self-righteous conviction that my own theory is spared that fate will surely deteriorate into self-advertising. (*Negative* 4)

9. Adorno recognizes that the "radical question that will destroy nothing but the doubt is itself illusory" (*Negative* 112). I will attempt to formulate a radical question towards the end of this reading of Adorno's metaphysics.

10. Adorno warns that "untruth is also lodged in the autonomous zones of [the] mind" because it "interprets this subjective incapacity as permitting a serene detachment with regard to objective truth" (*Metaphysics* 119).

11. Adorno reminds us that "the privileged are precisely those in whom the pursuit of interests has become second nature—they would not otherwise uphold privilege" (*Minima* 31).

12. The "notion of so-called everyday life . . . [is] bleating" (Adorno, *Metaphysics* 77).

13. In his fragmentary notes from his lectures on metaphysics, Adorno writes,

> While most metaphysics seek invariants, its subjects vary. E.g. the concept of <u>force</u> is hardly discussed in it today (natural science!), likewise that of life (largely replaced by existence). One speaks of <u>fashions</u>; but the so-called fashions of philosophy are indices of something deeper. Demonstrate by the example of *life*. (*Metaphysics* 10, emphasis added)

14. Adorno says, "Imagination gives offence to poverty. For shabbiness has charm only for the onlooker. And yet, imagination needs poverty, to which it does violence: the happiness it pursues is inscribed in the features of suffering" (*Minima* 170).

15. Adorno asserts, matter, "which for us is precisely the moment which decides the degree of reality, as that which is given by intuition, is demoted in [Aristotle's] philosophy to mere possibility" (*Metaphysics* 37). In Aristotle's system, the "concept of matter is extremely dematerialized" into "something very indefinite and general." For Aristotle, "[M]atter is not a solid entity one can hold on to but is just pure possibility; and that, by contrast, the real is actually form," but contemporary systems regard form as "that through which something existent, a τόδε τι . . . must . . . be formed" (49).

16. The Center for Biological Diversity informs:

> Species diversity ensures ecosystem resilience, giving ecological communities the scope they need to withstand stress. While conservationists often justifiably focus their efforts on species-rich ecosystems like rainforests and coral reefs—which have a lot to lose—a comprehensive strategy for saving biodiversity must also include habitat types with fewer species, like grasslands, tundra, and polar seas—for which any loss could be irreversibly devastating. And while much concern over extinction focuses on globally lost species, most of biodiversity's benefits take place at a local level, and conserving local populations is the only way to ensure genetic diversity critical for a species' long-term survival. / In the past 500 years, we know of approximately 1,000 species that have gone extinct—but this doesn't account for thousands of species that disappeared before scientists had a chance to describe them. Nobody really knows how many species are in danger of becoming extinct. Noted conservation scientist David Wilcove estimates that there are 14,000 to 35,000 endangered species in the United States, which is 7 to 18 percent of U.S. flora and fauna. The IUCN [The International Union for the Conservation of Nature] has assessed roughly 3 percent of described species and identified 16,928 species worldwide as being threatened with extinction, or roughly 38 percent of those assessed.

In its latest four-year endangered species assessment, the IUCN reports that the world won't meet a goal of reversing the extinction trend toward species depletion by 2010. (http://www.biologicaldiversity.org/programs/biodiversity/elements_of_biodiversity/extinction_crisis/)

17. The reference here to "going outside . . . and perhaps *being* some time" invokes the essay's epigraph drawn from Derek Mahon's villanelle "Antarctica." This remarkable poem from Mahon's *Antarctica* (1985) is constructed around the final utterance of Captain Lawrence Oates, one of Robert Falcon Scott's comrades on the disastrous 1912 English expedition to the South Pole. Scott's posthumously recovered journal records the decision of Captain Oates to commit suicide because his suffering from severe frostbite was slowing the progress of the few remaining men on the expedition. Wearing only his socks, Oates left the tent—a final figure for the entirety of human culture/civilization—in the middle of a blizzard, stating to his fellows: "I am just going outside and may be some time." Derek Mahon uses this posthumously recorded utterance as the crucially repeated line of his poem attempting to apprehend the instant of Oates's encounter with the sublimity of his life's dissipation into the white out of the frozen continent. The poem considers the telling insignificance of this one man's final hot words literally lost to an utterly other nature, and yet, by emphasizing these words' posthumous recovery (first by Scott and then by Mahon), "Antarctica" asserts that these words spoken from the very cusp of the individual's death might tell us something about the human relationship with both limit and otherness itself. The haunting key to Oates's utterance is that he steps open-eyed into his own death and overtly connects himself to not just a being *in* time but his *being* as "some" (an instant in) time.

18. See Brendan Corcoran's "'Antarctica' and Derek Mahon's 'Topography of the Void,'" *CR: New Centennial Review* 15, no. 3 (Winter 2015): 17–48.

19. Wilson created *The Encyclopedia of Life (EOL)* (http://www.eol.org/index/) as an attempt to "organize and make available . . . virtually all information about life present on Earth . . . approximately 1.8 million known species . . . including their taxonomy, geographic distribution, collections, genetics, evolutionary history, morphology, behavior, ecological relationships, and importance for human well being" (http://www.eol.org/content/page/who_we_are).

20. Here, Adorno casts consciousness itself as "a kind of derivative, a diverted *energy*" of our biological life (*Metaphysics* 132).

21. On May 10, 2013, the Earth passed four hundred parts per million (ppm) of atmospheric carbon dioxide (the primary greenhouse gas pollutant) for the first time in likely several million years—and definitively for the first time in over eight hundred thousand years. As of January 13, 2018, the atmosphere was at 408 ppm. https://scripps.ucsd.edu/programs/keelingcurve/.

22. Adorno vouches, "Dialectics—literally: language as the *organon* of thought—would mean to attempt a critical rescue of the rhetorical element, a mutual approximation of thing and expression, to the point where the difference fades. . . . It is in the rhetorical quality that culture, society, and tradition animate the thought" (*Negative* 56, emphasis added).

23. I will not delve into a fuller examination of Adorno's criticisms of Heidegger, as other scholars have already addressed these issues. Adorno argues against the naturalization of culture, which preempts the historic reality of suffering:

> Showing up, along with Heidegger's concept of Being, is the mythical concept of fate. . . . The eulogized undividedness of existence and essence in Being is thus called by name as what it is: the blind context of nature; the doom of concatenation; the absolute negation of the transcendence whose tremolo notes quiver in the talk of Being. The illusion in the concept of Being is this transcendence; but the reason for it is that Heidegger's definitions—deducted from Dasein, *from the miseries of real human history to this day*—dispense with the memory of those miseries. His definitions turn into moments of Being itself, and thus into things superior to that existence. Their astral power and glory is as cold to the infamy and fallibility of historic reality as that reality is sanctioned as immutable. The celebration of senselessness as sense is mythical; so is the ritualistic repetition of natural contexts in symbolic individual actions, as if that made these contexts supernatural. (*Negative* 118–19, emphases added)

24. Andrew Revkin reports that E.O. Wilson's chief concern is that "while the fight for progress on daunting issues like curbing greenhouse gases grinds on, the battle could be lost if Earth's last rich nodes of biological bounty dwindle and blink out in the meantime." Wilson says, "If you save the living environment . . . you will also automatically save the physical environment, too. . . . If you only save the physical environment, you will ultimately lose both." Andrew Revkin, "Wilson's Law (and Carlin's Rant)," *New York Times*, DOT EARTH, July 11, 2008 (http://dotearth.blogs.nytimes.com/2008/07/11/wilsons-law-and-carlins-rant/).

25. See Simone Weil's analysis of the "logic of force" and the creation of an "extraordinary entity"—that is, "a thing that has a soul" (165). This entity is characterized by loss of thinking, loss of galvanic responses, and reduction to and imitation of nothingness for self-preservation (163–68). In such manner, "here, surely, is death but death strung out over a whole lifetime; here, surely, is life, but life that death congeals" (168).

26. Adorno criticizes Heidegger: "By means of the authenticity of death as he flees from it, whatever announces itself as 'higher' than mere empirical certainty, in this attitude, falsely cleanses death from its misery and stench—from being an *animalistic* kicking of the bucket" (*Jargon* 158).

27. Adorno's famous criticism of Hannah Arendt enjoins that it is not evil that is banal, but the banal that is evil (*Industry* 115).

28. Adorno admonishes:

> If we—each of us sitting here—knew at every moment what has happened and to what concatenations we owe our own existence, and how our

own existence is interwoven with calamity, even if we have done nothing wrong, simply by having neglected, through fear, to help other people at a crucial moment[,] . . . if one were fully aware of all these things at every moment, one would really be unable to live. One is pushed, as it were, into forgetfulness, which is already a form of guilt. By failing to be aware at every moment of what threatens and what has happened, one also contributes to it; one resists it too little; and it can be repeated and reinstated at any moment. (*Metaphysics* 113)

29. This is the title of a song written by Paul Kelly and Kev Carmody about the story of Vincent Lingiari and the eight-year Gurindji strike (1966) at the Wave Hill cattle station in Western Australia for Aboriginal rights, which led to the return of land to the Gurindji people. Paul Kelly and Kev Carmody, along with Missy Higgins and John Butler, also performed this song during Live Earth Australia in Sydney on July 7, 2007.

30. The Nobel Prize-winning atmospheric chemist, Paul J. Crutzen, coined the term "anthropocene" in a 2000 paper co-written with Eugene Stoermer. At Yale Environment 360, Crutzen and Christian Schwägerl, in 2011, write:

It's a pity we're still officially living in an age called the Holocene. The Anthropocene—human dominance of biological, chemical and geological processes on Earth—is already an undeniable reality. Evidence is mounting that the name change suggested by one of us more than ten years ago is overdue. It may still take some time for the scientific body in charge of naming big stretches of time in Earth's history, the International Commission on Stratigraphy, to make up its mind about this name change. But that shouldn't stop us from seeing and learning what it means to live in this new Anthropocene epoch, on a planet that is being anthroposized at high speed. . . . We humans are becoming the dominant force for change on Earth. A long-held religious and philosophical idea—humans as the masters of planet Earth—has turned into a stark reality. What we do now already affects the planet of the year 3000 or even 50,000. (http://e360.yale.edu/feature/living_in_the_anthropocene_toward_a_new_global_ethos/2363/)

31. See Susan Sontag's discussion of torture throughout *Regarding the Pain of Others*, New York, NY: Picador, 2002.

Chapter Seven

1. Adorno acknowledges, "Zoological gardens . . . are laid out on the pattern of Noah's Ark. . . . [Zoo's] are allegories of the specimen or the pair who defy the disaster that befalls the species *qua* species. . . . The more purely nature is preserved and transplanted by civilization, the more implacably it is dominated" (*Minima* 115).

2. See Shaun A. Marcott, Jeremy D. Shakun, Peter U. Clark, and Alan C. Mix, "A Reconstruction of Regional and Global Temperature for the Past 11,300 Years," *Science* 339:6124, March 8, 2013, 1198–1201. [DOI: 10.1126/science.1228026] What this and other studies show is that due to human-produced greenhouse gas emissions, we are effectively leaving the Holocene, that ten thousand to twelve thousand year period of remarkable climactic stability during which human cultures and civilizations around the globe developed. Global warming at present is altering to some degree virtually every ecosystem of the planet and it is increasingly affecting directly—and disastrously—millions of human lives. A world of increasingly harsh climactic instability awaits us in the near future; the more distant future (of decades as opposed to years) betokens potentially cataclysmic transformations—unless humanity collectively chooses to seriously and substantively address this existential threat to human civilization and the biosphere.

3. Rajendra Pachauri, 2007 Nobel Peace Prize laureate, as Chairman of the IPCC (Intergovernmental Panel on Climate Change) wrote on May 29, 2009 in *The Guardian* ("This Silent Suffering") that "99% of the casualties linked to climate change occur in developing countries. Worst hit are the world's poorest groups. While climate change will increasingly affect wealthy countries, the brunt of the impact is being borne by the poor, whose plight simply receives less attention" (http://www.theguardian.com/commentisfree/cif-green/2009/may/29/climate-change-poor).

4. On February 14, 1990, NASA granted the request of astronomer Carl Sagan to turn the Voyager 1 spacecraft's camera back towards the Earth. What resulted was the iconic photo known as the "pale blue dot," an image of planet Earth taken from a distance of 6.4 billion kilometers. Sagan says:

> That's us. . . . Our posturings, our imagined self-importance, the delusion that we have some privileged position in the Universe, are challenged by this . . . lonely speck in the great enveloping cosmic dark. In our obscurity, in all this vastness, there is no hint that help will come from elsewhere to save us from ourselves. . . . To me, [this distant image] underscores our responsibility to deal more kindly with one another, and to preserve and cherish . . . the only home we've ever known. (6–7)

5. The environmental critique of urbanization is complex from a climate standpoint. With half the world's population living in cities today, urban population centers present acute vulnerabilities in a climatologically changing world, just as they also present opportunities both in terms of climate change mitigation and ultimately adaptation to climate change. The global billions living in cities could not suddenly move to rural lands without destroying virtually much of the remaining wild habitat. Cities in and of themselves may be necessary at this point simply to provide more efficient living/transport/distribution of services, etc. Cities can be designed to be even less inefficient—but this takes resources that too many nations lack. See http://www.unhabitat.org/content.asp?cid=10192&catid=550&typeid=24&subMenuId=0. But, writ-large, urbanism remains the ultimate by-product of our industrial society that continues to be ever more wasteful, even as we know what we have to do to live in much greater harmony with Nature and the planet's natural systems.

6. Gilroy refers to "hopeful despair" as an aspect of postmodern planetary consciousness, but he does not explain the relationship between postmodernism and postcolonialism (*Melancholia* 75).

7. Dr. Rajendra Pachauri, chair of the United Nations Intergovernmental Panel on Climate Change, highlighted that, as per the United Nation's Food and Agriculture Organization, global meat production is responsible for 18 percent of global greenhouse gas emissions, when deforestation for silage crops and rangeland, and petroleum use for pesticides, herbicides, fertilizers, and machinery operation are factored. See http://www.guardian.co.uk/environment/2008/sep/07/food.foodanddrink and http://www.fao.org/ag/magazine/0612sp1.htm.

Furthermore, Michael Pollan intones:

> Organic farmers . . . have also rejected what is perhaps the cornerstone of industrial agriculture: the economies of scale that only a monoculture can achieve. Monoculture—growing vast fields of the same crop year after year—is probably the single most powerful simplification of modern agriculture. But monoculture is poorly fitted to the way nature seems to work. Very simply, a field of identical plants will be exquisitely vulnerable to insects, weeds and disease. Monoculture is at the root of virtually every problem that bedevils the modern farmer, and that virtually every input has been designed to solve. ("Playing God in the Garden," *New York Times Magazine*, October 25, 1998, http://michaelpollan.com/articles-archive/playing-god-in-the-garden)

To address the vulnerabilities of the monoculture, required to yield the volume of produce needed to satisfy the global commercial food industries, vast quantities of pesticides, herbicides, and fungicides, not to mention fertilizers, have been used—to the point that many of these exotic chemicals are no longer effective, nature (weeds, pests, diseases) having evolved in short order defenses to these human assaults. The human response has been bioengineering of the monocultured crops themselves to either protect themselves or survive evermore potent chemical applications. What the creation of never-before-seen-in-nature genomes means for nature itself is of grave concern on multiple fronts.

8. I refer to Homi Bhabha's *Nation and Narration*, New York, NY: Routledge, 1990.

9. When critiquing "anodyne forms of nationalism," Gilroy focuses on the "subtleties and evasions characteristic of the racializing discourse to which 'culture talk' gives enduring expression" (*Melancholia* 141). In this metonymic chain, or "culture talk," nation becomes culture becomes race. Such discourse actively suppresses the "denial, guilt, and shame" induced by actual history (141).

10. Gilroy reinforces,

> The growing band of people who opt to bear active witness to distant suffering and even to place their lives at risk in many parts of the world as human shields thankfully represent the undoing of identity

politics. . . . Theirs is a translocal commitment to the alleviation of suffering and to the practical transfiguration of democracy which is incompatible
with racism and ethnic absolutism. It is only racism that acknowledges
the difference between their rights-bearing bodies and those of the rights-
less people they protect by their presence. These gestures of solidarity
proceed from the assumption that translation will be good enough to
make the desired existential, political, and ethical leap. (*Melancholia*
79)

11. Adorno impresses,

If there is any way out of this hellish circle . . . it is probably the ability
of mind to assimilate, to think the last extreme of horror and, in face
of this spiritual experience, to gain mastery over it. . . . [T]o feel that
one has gone relentlessly to the furthest extreme, there lies . . . the possibility of the mind, everything, to raise itself slightly above that which
is[,] . . . that even the worst is something which can be thought and,
because it falls within reflection, does not confront me as something
absolutely alien and different. (*Metaphysics* 125)

12. In his discussion of post-imperial England, Gilroy bemoans,

The invitation to revise and reassess [imperial history] often triggers a
chain of defensive argumentation that seeks firstly to minimize the extent
of the empire, then to deny or justify its brutal character, and, finally,
to present the British themselves as the ultimate tragic victims of their
extraordinary imperial successes. (*Melancholia* 94)

Practitioners of "culture talk" assign "a large measure of blame for the empire to
its victims and then seek to usurp their honored place of suffering, winning many
immediate political and psychological benefits in the process. Much of this embarrassing sentiment is today held captive by an unhealthy and destructive postimperial
hungering for renewed greatness" (95). As war seems to instantaneously grant moral
legitimacy, the absence of war leads to "a depressed reaction that inhibited any capacity
for responsible reconstructive practice" (98). Gilroy sees "culture talk" as the "debris
of . . . broken narcissism" (99).
     13. In Gilroy's estimation,

[H]istorians of . . . [our] repressed, denied, and disavowed blackness
must become willing to say the same things over and over again in the
hope that a climate will eventually develop in which we will be able to
find a hearing, and, secondly, that we must be prepared to step back
audaciously into the past. This should be done not just to establish
where the boundaries of the postcolonial present should fall but also to
enlist [our] largely untapped heterological and imperial histories in the

urgent service of contemporary multiculture and future pluralism. The little-known historical facts of [our] openness to the colonial worlds [we] helped to make must be employed to challenge fantasies of the newly embattled [Earth] . . . as a culturally bleached or politically fortified space. (*Melancholia* 141)

14. See http://thinkprogress.org/climate/2013/09/06/2522511/clive-hamilton-anthropocene/.

15. Adorno's original passage refers to "African" and "Siamese" students along with "diligent art-musicians and musicologists of petty-bourgeois origins" who have "an inordinate respect for all that is established, accepted, acknowledged. . . . It has been observed time and again how those recruited young and innocent to radical groups have defected once they felt the force of tradition. One must have tradition in oneself, to hate it properly" (*Minima* 52). There is much ambivalence about this passage as it proclaims, "*Savages are not more noble.*" Is Adorno mocking racist assumptions, or is he perpetuating them?

16. Contra static ontology, Adorno offers "some reflections on metaphysics which are located at the opposite historical extreme" (*Metaphysics* 98). Here, "metaphysical thinking [must] think against itself[,] . . . must measure itself against the ultimate, the absolutely unthinkable, to have any right to be a thinking at all" (115). He provides the name culture gives to the absolutely unthinkable: "I used only the name Auschwitz, although, of course that name stands for something unthinkable beyond the unthinkable, namely, a whole historical phase" (115–16).

17. When delineating the "logic of force," Simone Weil explains the distortions experienced by the victor's soul:

> To respect life in somebody else when you have had to castrate yourself for all yearning for it demands a truly heartbreaking assertion of the powers of generosity. . . . Lacking this generosity, the conquering soldier is like a scourge of nature. Possessed by war, he, like the slave, becomes a thing, though his manner of doing so is different—over him too, words are as powerless as over matter itself. And both, at the touch of force, experience its inevitable effects: they become deaf and dumb. (184)

Chapter Eight

1. In "Postcolonial Identity," Matilda Gabrielpillai argues that Euro-US postcolonial feminists appropriate and displace subaltern women to "indigeniz[e] . . . their [intellectual] postcolonial feminist struggle" (292). She also seems to suggest that the subject of *sati* marks an undomesticated or unincorporated space in postcolonial feminist subjectivity; postcolonial feminists exteriorize this conflict via this indigenization (293). Reformist efforts become simultaneously atonement (for one's culture) and homage (to one's culture). Insofar as the postcolonial feminist is no longer *that* culturally bound woman anymore, her cultural overdetermination can be transmogrified into a cultural

difference that fits US multiculturalism. Under the auspices of this postcoloniality, culture is an icon of both nostalgia and negation; decolonizing space is an abject and ironic realm of disruption and threat; and the subaltern woman is ontologically bound to her absence and disfigurement.

2. In *A Critique of Postcolonial Reason*, Spivak discusses two specific critiques: Leerom Medovoi, et al., "Can the Subaltern Vote?," *Socialist Review* 20, no. 3 (July–Sept. 1990): 133–49; and Abena Busia, "Silencing Sycorax: On African Colonial Discourse and the Unvoiced Female," *Cultural Critique*, The Construction of Gender and Modes of Social Division 2, no. 14 (Winter 1989–1990): 81–104.

3. See, for example, Sitansu Chakravarti, *Hinduism, A Way of Life*, New Delhi, India: Motilal Banarsidas Publishers, 1991; Doranne Jacobson and Susan Snow Wadley, *Women in India: Two Perspectives*, Columbia, MO: South Asia Publications, 1992; Julia Leslie, *The Perfect Wife: The Orthodox Hindu Woman to the Stridharmapaddhati of Tryambakayajvan*, New Delhi, India: Oxford University Press, 1989; and Wendy Doniger, *The Hindus: An Alternative History*, New York NY: Penguin Books, 2010.

4. As Sinha mentions, this letter ended up being a hoax and was written by two Hindu middle-class Bengali men (*Masculinity* 61–62).

5. See V.N. Datta, *Sati: A Historical, Social and Philosophical Enquiry into the Hindu Rite of Widow Burning*, Riverdale, MD: Riverdale, 1988; Romila Thapar, "Traditions Versus Misconceptions," *Manushi: A Journal about Women and Society* 42–43 (1987): 2–15; and Krupa Shandilya, "Desire, Death, and the Discourse of *Sati*: Bankimchandra Chatterjee's *Krishnakanter Uil* and Rabindranath Tagore's *Chokher Bali*" in *Intimate Relations: Social Reform and the Late Nineteenth Century South Asian Novel*, 20–37, Chicago, IL: Northwestern University Press, 2017.

6. Scholars such as Richard King have attempted to make postcolonial criticism of Orientalist discourse relevant to contemporary area studies and religious studies. See *Orientalism and Religion: Post-Colonial Theory, India and 'The Mystic East,'* London, UK: Routledge, 1999.

7. I have analyzed this particular *sati* in detail in "Who was Roop Kanwar? *Sati*, Law, Religion, and Post-Colonial Feminism," *Religion and Personal Law in Secular India: A Call to Judgment*, edited by Gerald J. Larson, 200–25, Bloomington, IN: Indiana University Press, 2001. This essay was co-authored with Paul Courtright; and, "De-Liberating Traditions: The Female Bodies of *Sati* and Slavery" in *Asian and Feminist Philosophies in Dialogue: Liberating Traditions*, edited by Ashby Butnor and Jen McWeeny, 247–70, New York, NY: Columbia University Press, 2014.

8. Spivak mentions this family relation in her 1992 interview with Leon De Kock, "Interview with Gayatri Chakravorty Spivak: New Nation Writers Conference in South Africa," *ARIEL: A Review of International English Literature* 23, no. 3 (July 1992): 29–47.

9. Spivak makes clear, "the 'singular' as it combats the universal-particular binary opposition, is not an individual, a person, an agent" (*Aesthetic* 437).

10. I refer to Bhabha's notions of the performative and the pedagogical. For Bhabha, "the repetitious, recursive strategy of the performative" accompanies the "continuist, accumulative temporality of the pedagogical" (*Location* 145).

11. In her talk "If Only," Spivak also refers to her niece, her sister's daughter, who is helping her with her biography.

Chapter Nine

1. Spivak does not position the *Dharmasastra* and *Rg-Veda* as more authentic but shows how far Foucault and Deleuze are off the mark concerning the problems of representation. Presuming transparency ideologically portrays hegemonic western selfhood as inclusivity.

2. Salman Rushdie, *The Ground Beneath Her Feet: A Novel*, New York, NY: Henry Hold, 1999. Rushdie uses the myth of Orpheus and Eurydice as the governing conceit of a story about (among a myriad of issues) the jet-setting world of globally ascendant rock musicians confronting ground level actualities of life, love, and death, albeit from what is quite literally a parallel universe.

3. Narayan points out that nationalists have also been involved in reinforcing these static images of third world culture, in their endeavors to establish independence as well as in post-independence communitarian politics.

4. See Narayan, *Dislocating*, 41–80.

5. In "Harlem," Spivak remonstrates that "archivization . . . attempts not only to restrain but also to arrest the speed of the vanishing present, alive and dying" (116). In keeping with this charge, "culturally inscribed dominant mindsets that are *defective* for capitalism should be nurtured for grafting into our dominant" (118).

6. See Spivak's discussion of how "empire messes with identity" wherein she criticizes the performative (read: virtual) aspect of the postcolonial scene, which embodies that "peculiar felicity of postcoloniality" where "good and evil" become "reactive simulation." At this site/sight, "[p]ostcolonial women and men, in many different ways, utter metropolitan performatives on the stage of migrancy as they utter 'cultural-origin' performatives in a simultaneously shadow play; perhaps revealing the constitutive theatricality of all performatives." Yet, she is called out for giving resistance "no speaking part" (*Outside* 226). I attempt to invert the theatricality of the postcolonial performative so that postcoloniality can actually make a difference instead of blending into the cultural landscape of neocolonial first world migrancy.

7. Spivak's fleshing out of the possibility for non-Eurocentric ecological justice finds one of its most poignant articulations in her essay, "Righting Wrongs," *The South Atlantic Quarterly* 103, no. 2/3 (Spring/Summer 2004): 523–81.

8. Spivak commiserates, "What is it to ask the question of psychobiography? I should need much greater learning to be a real player here. But it is part of the tragic narrative of the atrophy of classical learning that the scholar cannot ask the radical questions" (*Critique* 291–92).

9. Shetty and Bellamy are citing Derrida ("Postcolonialism's Archive" 35, 36).

10. Spivak, "Can the Subaltern Speak?," 303. Shetty and Bellamy also cite this phrase ("Postcolonialism's Archive" 32).

11. I refer, of course, to the repeated refrain that ends *Beloved*, as a little girl becomes family legend. In so doing, she broadens the domestic outline of US history.

12. The Goddess Durga preserves the moral order and combats evil forces. She is adorned with weapons including a trident, mace, sword, arrow, and disc. Each weapon empowers her to fight distinct enemies.

13. See "Gayatri Spivak on the Politics of the Subaltern," Interview with Howard Winant, *Socialist Review* 20, no. 3 (1990): 95 (first emphasis added). Shetty and Bellamy also use this phrase ("Postcolonialism's Archive" 47).

14. The subaltern's foreclosed native informancy of her actions, by "inhabiting us," prevents us from "claim[ing] the credit for our proper name" (Spivak, *Critique* 111).

15. See Shetty and Bellamy's discussion of Spivak's reading of Derrida's *Glas* (46). For Spivak, *Sa*, which is Derrida's acronym for Hegel's *savoir absolu*, is a "miring movement of autobiography that will not allow 'analytical distance'" ("Glas-Piece" 36). See Spivak, "Glas-Piece: A Compte Rendu," *Diacritics* (September 1977): 22–43.

16. James Hansen, Makiko Sato, Gary Russell, and Pushker Kharecha, "Climate Sensitivity, Sea Level and Atmospheric Carbon Dioxide," *Philosophical Transactions of the Royal Society*, A 2013 371, 20120294, September 16, 2013, 24. Hansen and his team confirm:

> The human body generates about 100W of metabolic heat that must be carried away to maintain a core body temperature near 37°C, which implies that sustained wet bulb temperatures above 35°C can result in lethal hyperthermia [132, 134]. Today, the summer temperature varies widely over the Earth's surface, but wet bulb temperature is more narrowly confined by the effect of humidity, with the most common value of approximately 26–27°C and the highest approximately of 31°C. A warming of 10–12°C would put most of today's world population in regions with a wet bulb temperature above 35°C [132]. (24)

Chapter Ten

1. See Lola Young's "Missing Persons: Fantasising Black Women in 'Black Skin, White Masks'" in *The Fact of Blackness: Frantz Fanon and Visual Representation*, edited by A. Read, 86–101, Seattle, WA: Bay Press, 1996.

2. The March 1965 Moynihan Report was titled *The Negro Family: The Case for National Action*. Authored by Daniel Patrick Moynihan, a sociologist at the time, the report placed the blame for black poverty on the Negro family. Lack of nuclear family structures resulted in single-mother families that hindered economic progress. The report went further and blamed the matriarchal family structure on "ghetto culture," which has its origins in slavery and Jim Crow. Moynihan served as Assistant Secretary of Labor under President Lyndon B. Johnson and later became a US senator. The full report is available at: http://www.stanford.edu/~mrosenfe/Moynihan's%20 The%20Negro%20Family.pdf.

3. In the lexicon of total objectification, "diseased, damaged, and disabled" slaves are a living laboratory of specimens for medical research *after* they are "*otherwise* worthless" (Spillers, "Mama's Baby" 388, emphasis added).

4. This is obviously a very limited telling of the raping and mutilation of the black body. See Tommy Curry's *The Man-Not: Race, Class, Genre, and the Dilemmas of Black Manhood*, Philadelphia, PA: Temple University Press, 2017.

5. Spillers's mention of the climate recalls the company's chief accountant in *Heart of Darkness* who was of "faultless appearance (and even slightly scented)." His office served as respite for Marlow from the chaos (flies, heads, things, buildings, splay feet, rubbishy manufactured goods, precious ivory) of the way station (Conrad 18).

6. Spivak explicates,

> "Iterability" is cutting and pasting—here cutting and sewing on (*couture et coupure*), and the cuts bleed. The necessary yet impossible first "cut" is difference from the "original," the primordial wound of living-in-time, for example. . . . [T]he wounds of all this cutting would bleed[,] . . . [marking] a shift from a masculist (the absent reference in the patronym) to a feminist (the bleeding of preemergence) model of explanation. (*Critique* 333, note 31)

7. I address this problematic assumption of free will in "De-Liberating Traditions: The Female Bodies of *Sati* and Slavery" in *Asian and Feminist Philosophies in Dialogue: Liberating Traditions*, edited by Ashby Butnor and Jen McWeeny, 247–70, New York, NY: Columbia University Press, 2014.

8. In one of his poems describing a "bog body" (a Neolithic corpse uncannily preserved by the bog only to surface into our time as the Jutland bog containing the body was excavated for turf), Seamus Heaney, in "The Grauballe Man" from *North* (1975), writes: "The head lifts, / the chin is a visor / raised above the vent / of his slashed throat / that has tanned and toughened. / The cured wound / opens inwards to a dark / elderberry place" (*Opened Ground* 110). While the "cured wound" serves as a synecdoche for the unburied corpse itself, the literal fact is that this particular body was killed by having had its throat slit before being pinned to the bottom of a bog hole. The preservative qualities of the water have "cured" the wound, preserving it in perpetuity. Heaney's use of the word "cured" to describe the death-dealing wound suspends the physical fact of death before us at the same time that the poem inquires into the capacity for human arts to "cure" or heal the wounds of loss and death.

9. See Spivak's discussion of this term in *Imaginary Maps* (2001) when she speaks to the ethos of Mahasweta Devi's fiction:

> [A] strong connection, a complicity, between the bourgeoisie of the Third World and migrants in the First cannot be ignored. . . . Is it more or less "Indian" to insist on this open secret? . . . What we are dreaming of here is not how to keep the tribal in a state of excluded cultural conformity but how to construct a sense of sacred Nature which can help mobilize a general ecological mind-set beyond the reasonable and self-interested grounds of long-term global survival. . . . [T]he preparation of "technical

papers" that . . . extract methods from so-called "indigenous knowledge" [are] not . . . accompanied by any change of mind-set in the researchers. By contrast, we draw out from literary and social texts some impossible yet necessary project of changing the minds that innocently support a vicious system. (201–2)

She adds, "Nature 'is' also super-nature in this way of thinking and knowing . . . [as we seek] the inter-nationality of ecological justice in that impossible undivided world" (203).

10. Nanna Nungala Fejo, an Aboriginal woman stolen from her mother when she was four years old, spoke these words to Kevin Rudd, Prime Minister of Australia, when asked what lesson he should convey to the nation regarding forced separation of "half-caste" children from their mothers to eradicate all Aboriginal peoples. In his "Sorry Speech," that opened the forty-second parliament with a formal apology to the stolen generations, he stated: "She thought for a few moments then said that what I should say today was that all mothers are important." ("Kevin Rudd's sorry speech," *Sydney Morning Herald*, February 13, 2008, http://www.smh.com.au/articles/2008/02/13/1202760379056.html.)

Conclusion

1. See Gayatri Spivak, "Three Women's Texts and a Critique of Imperialism," *Critical Inquiry* 12, no. 1, "'Race,' Writing, and Difference" (Autumn 1985): 243–61.

2. Spivak uses this phrase to describe the inverted *telos* of modernity, a double bind, inasmuch as agency is self-destruction (*Aesthetic* 3, 504).

3. http://www.globalcoralbleaching.org

4. https://www.climateinteractive.org/programs/scoreboard/

5. Quoted in Joe Romm, *Climate Change: What Everyone Needs to Know*, Oxford, UK: Oxford University Press, 2015, 152.

6. Eric Rignot, "Global Warming: It's a Point of No Return in West Antarctica. What Happens Next?," *Guardian*, May 17, 2014. https://www.theguardian.com/commentisfree/2014/may/17/climate-change-antarctica-glaciers-melting-global-warming-nasa?utm_source=Daily+Carbon+Briefing&utm_campaign=dff569c0ec-DAILY_BRIEFING&utm_medium=email&utm_term=0_876aab4fd7-dff569c0ec-303421297

7. See the *Nature* study, "Repeated Large-Scale Retreat and Advance of Totten Glacier Indicated by Inland Bed Erosion" by A.R.A. Aitken, et al. mentioned in "Antarctica's Totten Glacier Has Become 'Dangerously Unstable': Research Suggests We Are Slowly Awakening a Process That, in the Past, Has Utterly Transformed One of The Biggest Ice Sources on Earth," by Chris Mooney, *Independent*, May 22, 2016. http://www.independent.co.uk/environment/antarcticas-totten-glacier-has-become-dangerously-unstable-a7041951.html

8. See *Climate Change*, 121.

9. See http://www.biologicaldiversity.org/programs/biodiversity/elements _of_ biodiversity/extinction_crisis/; Romm 122–23.

10. See E.O. Wilson's *Half-Earth: Our Planet's Fight for Life*, New York, NY: Norton, 2016, 8.

11. http://www.theatlantic.com/international/archive/2015/12/brackets-climate-agreement-paris/418041/

12. 3+ = possible runaway greenhouse effect, inundation of coasts, loss of forest and oceanic food chains; 2 = catastrophe for us and life; 1.5 = massive loss that over time we and life might manage; survivability possible; 1. 2 + = what we have already built into the climate system; 1 = where we are now, witness to increasing systemic changes that get worse and amplified.

13. We are not talking about the survival of the fittest against a random and hostile nature, but the essential survival of a familiar nature and a familiar civilization. The use of familiar makes it seem that we are the subject of this struggle but that is not the case. Everything alive today has evolved for these and only these conditions. As Wilson says:

> Like it or not, we remain a biological species in a biological world, wondrously well adapted to the peculiar conditions of the planet's former living environment, albeit tragically not this environment or the one we are creating. In body and soul we are children of the Holocene [the geologic epoch extending back 11,700 years], the epoch that created us, yet far from well adapted to its successor, the Anthropocene. (*Half-Earth* 2)

14. See "Ascending to Nature" in E.O. Wilson's *The Creation: An Appeal to Save Life on Earth*, 9–14, New York, NY: Norton, 2006.

15. Spivak elaborates what going native might actually mean as an allegory of knowing and doing in her chapter "Collectivities" in *Death of a Discipline*, 25–70.

16. This is not a psychoanalytic claim regarding the uncanny and the indeterminate. Mother Right is used far more literally as (for example) ecosystem, Earth, or the unknown origins of life.

17. The impossible and the real are intrinsically intertwined. Although the square root of minus one is called "the imaginary number" because logically it cannot exist, all parts of physics (like quantum mechanics) necessarily use this number.

18. Also, if the Anthropocene began with the steam engine (1781), then the alleged gratitude Indians should feel towards British colonization for the Indian railways becomes quite the contrary.

19. http://www.joelsartore.com/about-the-photo-ark/

20. http://nationalgeographic.org/projects/photo-ark/about/

Coda

1. I seek to echo Tim Robinson's mapping of the Aran Islands here. He begins with Pangaea, or all-earth: "Two hundred million years ago the Atlantic did not exist and all the land-masses of today were clasped together in one continuity, in pre-Adamite

innocence of the fact that one day scientists inhabiting its scattered fragments would give it the lovely name of Pangaea, all-earth, and that its unbounded encircling ocean was Panthalassa, all-sea" (2).

Bibliography

Abel, Elizabeth. "White Reading: Race and the Politics of Feminist Interpretation." *Critical Inquiry* 19, no. 3 (Spring 1993): 470–98.

"About Photo Ark: Saving Species Through the Power of Photography." *National Geographic.* www.nationalgeographic.org/projects/photo-ark/about/

Abraham, Susan. "The Pterodactyl in the Margins: Detranscendentalizing Postcolonial Theology." In *Planetary Loves: Spivak, Postcoloniality, and Theology*, edited by Stephen D. Moore and Maya Rivera, 79–101. New York, NY: Fordham University Press, 2011.

Adorno, Theodor. "The Actuality of Philosophy." In *The Adorno Reader*, edited by Brian O'Conner, 23–39. Malden, MA: Wiley Blackwell, 2000.

———. *The Culture Industry: Selected Essays on Mass Culture.* New York, NY: Routledge, 2001.

———. *History and Freedom: Lectures 1964–1965.* Malden, MA: Polity, 2006.

———. *Jargon of Authenticity.* Chicago, IL: Northwestern University Press, 1973.

———. *Lectures on Negative Dialectics: Fragments of a Lecture Course 1965/1966.* Malden, MA: Polity, 2008.

———. "Meditations on Metaphysics: After Auschwitz." In *The Adorno Reader*, edited by Brian O'Conner, 84–88. Malden, MA: Wiley Blackwell, 2000.

———. *Metaphysics: Concept and Problems.* Redwood City, CA: Stanford University Press, 2000.

———. *Minima Moralia: Reflections from Damaged Life.* New York, NY: Verso Books, 1978.

———. *Negative Dialectics.* New York, NY: Continuum, 1973.

———. "Why Philosophy." In *The Adorno Reader*, edited by Brian O'Conner, 40–53. Malden, MA: Wiley Blackwell, 2000.

Adorno, Theodor, and Max Horkheimer. *Dialectic of Enlightenment.* New York, NY: Continuum, 1997.

Agnes, Flavia. "Redefining the Agenda of the Women's Movement Within a Secular Framework." In *Women and Right-Wing Movements: Indian Experiences*, edited by Tanika Sarkar and Urvashi Butalia, 138–57. London and New Jersey: Zed Books, 1995.

Ahmad, Aijaz. *In Theory: Classes, Nations, Literatures*. New York, NY: Verso, 1994.

Aitken, A.R.A., et al. "Repeated Large-Scale Retreat and Advance of Totten Glacier Indicated by Inland Bed Erosion." *Nature: International Journal of Science* 533 (May 19, 2016). DOI: 10.1038/nature17447. www.nature.com/articles/nature17447

Alexander, Jacqui, and Chandra Mohanty, eds. *Feminist Genealogies, Colonial Legacies, Democratic Futures*. New York, NY: Routledge, 1997.

Allen, Amy. *The End of Progress: Decolonizing the Normative Foundations of Critical Theory*. New York, NY: Columbia University Press, 2016.

Anzaldúa, Gloria, ed. *Making Face, Making Soul/Haciendo Caras: Creative and Critical Perspectives by Feminists of Color*. San Francisco, CA: Aunt Lute Books, 1990.

Appiah, Kwame Anthony. "Is the Post- in Postmodernism the Post- in Postcolonial?" *Critical Inquiry* 17, no. 2 (Winter 1991): 336–57.

Arnold, Matthew. "Dover Beach." In *The Norton Anthology of Poetry*, Fifth Edition, edited by Margaret Ferguson, Mary Jo Salter, and Jon Stallworthy, 1101. New York, NY: W.W. Norton and Company, 2004.

Awkward, Michael. "Appropriative Gestures: Theory and Afro-American Literary Criticism." In *Gender and Theory: Dialogues in Feminist Criticism*, edited by Linda Kauffman, 238–45. New York, NY: Basil Blackwell, 1989.

Bennington, Geoffrey. "Embarrassing Ourselves." *Los Angeles Review of Books*, March 20, 2016. https://lareviewofbooks.org/article/embarrassing-ourselves/#

Bahri, Deepika. *Native Intelligence: Aesthetics, Politics, and Postcolonial Literature*. Minneapolis, MN: University of Minnesota Press, 2003.

———. "Once More with Feeling: What Is Postcolonialism?" *Ariel* 26, no. 1 (1991): 51–82.

Baker, Pauline. *The United States and South Africa: The Reagan Years*. New York, NY: Ford Foundation, 1989.

Bambara, Toni Cade, ed. *The Black Woman: An Anthology*. New York, NY: New American Library, 1970.

Bartolovich, Crystal. "Global Capital and Transnationalism." In *A Companion to Postcolonial Studies*, edited by Henry Schwarz and Sangeeta Ray, 238–45. Malden, MA: Blackwell, 2000.

Basu, Amrita. "Feminism Inverted: The Gendered Imagery and Real Women of Hindu Nationalism." In *Women and Right-Wing Movements: Indian Experiences*, edited by Tanika Sarkar and Urvashi Butalia, 158–80. London, UK: Zed Books, 1995.

Bhabha, Homi. *The Location of Culture*. New York, NY: Routledge, 1994.

———. *Nation and Narration*. New York, NY: Routledge, 1990.

Birla, Ritu. "Postcolonial Studies: Now That's History." In *Can the Subaltern Speak?: Reflections on the History of an Idea*, edited by Rosalind C. Morris, 87–99. New York, NY: Columbia University Press, 2010.

Bonner, Raymond. "A Challenge in India Snarls Foreign Adoptions." *New York Times*, June 23, 2003. www.nytimes.com/2003/06/23/world/a-challenge-in-india-snarls-foreign-adoptions.html

Bordo, Susan. "Feminism, Postmodernism, and Gender-Scepticism." In *Feminism/Postmodernism*, edited by Linda J. Nicholson, 133–56. New York, NY: Routledge, 1990.

Breaking Bad. "Ozymandias." Directed by Rian Johnson. Written by Moira Walley-Beckett. *AMC*, 2013.

Brontë, Charlotte. *Jane Eyre*. London, UK: Penguin Classics, 1985.

Bryson, Bill. *A Short History of Nearly Everything*. London, UK: Doubleday, 2003.

Busia, Abena. "Silencing Sycorax: On African Colonial Discourse and the Unvoiced Female." *Cultural Critique*, no. 14 (Winter 1989–1990): 81–104.

Butler, Judith. *Undoing Gender*. New York, NY: Routledge, 2004.

———. *Gender Trouble: Feminism and the Subversion of Identity*. Thinking Gender. New York, NY: Routledge, 1990.

Carby, Hazel. "The Multicultural Wars." *Radical History Review* 54 (1992): 7–18.

Center for Biological Diversity. "The Extinction Crisis." www.biologicaldiversity.org/programs/biodiversity/elements_of_biodiversity/extinction_crisis/

Chakrabarty, Dipesh. "The Climate of History: Four Theses." *Critical Inquiry* 35, no. 2 (Winter 2009): 197–222.

———. "Postcolonial Studies and the Challenge of Climate Change." *New Literary History* 43, no. 1 (Winter 2012): 1–18.

———. *Provincializing Europe: Postcolonial Thought and Historical Difference*. Princeton, NJ: Princeton University Press, 2000.

Chakravarti, Sitansu. *Hinduism, A Way of Life*. New Delhi, India: Motilal Banarsidass Publishers, 1991.

Chatterjee, Partha. *The Nation and Its Fragments: Colonial and Postcolonial Histories*. Princeton, NJ: Princeton University Press, 1993.

Chow, Rey. *Writing Diaspora: Tactics of Intervention in Contemporary Cultural Studies*. Bloomington, IN: Indiana University Press, 1993.

Christian, Barbara. "The Highs and Lows of Black Feminist Criticism." In *Reading Black, Reading Feminist: A Critical Anthology*, edited by Henry Louis Gates, Jr., 44–51. New York, NY: Meridian, 1990.

———. "The Race for Theory." *Cultural Critique*, special issue of *The Nature and Context of Minority Discourse* 6 (Spring 1987): 51–63.

Climate Interactive: Tools for a Thriving Universe. Climate Scoreboard. www.climateinteractive.org/programs/scoreboard/

"Compensation Case against South African Miners Thrown Out." *Metal Bulletin*, November 30 2004. www.minesandcommunities.org/article.php?a=156

"Conan O'Brien Compares Correspondents' Dinner to 'School Cafeteria.'" ABC News, April 27, 2013. www.abcnews.go.com/Politics/video/conan-obrien-compares-correspondents-dinner-school-cafeteria-19059465

Conrad, Joseph. *Heart of Darkness*, edited by Paul B. Armstrong, 3–77. New York, NY: W.W. Norton and Company, 2006.

Cooper, Anna Julia. *A Voice from the South*. New York, NY: Oxford University Press, 1988.

"Coral Bleaching." Coral Reef Image Bank. www.coralreefimagebank.org/coral-bleaching/

Corcoran, Brendan. "'Antarctica' and Derek Mahon's 'Topography of the Void.'" *CR: The New Centennial Review* 15, no. 3 (Winter 2015): 17–48.

———. "'Stalled in the Pre-Articulate': Heaney, Poetry, and War." In *The Oxford Handbook of British and Irish Poetry*, edited by Tim Kendall, 684–705. Oxford, UK: Oxford University Press, 2007.

Courtright, Paul, and Namita Goswami. "Who was Roop Kanwar? *Sati*, Law, Religion, and Post-Colonial Feminism." In *Religion and Personal Law in Secular India: A Call to Judgment*, edited by Gerald J. Larson, 200–25. Bloomington, IN: Indiana University Press, 2001.

Curry, Tommy. *The Man-Not: Race, Class, Genre, and the Dilemmas of Black Manhood*. Philadelphia, PA: Temple University Press, 2017.

Dallmayr, Fred. "The Politics of Nonidentity: Adorno, Postmodernism—and Edward Said." *Political Theory* 25, no. 1 (1997): 33–56.

Datta, V.N. *Sati: A Historical, Social and Philosophical Enquiry into the Hindu Rite of Widow Burning*. Riverdale, MD: Riverdale, 1988.

Davies, Carol Boyce. *Black Women, Writing, and Identity: Migrations of the Subject*. New York, NY: Routledge, 1994.

de Beauvoir, Simone. *The Second Sex*. New York, NY: Vintage, 1974.

de Man, Paul. "Allegory of Reading: (*Profession de Foi*)." In *Allegories of Reading: Figural Language in Rousseau, Nietzsche, Rilke, and Proust*, 221–245. New Haven, CT: Yale University Press, 1979.

Descartes, René. *Meditations on First Philosophy*, translated by Donald Cress. Indianapolis, IN: Hackett Publishing Company, 1979.

Devi, Mahasweta. "Douloti the Bountiful." In *Imaginary Maps: Three Stories by Mahasweta Devi*, translated by Gayatri Spivak, 19–93. Kolkata, India: Thema, 2001.

Dhagamwar, Vasudha. "Saints, Victim, or Criminal." *Seminar* 342 (1988): 34–39.

Dirlik, Arif. *The Postcolonial Aura: Third World Criticism in the Age of Global Capitalism*. Boulder, CO: Westview Press, 1997.

———. "The Postcolonial Aura: Third World Criticism in the Age of Global Capitalism." *Critical Inquiry* 20 (Winter 1994): 328–56.

Doniger, Wendy. *The Hindus: An Alternative History*. New York, NY: Penguin Books, 2010.

DuCille, Ann. "The Occult of True Black Womanhood: Critical Demeanor and Black Feminist Studies." *Signs: Journal of Women in Culture and Society* 19, no. 3 (1994): 591–629.

———. *Skin Trade*. Cambridge, MA: Harvard University Press, 1996.

Dugard, John, Nicholas Haysom, and Gilbert Marcus. *The Last Years of Apartheid: Civil Liberties in South Africa*. New York, NY: Ford Foundation and Foreign Policy Association, 1992.

Edgar, Robert. *Sanctioning Apartheid*. Trenton, NJ: Africa World, 1990.

Ellis, Stephen, and Sechaba Tsepo. *Comrades Against Apartheid: The ANC and the South African Communist Party in Exile*. Bloomington, IN: Indiana University Press, 1992.

Encyclopedia of Life: Global Access to Knowledge About Life on Earth. www.eol.org

Eze, Emmanuel C. "Toward a Critical Theory of Postcolonial African Identities." In *Postcolonial African Philosophy: A Critical Reader*, edited by Emmanuel C. Eze, 339–44. Oxford, UK: Blackwell Publishers, 1997.

Fanon, Frantz. *Black Skin, White Masks*. London, UK: Pluto, 1986.

Foucault, Michel. *The Order of Things: An Archaeology of the Human* Sciences. New York, NY: Vintage, 1973.

———. *Power (The Essential Works of Foucault, 1954–1984, vol. 3)*. New York, NY: New Press, 2001.

———. *"Society Must Be Defended": Lectures at the Collège de France, 1975–1976*. New York, NY: Picador, 2003.

Fredrickson, George M. "African Americans and African Africans." *New York Review of Books*, September 26, 1991, 32–33.

Friedman, Uri. "The Fate of the World Lies in Between Brackets: A Guide to the Most Important Climate Deal in Years. (Possibly.)." *The Atlantic*, December 1, 2015. www.theatlantic.com/international/archive/2015/12/brackets-climate-agreement paris/418041/

Freud, Sigmund. *Beyond the Pleasure Principle*, translated by James Strachey. New York, NY: W.W. Norton and Company, 1961.

Gabrielpillai, Matilda. "Postcolonial Identity as Feminist Fantasy: A Study of Tamil Women's Short Fiction on Dowry." In *Faces of the Feminine in Ancient, Medieval, and Modern India*, edited by Mandakranta Bose, 287–96. New York, NY: Oxford University Press, 2000.

Ganguly, Keya. "Adorno, Authenticity, Critique." In *Marxism, Modernity, and Postcolonial Studies*, edited by Crystal Bartolovich and Neil Lazarus, 240–56. Cambridge, UK: Cambridge University Press, 2002.

Gates, Jr., Henry Louis. "Authority, (White) Power and the (Black) Critic; It's All Greek to Me." *Cultural Critique*, special issue of *The Nature and Context of Minority Discourse II* 7 (Autumn 1987): 19–46.

Gilroy, Paul. *Black Atlantic: Modernity and Double Consciousness*. Cambridge, MA: Harvard University Press, 1993.

———. *Postcolonial Melancholia*. New York, NY: Columbia University Press, 2006.

———.*'There Ain't no Black in the Union Jack': The Cultural Politics of Race and Nation*. Chicago, IL: University of Chicago Press, 1991.

Gore, Al. *An Inconvenient Truth: The Planetary Emergency of Global Warming and What We Can Do About It*. Emmaus, PA: Rodale Books, 2006.

Goswami, Namita. "De-Liberating Traditions: The Female Bodies of *Sati* and Slavery." In *Asian and Feminist Philosophies in Dialogue: Liberating Traditions*, edited by Ashby Butnor and Jen McWeeny, 247–70. New York, NY: Columbia University Press, 2014.

Gumbs, Alexis Pauline. "The Shape of My Impact." *The Feminist Wire*, October 29, 2012. www.thefeministwire.com/2012/10/the-shape-of-my-impact/

Guy-Sheftall, Beverly, ed. *Words of Fire: An Anthology of African-American Feminist Thought*. New York, NY: New Press, 1995.

Hamilton, Carol. "All That Jazz Again: Adorno's Sociology of Music." *Popular Music and Society* 15, no. 3 (Fall 1991): 31–40.

Hammond, Evelyn. "Black (W)holes and the Geometry of Black Female Sexuality." *differences: A Journal of Feminist Cultural Studies* 6, no. 2–3 (1995): 126–45.

Hansen, James, et al. "Climate Sensitivity, Sea Level and Atmospheric Carbon Dioxide." *Philosophical Transactions of the Royal Society*, September 16, 2013. DOI: 10.1098/ rsta.2012.0294.rsta.royalsocietypublishing.org/content/371/2001/20120294

Haraway, Donna. "Anthropocene, Capitalocene, Plantationocene, Chthulucene: Making Kin." *Environmental Humanities* 6 (2015): 159–65.

Harris, Angela P. "Race and Essentialism in Feminist Legal Theory." *Stanford Law Review* 42, no. 3 (1990): 235–62.

Hartman, Saidiya. *Lose Your Mother: A Journey Along the Atlantic Slave Route.* New York, NY: Farrar, Straus and Giroux, 1998.

Hartsock, Nancy. "Rethinking Modernism: Minority vs. Majority Theories." *Cultural Critique*, special issue of *The Nature and Context of Minority Discourse II* 7 (Autumn 1987): 187–206.

Heaney, Seamus. "The Early Purges." In *Death of a Naturalist*, 11. London, UK: Faber and Faber, 1966.

———. "The Grauballe Man." In *North*, 28–29. London, UK: Faber and Faber, 1975.

———. "Making Strange." In *Station Island*, 32–33. New York, NY: Farrar, Straus and Giroux, 1985.

Hill Collins, Patricia. *Black Feminist Thought: Knowledge, Consciousness, and Empowerment.* New York, NY: Routledge, 1990.

Hodgson, Martin. "Lingiari's Legacy: From Little Things Big Things Grow." ABC News, August 25, 2011. www.abc.net.au/news/2011-08-26/hodgson-from-little-things-big-things-grow/2855942

hooks, bell. "Dialectically Down with the Critical Program." In *Black Popular Culture: A Project by Michele Wallace*, edited by Gina Dent, 48–55. New York, NY: Bay Press, 1992.

———. *Talking Back: Thinking Feminist, Thinking Black.* Boston, MA: South End Press, 1989.

———. *Yearning: Race, Gender, and Cultural Politics.* Boston, MA: South End Press, 1990.

Hull, Gloria T., Patricia Bell-Scott, and Barbara Smith, eds. *All the Women Are White, All the Men Are Black, but Some of Us Are Brave: Black Women's Studies.* New York, NY: Feminist Press at CUNY, 1982.

Irigaray, Luce. *An Ethics of Sexual Difference.* Ithaca, NY: Cornell University Press, 1993.

Jacobson, Doranne, and Susan Snow Wadley. *Women in India: Two Perspectives.* Columbia, MO: South Asia Publications, 1992.

James, C.L.R. *The Black Jacobins: Toussaint L'Ouverture and the San Domingo Revolution.* New York, NY: Vintage Books, 1989.

JanMohamed, Abdul, and David Lloyd. "Introduction: Minority Discourse: What Is to Be Done?" *Cultural Critique*, special issue of *The Nature and Context of Minority Discourse II* 7 (Autumn 1987): 5–17.

————. "Introduction: Toward a Theory of Minority Discourse." *Cultural Critique*, special issue of *The Nature and Context of Minority Discourse* 6 (Spring 1987): 5–12.

Johnson, Lyndon B. "Special Message to the Congress on Immigration." The American Presidency Project, January 13, 1965. www.presidency.ucsb.edu/ws/index.php?pid=26830

"Kevin Rudd's Sorry Speech." *Sydney Morning Herald*, February 13, 2008, 1–9. www.smh.com.au/articles/2008/02/13/1202760379056.html

King, Richard. *Orientalism and Religion: Post-Colonial Theory, India and 'The Mystic East.'* London, UK: Routledge, 1999.

Kishwar, Madhu, and Ruth Vanita. "The Burning of Roop Kanwar." *Manushi: A Journal About Women and Society*, no. 42–43 (1988): 15–25.

Kitch, Sally, and Mary Fonow. "Analyzing Women's Studies Dissertations: Methodologies, Epistemologies, and Field Formation." *SIGNS: Journal of Women in Culture and Society* 38, no. 1 (2012): 99–126.

Krauss, Lawrence. *A Universe From Nothing: Why There Is Something Rather Than Nothing.* New York, NY: Atria Books, 2013.

Kumar, Radha. *The History of Doing: An Illustrated Account of Movements for Women's Rights and Feminism in India, 1800–1990.* London, UK: Verso, 1993.

LaCapra, Dominick. *History and Criticism.* Ithaca, NY: Cornell University Press, 1987.

Laub, Dori. "Reestablishing the Internal 'Thou' in Testimony of Trauma." *Psychoanalysis, Culture & Society* 18 (2013): 184–98.

Lambertini, Marco. *WWF Living Planet Report 2016: Risk and Resilience in a New Era*, 6–7. www.wwf.gr/images/pdfs/LPR_2016_full%20report_low-res_embargo.pdf

Lazarus, Neil. "Hating Tradition Properly." *New Formations* 38 (1999): 9–30.

————. "Modernism and Modernity: T.W. Adorno and White South African Literature." *Cultural Critique* 5 (1986–1987): 131–55.

LeDœuff, Michèle. *Hipparchia's Choice: An Essay Concerning Women, Philosophy, etc.*, translated by Trista Selous. Oxford, UK: Blackwell, 1991.

Leslie, Julia. *The Perfect Wife: The Orthodox Hindu Woman According to the Stridharmapaddhati of Tryambakayajvan.* New Delhi, India: Oxford University Press, 1989.

Levi, Primo. *Survival in Auschwitz: The Nazi Assault on Humanity*, translated by Stuart Woolf. New York, NY: Simon and Schuster, 1958.

Loomba, Ania. "Dead Women Tell No Tales: Issues of Female Subjectivity, Subaltern Agency and Tradition in Colonial and Post-Colonial Writings on Widow Immolation in India." *History Workshop Journal: HWJ* 36 (1993): 209–27.

Lorde, Audre. "Apartheid U.S.A.," *Freedom Organizing Series #2*. New York, NY: Kitchen Table: Women of Color Press, 1986.

————. "For Each of You." In *The Collected Poems of Audre Lorde*, 59–60. London, UK: W.W. Norton and Company, 1997.

————. *Sister/Outsider: Essays and Speeches.* Trumansburg, NY: Crossing Press, 1984.

Loughlin, Sean. "Rumsfeld on Looting in Iraq: 'Stuff Happens.'" CNN.com/U.S., April 12, 2003. www.cnn.com/2003/US/04/11/sprj.irq.pentagon/

Ludden, Jennifer. "1965 Immigration Law Changed the Face of America." National Public Radio, Special Series: The Immigration Debate, May 9, 2006. www.npr. org/templates/story/story.php?storyId=5391395

Macaulay, Thomas. "Minute on Indian Education (1835)." *The Norton Anthology of English Literature*. www.wwnorton.com/college/english/nael/victorian/topic_4/ macaulay.htm

Mahon, Derek. "Antarctica." In *Antarctica*, 33. Oldcastle, Co. Meath: The Gallery Press, 1985.

Mani, Lata. *Contentious Traditions: The Debate on Sati in Colonial India*. Berkeley, CA: University of California Press, 1998.

———. "Contentious Traditions: The Debate on Sati in Colonial India." *Cultural Critique*, special issue of *The Nature and Context of Minority Discourse II* 7 (Autumn 1987): 119–56.

Marcott, Shaun A., et al. "A Reconstruction of Regional and Global Temperature for the Past 11,300 Years." *Science* 339, no. 6124 (March 8, 2013): 1198–1201. DOI: 10.1126/science.1228026. www.science.sciencemag.org/content/339/6124/1198?s id=560b01f9-562d-491a-9a30-16222b025ee6

Martín-Alcoff, Linda. *Visible Identities: Race, Gender, and the Self*. Oxford, UK: Oxford University Press, 2005.

McClintock, Ann. "The Angel of Progress: Pitfalls of the Term Post-Colonialism." *Social Text*, no. 31 and 32 (Spring 1992): 84–98.

———. *Imperial Leather: Race, Gender, and Sexuality in the Colonial Contest*. London, UK: Routledge, 1995.

Medovoi, Leerom, et al. "Can the Subaltern Vote?" *Socialist Review* 20, no. 3 (July–September 1990): 133–49.

Milosz, Czeslaw. "That." In *Road-Side Dog*, 51. New York, NY: Farrar, Straus and Giroux, 1998.

Min-Ha, Trinh T. *Woman, Native, Other: Writing Postcoloniality and Feminism*. Bloomington, IN: Indiana University Press, 1989.

Mohanty, Chandra, Lourdes Torres, and Ann Russo, eds. *Third World Women and the Politics of Feminism*. Bloomington, IN: Indiana University Press, 1991.

———. "Under Western Eyes: Feminist Scholarship and Colonial Discourses." In *Third World Women and the Politics of Feminism*, edited by Chandra Mohanty, Lourdes Torres, and Ann Russo, 51–80. Bloomington, IN: Indiana University Press, 1991.

Mongia, Padmini. "Introduction." In *Contemporary Postcolonial Theory: A Reader*, edited by Padmini Mongia, 1–19. London, UK: Arnold, 1996.

Montaigne, Michel de. "Of Cruelty." In *The Complete Essays of Montaigne*, translated by Donald Frame, 306–18. Stanford, CA: Stanford University Press, 1965.

Mooney, Chris. "Antarctica's Totten Glacier Has Become 'Dangerously Unstable': Research Suggests We are Slowly Awakening a Process That, in the Past, Has Utterly Transformed One of The Biggest Ice Sources on Earth." *Independent*, May 22, 2016. www.independent.co.uk/environment/antarcticas-totten-glacier-has-become-dangerously-unstable-a7041951.html

Moraga, Cherríe, and Gloria Anzaldúa, eds. *This Bridge Called My Back: Writings by Radical Women of Color*. Watertown, MA: Persephone Press, 1981.

Morrison, Toni. *Beloved: A Novel.* New York, NY: Plume, 1987.

Moynihan, Daniel Patrick. *The Negro Family: The Case for National Action.* Office of Policy Planning and Research, United States Department of Labor, March 1965. www.stanford.edu/~mrosenfe/Moynihan's%20The%20Negro%20Family.pdf

Narayan, Uma. *Dislocating Cultures: Identities, Traditions, and Third-World Feminism.* London, UK: Routledge, 1997.

Nicholson, Linda J., and Nancy Fraser. "Social Criticism Without Philosophy: An Encounter Between Feminism and Postmodernism." In *Feminism/Postmodernism,* edited by Linda J. Nicholson, 19–38. London, UK: Routledge, 1990.

Nussbaum, Felicity A. *Torrid Zones: Maternity, Sexuality, and Empire in Eighteenth-Century English Narratives.* Baltimore, MA: Johns Hopkins University Press, 1995.

Nye, William P. "Theodor Adorno on Jazz: A Critique of Critical Theory." *Popular Music and Society* 12, no. 4 (Winter 1988): 69–73.

Pachauri, Rajendra. "Petroleum Use for Pesticides, Herbicides, Fertilizers, and Machinery Operation Are Factored." *The Guardian,* September 7, 2008. www.guardian.co.uk/environment/2008/sep/07/food.foodanddrink

———. "This Silent Suffering." *The Guardian,* May 29, 2009. www.theguardian.com/commentisfree/cif-green/2009/may/29/climate-change-poor

Parry, Benita. "The Institutionalization of Postcolonial Studies." In *The Cambridge Companion to Postcolonial Literary Studies,* edited by Neil Lazarus, 66–80. Cambridge, UK: Cambridge University Press, 2004.

Pauw, Jacques. *In the Heart of the Whore: The Story of Apartheid's Death Squads.* Halfway House, South Africa: Southern Press, 1991.

Phillips, Ari. "Climate Change's Silver Bullet? Our Interview with One of the World's Top Geoengineering Scholars." *Think Progress,* September 6, 2013. www.thinkprogress.org/climate-changes-silver-bullet-our-interview-with-one-of-the-worlds-top-geoengineering-scholars-a02fad9e612f/

Plato. *Phaedo.* In *Five Dialogues: Euthyphro, Apology, Crito, Meno, Phaedo,* translated by G.M.A. Grube, 93–155. Indianapolis: IN: Hackett Publishing Company, 1981.

Pollan, Michael. "Playing God in the Garden." *New York Times Magazine,* October 25, 1998. www.michaelpollan.com/articles-archive/playing-god-in-the-garden/

"Poor Countries' Brain Drain." *The Economist,* November 3, 2005.

Pressly, Donwald. "Mandela's Triumphant Walk." *News* 24, July 18, 2003.

Psihoyos, Louie, director. *Racing Extinction.* Discovery, 2015.

Puar, Jasbir K., and Amit S. Rai. "The Remaking of a Model Minority: Perverse Projectiles Under the Threat of (Counter) Terrorism." *Social Text* 80 22, no. 3 (Fall 2004): 75–104.

Radhakrishnan, R. "Ethnic Identity and Post-Structuralist Difference." *Cultural Critique,* special issue of *The Nature and Context of Minority Discourse* 6 (Spring 1987): 199–220.

Ray, Sangeeta. *Gayatri Chakravorty Spivak: In Other Words.* Oxford, UK: Wiley Blackwell, 2009.

Reid, Frances, and Deborah Hoffmann, directors. *Long Night's Journey Into Day.* Iris Films, 2000.

Revkin, Andrew. "Wilson's Law (and Carlin's Rant)." *New York Times*, DOT EARTH, July 11, 2008. www.dotearth.blogs.nytimes.com/2008/07/11/wilsons-law-and-carlins-rant/

Rhys, Jean. *Wide Sargasso Sea*. London, UK: W.W. Norton and Company, 1966.

Robinson, J. Bradford. "The Jazz Essays of Theodor Adorno: Some Thoughts on Jazz Reception in Weimar Germany." *Popular Music* 13, no. 1 (January 1994): 1–25.

Robinson, Tim. *Stones of Aran: Pilgrimage*. New York, NY: New York Review of Books Classics, 2008.

Rockstrom, Johan. *WWF Living Planet Report 2016: Risk and Resilience in a New Era*, 4–5. www.wwf.gr/images/pdfs/LPR_2016_full%20report_low-res_embargo.pdf

Romm, Joe. *Climate Change: What Everyone Needs to Know*. Oxford, UK: Oxford University Press, 2015.

Rignot, Eric. "Global Warming: It's a Point of No Return In West Antarctica. What Happens Next?" *The Guardian*, May 17, 2014. www.theguardian.com/commentisfree/2014/may/17/climate-change-antarctica-glaciers-melting-global-warming-nasa

Rushdie, Salman. *The Ground Beneath Her Feet: A Novel*. New York, NY: Henry Holt, 1999.

———. *The Moor's Last Sigh*. New York, NY: Vintage, 1997.

Said, Edward. "Adorno as Lateness Itself." In *Adorno: A Critical Reader*, edited by Nigel Gibson and Andrew Rubin, 193–208. Oxford, UK: Blackwell, 2002.

———. *Culture and Imperialism*. New York, NY: Vintage, 1994.

———. *Power, Politics, Culture: Interviews with Edward W. Said*. New York, NY: Vintage, 2002.

———. *Reflections on Exile and Other Essays*. Cambridge, MA: Harvard University Press, 2000.

———. *The World, the Text, and the Critic*. Cambridge, MA: Harvard University Press, 1983.

Sagan, Carl. *Pale Blue Dot: A Vision of the Human Future in Space*. New York, NY: Random House, 1994.

Sangari, Kumkum. *Politics of the Possible: Essays on Gender, History, Narrative, Colonial English*. New Delhi, India: Tulika, 2000.

———. "The Politics of the Possible." *Cultural Critique*, special issue of *The Nature and Context of Minority Discourse II* 7 (Autumn 1987): 157–86.

Sangari, Kumkum, and Sudesh Vaid. "Institutions, Ideologies, Beliefs." In *Embodied Violence: Communalising Women's Sexuality in South Asia*, edited by Kumari Jayawardena and Malathi de Alwis, 240–96. London, UK: Zed Books, 1996.

Sarkar, Tanika. "Heroic Women." In *Women and the Hindu Right: A Collection of Essays*, edited by Tanika Sarkar and Urvashi Butalia, 181–215. New Delhi, India: Kali for Women, 1995.

Sartore, Joel. "About the Photo Ark." www.joelsartore.com/about-the-photo-ark/

Scripps Institution of Oceanography. "The Keeling Curve: A Daily Record of Atmospheric Carbon Dioxide from Scripps Institution of Oceanography at UC San Diego." www.scripps.ucsd.edu/programs/keelingcurve/

"Security Council Calls on South Africa to Lift State of Emergency." *UN Chronicle* 23 (August 1986): 33–35.

Seuss, Theodor. *McElligot's Pool*. New York, NY: Random House Books for Young Readers, 1947.

Schwägerl, Christian. "Living in the Anthropocene: Toward a New Global Ethos." *Yale Environment 360: Published at the Yale School of Forestry & Environmental Studies*, January 24, 2011. www.e360.yale.edu/features/living_in_the_anthropocene _toward_a_new_global_ethos

Shandilya, Krupa. "Desire, Death, and the Discourse of *Sati*: Bankimchandra Chatterjee's *Krishnakanter Uil* and Rabindranath Tagore's *Chokher Bali*." In *Intimate Relations: Social Reform and the Late Nineteenth Century South Asian Novel*, 20–37. Chicago, IL: Northwestern University Press, 2017.

Sharpe, Jenny. "Postcolonial Studies in the House of US Multiculturalism." In *A Companion to Postcolonial Studies*, edited by Henry Schwarz and Sangeeta Ray, 112–25. Malden, MA: Blackwell, 2000.

———. *Allegories of Empire: The Figure of Woman in the Colonial Text*. Minneapolis and St. Paul, MN: University of Minnesota Press, 1993.

Shelley, Mary. *Frankenstein*. London, UK: Penguin Books, 2007.

Shelley, Percy Bysshe. "Ozymandias." In *The Norton Anthology of Poetry*, Fifth Edition, edited by Margaret Ferguson, Mary Jo Salter, and Jon Stallworthy, 870. London, UK: W.W. Norton and Company, 2004.

Shetty, Sandhya, and Elizabeth Bellamy. "Postcolonialism's Archive Fever." *Diacritics* 30, no. 1 (Spring 2000): 25–48.

Shohat, Ella. "Notes on the 'Postcolonial.'" *Social Text*, no. 31 and 32 (Spring 1992): 99–113.

Sinha, Mrinalini. *The "Manly Englishman" and the "Effeminate Bengali" in the Late Nineteenth Century*. Manchester, UK: Manchester University Press, 1995.

Smith, Barbara. "Toward a Black Feminist Criticism." *The Radical Teacher*, no. 7 (March 1978): 20–27.

Sontag, Susan. *Regarding the Pain of Others*. New York, NY: Farrar, Straus and Giroux, 2002.

"Species Extinction—The Facts." The IUCN Red List of Threatened Species, Species Survival Commission, The International Union for the Conservation of Nature. www.cmsdata.iucn.org/downloads/species_extinction_05_2007.pdf

Spencer, Robert. "Thoughts from Abroad: Theodor Adorno as Postcolonial Theorist." *Culture, Theory, Critique* 51, no. 3 (2010): 207–21.

Spillers, Hortense J. *Black, White, and in Color*. Chicago, IL: University of Chicago Press, 2003.

———. "Mama's Baby, Papa's Maybe: An American Grammar Book." In *Feminisms: An Anthology of Literary Theory and Criticism*, edited by Robyn R. Warhol and Diane Price Herndl, 384–405. New Brunswick, NJ: Rutgers University Press, 1997.

Spivak, Gayatri. *An Aesthetic Education in the Era of Globalization*. Cambridge, MA: Harvard University Press, 2013.

———. "At the Planchette of Deconstruction is/in America." In *Deconstruction Is/In America: A New Sense of the Political*, edited by Anselm Haverkamp, 237–49. New York, NY: New York University Press, 1995.

————. "Can the Subaltern Speak?" In *Marxism and the Interpretation of Culture*, edited by Cary Nelson and Lawrence Grossberg, 271–313. Urbana, IL: University of Illinois Press, 1988.

————. *A Critique of Postcolonial Reason: Toward a History of the Vanishing Present.* Cambridge, MA: Harvard University Press, 1999.

————. "Culture Alive." *Theory, Culture & Society* 23, no. 2–3 (May 2006): 359–60.

————. *Death of a Discipline.* New York, NY: Columbia University Press, 2005.

————. "Foreword: Upon Reading the Companion to Postcolonial Studies." In *A Companion to Postcolonial Studies,* edited by Henry Schwarz and Sangeeta Ray, xv–xxii. Malden, MA: Blackwell, 2000.

————. "Gayatri Spivak on the Politics of the Subaltern." Interview with Howard Winant. *Socialist Review* 20, no. 3 (1990): 85–97.

————. "Glas-Piece: A Compte Rendu," *Diacritics* (September 1977): 22–43.

————. "Globalicities: Terror and its Consequences." *CR: The New Centennial Review* 4, no. 1 (2004): 73–94.

————. "Harlem." *Social Text* 22, no. 4 (2004): 113–39.

————. "How to Teach a Culturally Different Book." In *The Spivak Reader: Selected Works of Gayatri Chakravorty Spivak,* edited by Donna Landry and Gerald Maclean, 237–66. London, UK: Routledge, 1996.

————. "If Only." *The Scholar & Feminist Online* 4, no. 2 (Spring 2006): 1–3. www.sfonline.barnard.edu/heilbrun/spivak_02.htm

————. *In Other Worlds: Essays in Cultural Politics.* London, UK: Routledge, 1988.

————. "In Response: Looking Back, Looking Forward." In *Can the Subaltern Speak?: Reflections on the History of an Idea,* edited by Rosalind C. Morris, 227–36. New York, NY: Columbia University Press, 2010.

————. "Interview with Gayatri Chakravorty Spivak: New Nation Writers Conference in South Africa." *ARIEL: A Review of International English Literature* 23, no. 3 (July 1992): 29–47.

————. "An Interview with Gayatri Spivak." *Women in Performance* 5, no. 1 (1990): 80–92.

————. "Love, Cruelty, and Cultural Talks in the Hot Peace." *Parallax: A Journal of Metadiscursive Theory and Cultural Practices* 1 (1995): 1–31.

————. "A Moral Dilemma." *Theoria: A Journal of Social and Political Theory,* special issue of *Trust, Democracy and Justice,* no. 96 (December 2000): 99–120.

————. "The New Subaltern: A Silent Interview." In *Mapping Subaltern Studies and the Postcolonial,* edited by Vinayak Chaturvedi, 324–40. London, UK: Verso, 2000.

————. "'On the Cusp of the Personal and the Impersonal': An Interview with Gayatri Chakravorty Spivak." *Biography,* special issue of *Personal Effects: The Testimonial Uses of Life Writing* 27, no. 1 (Winter 2004): 203–21.

————. *Outside in the Teaching Machine.* London, UK: Routledge, 1993.

————. *The Post-Colonial Critic: Interviews, Strategies, Dialogues,* edited by Sara Harasym. London, UK: Routledge, 1990.

————. "Rani of Sirmur: An Essay in Reading the Archives." *History and Theory* 24, no. 3 (October 1985): 247–72.

———. "Righting Wrongs." *The South Atlantic Quarterly* 103, no. 2/3 (Spring/Summer 2004): 523–81.

———. "Subaltern Talk: Interview with the Editors." In *The Spivak Reader: Selected Works of Gayatri Chakravorty Spivak*, edited by Donna Landry and Gerald Maclean, 287–308. London, UK: Routledge, 1996.

———. "Teaching for the Times." *Journal of the Midwest Modern Language Association* 25, no. 1 (1992): 3–22.

———. "Three Women's Texts and a Critique of Imperialism." *Critical Inquiry* 12, no. 1 (1985): 243–61.

———. "Translator's Preface." In *Imaginary Maps*, translated by Gayatri Spivak, xvii–xxvii. Kolkata, India: Thema 2001.

———. "Transnationality and Multiculturalist Ideology: Interview with Gayatri Spivak." In *Between the Lines: South Asians and Postcoloniality*, edited by Deepika Bahri and Mary Vasudeva, 64–92. Philadelphia, PA: Temple University Press, 1996.

Suleri, Sara. "Woman Skin Deep: Feminism and the Postcolonial Condition." *Critical Inquiry* 18 (1992): 757–69.

Sunder Rajan, Rajeswari. "Death and the Subaltern." In *Can the Subaltern Speak?: Reflections on the History of an Idea*, edited by Rosalind C. Morris, 117–38. New York, NY: Columbia University Press, 2010.

———. *Real and Imagined Women: Gender, Culture, and Postcolonialism*. London, UK: Routledge, 1993.

Sunder Rajan, Rajeswari and You-me Park. "Postcolonial Feminism/Postcolonialism and Feminism." In *A Companion to Postcolonial Studies*, edited by Sangeeta Ray and Henry Schwarz, 53–71. Malden, MA and Oxford, UK: Blackwell Publishers, 2000.

Suskind, Ron. "Without a Doubt." *New York Times Magazine*, October 17, 2004. www.nytimes.com/2004/10/17/magazine/faith-certainty-and-the-presidency-of-george-w-bush.html

Thapar, Romila. "Traditions Versus Misconceptions." *Manushi: A Journal about Women and Society* 42–43 (1987): 2–15.

Thompson, Edward. *Suttee: A Historical and Philosophical Enquiry into the Hindu Rite of Widow-Burning*. London, UK: George Allen and Unwin, 1928.

Unhabitat for a Better Urban Future. www.unhabitat.org/content. asp?cid=10192&catid=550&typeid=24&subMenuId=0

Varadharajan, Asha. *Exotic Parodies: Subjectivity in Adorno, Spivak, and Said*. Minneapolis, MN: University of Minnesota Press, 1995.

———. " 'On the Morality of Thinking,' or Why Still Adorno." In *Adorno and the Need in Thinking: New Critical Essays*, edited by Donald Burke, et al., 316–45. Toronto, Canada: University of Toronto Press, 2007.

Walker, Alice. "Coming Apart." In *You Can't Keep a Good Woman Down*, 41–53. New York, NY: Harcourt Brace Jovanovich, 1981.

Wall, Cheryl A., ed. *Changing Our Own Words: Essays on Criticism, Theory, and Writing by Black Women*. New Brunswick, NJ: Rutgers University Press, 1989.

Weil, Simone. " 'The *Iliad*' or the Poem of Force." In *Simone Weil: An Anthology*, edited by Siân Miles, 162–95. New York, NY: Weidenfeld and Nicholson, 1986.

Wilcock, Evelyn. "Adorno, Jazz, and Racism: 'Über Jazz' and the 1934–7 British Jazz Debate." *Telos* 107 (Spring 1996): 63–80.

Wilson, Edward O. *Half-Earth: Our Planet's Fight for Life.* New York, NY: W.W. Norton and Company, 2016.

———. *The Creation: An Appeal to Save Life on Earth.* New York, NY: W.W. Norton and Company, 2006.

———. "Ascending to Nature." In *The Creation: An Appeal to Save Life on Earth,* 9–14. New York, NY: W.W. Norton and Company, 2006.

Witkin, Robert W. "Why Did Adorno 'Hate' Jazz?" *Sociological Theory* 18, no. 1 (March 2000): 145–70.

WWF Living Planet Report 2016: Risk and Resilience in a New Era, 4–144. www.wwf. gr/images/pdfs/LPR_2016_full%20report_low-res_embargo.pdf

Yeats, William Butler. "Man and the Echo." In *The Collected Works of W. B. Yeats: The Poems,* edited by Richard J. Finneran, 353–54. New York, NY: Scribner, 1997.

Young, Lola. "Missing Persons: Fantasising Black Women in 'Black Skin, White Masks.'" In *The Fact of Blackness: Frantz Fanon and Visual Representation,* edited by A. Read, 86–101. Seattle, WA: Bay Press, 1996.

Zack, Naomi. *Inclusive Feminism: A Third Wave Theory of Women's Commonality.* Lanham, MD: Rowman and Littlefield, 2005.

Index